The American Discovery
of the Norse

The American Discovery of the Norse

An Episode in Nineteenth-Century American Literature

Erik Ingvar Thurin

Lewisburg

Bucknell University Press

London: Associated University Presses

Associated University Presses
440 Forsgate Drive
Cranbury, NJ 08512

Associated University Presses
16 Barter Street
London WC1A 2AH, England

Associated University Presses
P.O. Box 338, Port Credit
Mississauga, Ontario
Canada L5G 4L8

The paper used in this publication meets the requirements
of the American National Standard for Permanence of Paper
for Printed Library Materials Z39.48–1984.

Library of Congress Cataloging-in-Publication Data

Thurin, Erik Ingvar.
    The American discovery of the Norse : an episode in nineteenth-century American Literature / Erik Ingvar Thurin.
        p.   cm.
    Includes bibliographical references and index.
    ISBN 0–8387–5412–0 (alk. paper)
    1. American literature—19th century—History and criticism. 2. Literature, Comparative—American and Scandinavian. 3. Literature, Comparative—Scandinavian and American. 4. Old Norse literature—Appreciation—United States. 5. American literature—Scandinavian influences. 6. Mythology, Norse, in literature. 7. Scandinavia—In literature. 8. Vikings in literature.
I. Title.
PS 159.S34T48   1999
810.9'003—dc21   99–15514
                                                                                    CIP

PRINTED IN THE UNITED STATES OF AMERICA

For Susan

Contents

The American Discovery
of the Norse

Preface

When I began working on *The American Discovery of the Norse* in the summer of 1996, my motivation was the need to fill a lacuna in the study of American literature. I was not particularly aware that the publication of my book, if I succeeded in writing one, would coincide with the national and international celebrations of the Norse discovery of America. I did not know that the postal services of the United States, Canada, and the Nordic countries were to issue commemorative stamps in August, 1999, and that the heads of state of these nations would issue proclamations for the Leif Ericsson Year. Nor did I know about the events planned for the millennial year itself: parade of tall ships, reenactment of Leif's voyage, Leif Ericsson Day, world Viking symposium at the University of Pennsylvania, to mention just a few.

This happy coincidence would hardly have been possible, had I not been sped on my way by friendly institutions and individuals. In the fall of 1996 I was able to spend some time working in the British Library, and I was impressed by the promptitude with which they produced the old and rare books I asked for. Closer to home, I am indebted to Faye Neuenfeldt in the interlibrary-loan section of the Pierce library in Menomonie; I believe Mrs. Neuenfeldt located and got for me every book and article I ordered. After my manuscript had been accepted for publication, I was pleased to get it back early in 1999, thoroughly and competently copyedited by Mr. Tom Riggs.

I also want to seize this opportunity to thank Dr. Domnhall Mitchell, of the Norwegian University of Science and Technology in Trondheim (the city founded by Olaf Tryggvason). Dr. Mitchell read the manuscript early on and made a number of valuable suggestions.

Throughout, I have benefitted from the expert help and advice of my wife, Dr. Susan Schoenbauer Thurin. Without her, this book might not have seen the light of day.

11

1

Introduction

THE ICELANDIC-NORSE BACKGROUND

The American discovery of the Norse is an avatar—in some respects the final avatar—of an array of Norse "revivals." The term "revival" has been used to denote related cultural movements in several countries of northern Europe as well as these movements taken as an ensemble. One may of course also speak of the "Norse revival in America"—I will occasionally do so—as long as it is understood that the reference then is to what happened to the European movement in the New World. The American discovery of the Norse is less direct, less of a rediscovery than the corresponding events in the European countries, the early national background of which is wholly or partially Norse. It would never have happened the way it did if it had not been for the Norse revival overseas.

Especially in Scandinavia the feeling of a direct historical connection was so strong that it generated hopes of national renewal through the resurrection of what was seen as old Norse virtues. However, even there the Norse revival remained largely a literary phenomenon (to some extent supported by art and archeology). The primary sources of my study of its American phase are basically literary. They are the works of well-known—or less well-known—American writers of the mid-nineteenth century.

The sources of inspiration of the American discoverers of the Norse are also mainly literary, whether they are primary or secondary. As for the former category, it is worth noting that Runic inscriptions play a rather insignificant role in spite of a certain tendency on the part of romantic poets to speak of "runic bards" and "runic rhymes." Again, medieval Scandinavian ballads, which regardless of their age have not come down to us in Norse, a tongue as different

13

from the modern Scandinavian languages as Old English is from today's English, will be considered of peripheral relevance even though some of the American writers involved—like several of the foreground figures of the Scandinavian Norse revival—took a keen interest in them and talked of them as if they were Norse.[1] The same thing holds for the famed Norwegian folktales often presented as "Norse" in America.[2]

At the center of our attention, so far as the Norse sources are concerned, stands a set of works written down in Iceland during that unique period of literary activity that began toward the end of the twelfth century and peaked during the following hundred years, thus coinciding, so far as the most prestigious works are concerned, with the highpoint of continental European civilization in the Middle Ages. The bulk of these works consists of prose: the family sagas; the chronicles of the kings of Norway in *Heimskringla,* composed by Snorri Sturluson; and the Younger *Edda,* by the same author, featuring manuals of mythology and poetic composition.[3] The chief poetic monument that has come down to us from Norse times is the Elder ("Saemund's") Edda, with its songs about gods and heroes, a kind of Norse Bible. There are also plenty of samples of a later school of poetry, the *skaldic* one, as quoted in the family sagas, *Heimskringla,* and Snorri's Edda. These primary texts were in various degrees accessible in translations from the Icelandic during the years of the American discovery of the Norse.

In spite of the Icelandic provenance of the literary inspiration, it would be inappropriate to speak of an Icelandic revival with reference to the European rediscovery of the Norse or the American discovery of them. Although written down in Iceland, some of the works are of pre-Icelandic origin, some may have been composed elsewhere, and the scene is often Scandinavia proper, the actors Norwegians, Swedes, and Danes. Norse literature as defined here reflects the lingering ideals of a heroic society that was once common to Scandinavia, although—ironically—already a thing of the past in Denmark and Sweden at the time Iceland was settled (beginning in 874). The settling of the country "of fire and ice" was orchestrated by Norwegian aristocrats who resented the introduction of a more feudal social and political order in Norway under Harald Fairhair, and Norse literature is in a sense the product of the nostalgia of their descendants for a way of life that in the long run could not be maintained even that far out in the Atlantic.[4]

The creative impetus of Icelandic literary activity grew weaker after the thirteenth century, but it did not vanish altogether, and the old texts continued to be copied throughout the Middle Ages until the age of book printing. Scandinavia proper, on the other hand, after the demise of its original pagan civilization and the end of the astounding period of raiding and/or settling in western and eastern Europe known as the Viking Age, settled down to absorb and digest the overwhelming foreign, continental European influences that came with the new religion. The Norse language, once relatively homogeneous, broke up into various local and national dialects. Denmark, Sweden, and Norway had been semiliterate ("runic") during the heyday of Norse power. At the beginning of the sixteenth century, these countries were sufficiently literate and Latinate, but it takes time to create a new identity, and as yet there were no signs of distinct vernacular literatures comparable to what Iceland had produced. Awareness of the Norse manuscripts preserved in that faraway place was scant.

THE NORSE REVIVALS IN EUROPE AND BRITAIN

The memory of the Norse was even vaguer in the British Isles, where in spite of sometimes intense colonization Norse had long ceased to be spoken, except in certain outlying areas; and this was a fortiori true of Germany, whose medieval literary connection with Scandinavia was relatively remote and mythical. Yet in all of these overseas countries there were to be Norse revivals, and they need to be reviewed briefly here before we can concentrate on the one that took place in America in the mid-nineteenth century. The significance of the American discovery of the Norse can only be fully appreciated in this larger context.

   Although Denmark took the lead in developing the field of Norse studies, it was perhaps inevitable that people from Iceland, where the language had not changed much since the saga period, should play an important role in getting things started by collecting and preserving old manuscripts. One Icelandic collector, Arni Magnússon, moved to Copenhagen, where he was employed as a copyist by Thomas Bartholin (*Bartholinus*), the publisher (in 1689) of *De causis contemptae mortis a Danis adhuc gentilibus* (Why the Danes did not fear death during the pagan period), a compilation that contains an anthology of texts. Before him, Magnús Oláfsson had reached the capital (Iceland and Norway being then under the Danish Crown) and become the collaborator of Ole Worm (*Wormius*), whose *Runir seu Danica literatura antiquissima, vulgo Gothica dicta* (On the oldest Danish literature, commonly called "Gothic") was first published in 1636.[5] Thormódhur

Torfason *(Torfaeus)*, likewise an Icelander by birth, wrote works such as *Orcades* (a History of the Orkneys), printed in 1697, and *Historia Vinlandiae* (1715). As these scholars wrote in Latin, their works could be read anywhere in Europe.[6]

In Sweden an Icelander taken prisoner in a war with Denmark helped create an interest in Norse literature in the 1600s; there was at least one collector of Icelandic manuscripts: Count de la Gardie. But on the whole the first Norse revival in that country took a rather different course. When Sweden emerged as a Protestant nation state in the 1520s, national pride seized upon the tradition that made it the original home of the Goths and the Gothic conquest of Rome in 410 as a symbol of Swedish superiority. In 1554 Johannes Magnus published *Historia de omnibus Gothorum Sueonumque regibus* (History of All Gothic and Swedish Kings), in which he claimed, among other things, that Sweden was literate long before Rome. The national chauvinism of scholars only got worse after Sweden under Gustavus Adolphus became a significant European power during the Thirty Years War. The transfer of the Codex Argenteus, the Gothic bible, from a Prague monastery to Sweden was fraught with symbolism.[7] This kind of nationalist fervor reached its non-plus-ultra climax in Olof Rudbeck's four-volume *Atlantica*, in which the Greek legend of the Hyperboreans is connected with Plato's story about Atlantis and both identified with Sweden (1679–1704). By means of fanciful etymology, Rudbeck (formerly a physician) showed that all culture was developed by Swedes and transmitted by them to the rest of Europe (with some difficulty because of the backwardness of southern nations).

The Enlightenment and the gradual triumph of a more critical and rational spirit in Europe put a stop to this kind of speculation. In *Svea rikes historia*, the publication of which began in 1747, Olof von Dalin ridicules the methods used by Rudbeck. The king of Denmark invited a Frenchman, a disciple of Montesquieu, to write a modern history of Denmark—in French, the language which was then rivaling Latin as vehicle of international communication. Jean-Paul Mallet's *Introduction à l'histoire de Dannemarc* was published in Copenhagen in 1855 and the companion volume, *Monuments de la mythologie et de la poésie des Celtes, et particulièrement des anciens Scandinaves*, in 1856. Mallet, while quoting Dalin as one of his sources, still has an uncertain grasp of the early history of the Germanic nations; among other things he tends to confuse them with the Celts, as shown already by the title of the latter volume. But his use of Montesquieu's ideas about the relation between climate and national spirit to explain the Norse love of liberty—the election of kings, the republic of Iceland, etc.—has proved very influential. There is also an account of the Norse explorations of North America (based on Torfaeus's *Historia Vinlandiae*). Yet the selections of Icelandic literature published in the companion volume to Mallet's history of Denmark may be his most important contribution: there, in easy-to-read French fashioned for the salons, the world could read the mythological part of the Prose Edda and various samples of verse, including the notorious "Ode of Ragnar Lodbrok."[8]

On the other hand, the ascendancy of France and French during the eighteenth century meant that the northern countries came to be dominated by a neoclassical taste according to which everything medieval was "Gothic" and "Gothic" a bad word. This French influence was particularly strong during the so-called "Gustavian" period in Sweden toward the end of the century. The Swedish Academy, founded by Gustavus III after the French model, frowned upon literary efforts based on Norse subjects even when the author formally adhered to the neoclassical esthetics. When the first real literary Norse revival got under way in Sweden, it meant the victory of new, "neoromantic" ideas emanating from England and Germany, but it took a national calamity—Sweden's defeat in the 1808–9 war with Russia and the resulting loss of Finland—to bring it about. *Götiska förbundet* (the Gothic Society) was founded in 1811 by a group of literati who attributed the debacle to the loss of the old "Gothic" *(götiska)* virtues—courage, constancy, honesty—that had once made Sweden great.[9] The members of this society, notably E. G. Geijer and A. A. Afzelius, also showed a certain interest in the folk ballads of a later period, but their main literary focus was the Eddas and sagas. The chief literary outlet for "Gothic" products was significantly called *Iduna* (goddess of youth and spring and wife of Bragi, god of poetry and eloquence). Geijer used it to publish a series of poems that became important to the nation. Some of his titles, such as "Den siste skalden" (The last Skald) and "Den siste kämpen" (The last Warrior) seem reminiscent of Thomas Gray's "The Last Bard" and Ossianic nostalgia in general. The title of the "program poem," "Manhem," is identical with the subtitle of Rudbeck's *Atlantica*. However, Geijer (who was to become professor of Scandinavian history at Uppsala), was, even more than Dalin, capable of a more sober approach. "Vikingen" (The Viking) is reasonably convincing as a celebration of the Norse love of freedom and adventure at sea and in foreign lands;

"Odalbonden" (The Yeoman Farmer) glorifies the other, no less remarkable side of Norse life: the freeholder's patient and peaceful cultivation of the land. Both of these poems are useful reference points in the study of the American discovery of the Norse.[10]

Even more important as such a point is the other star of the neoromantic Norse revival in Sweden, Esaias Tegnér, who was a strong influence on Longfellow. He gained national notoriety in 1811 as the author of "Svea," a poem urging the reconquest of Finland so stridently that the academy had to ask him to tone it down, if he wanted an award, so that it would not embarrass the makers of foreign policy, who thought very differently about national needs. The work on which Tegnér's poetic reputation chiefly rests, however, is *Frithiofs Saga* (1825), a heroic poem in twenty-four stanzas inspired by one of the relatively late Icelandic *fornaldarsögur*, which it follows fairly closely in some respects while deviating widely from it in others.[11]

In a way Tegnér was an unlikely author of such a poem: he was professor of Greek at Lund before becoming bishop of Växsjö. Both Greek and Christian influences are undeniably present in *Frithiofs Saga*, but the chief intent of the author is clearly to imbue it with some of the dash and glamour of Norse life without getting too far ahead of contemporary taste. His hero is a hot-blooded young Norseman of wealthy *odalbonde* stock whose father is a close friend of the king and who is the foster-brother of the king's daughter, Ingeborg. The two fall in love while still children, and when the king dies Frithiof is ready to marry her. But her evil brother Helge prevents him from doing so on the pretext that he is not her social equal. In return, Frithiof refuses to help defend the realm against old King Ring, who threatens to invade unless he gets Ingeborg for queen (and stepmother for the small children he has from an earlier marriage). After consulting the gods, Helge places his sister in Balder's Meads for protection. Frithiof boldly goes to see her there and asks her to run away to Greece with him, but she refuses. As penalty for repeated trysts on the temple premises, Frithiof has to go to the Orkneys and collect a tax, a perilous undertaking. He returns safely only to find that his estate has been burned by the treacherous Helge. During the ensuing conflict with Ingeborg's brother, Frithiof accidentally sets the temple of Balder on fire; he flees abroad and for some time leads the life of a Viking. In the meantime, the princess is married off to her aggressive royal suitor. However, Frithiof betakes himself to King Ring's court and spends a winter there in (rather unsuccessful) disguise. After getting to know Frithiof's unmatched qualities and his great love for Ingeborg, the graybeard monarch obligingly commits ritual suicide and is received with enthusiasm in Valhalla. The people proclaim Frithiof regent of the realm. Returning to his own country, he learns that Helge has been slain battling the Finns. Frithiof, now a sadder and a wiser man, rebuilds the temple of Balder, and Ingeborg agrees to marry him there. On the recommendation of the High Priest, who refers to a peace-loving "Balder" in the south (that is, Christ) he is reconciled with Halfdan, Helge's (and Ingeborg's) childlike half-wit of a brother.[12]

While *Frithiofs Saga* is probably the outstanding poem of its kind to come out of the neoromantic Norse Revival in Scandinavia, Denmark had a slight chronological edge over Sweden (perhaps in part because its national pride received a jolt several years earlier: the English bombardment of Copenhagen in 1801 was a strong reminder of the decline of Danish power since the days of Canute).[13] A poem that may be said to mark the starting point of the Norse revival in Denmark was Adam Oehlenschläger's "Guldhornene" (The Gold Horns), published in 1803.[14] The inspiration of this poem was provided by the separate discoveries in the seventeenth and eighteenth centuries of two drinking horns made of gold and dating from the time of the migrations (one of them with a runic inscription) and the subsequent loss of this national treasure through theft. The poem develops the idea that the horns were two signs, two chances offered by the gods for humanity to redeem itself. The gods are obviously the pagan Norse gods worshiped by the makers of the horns. Oehlenschläger liked to see them not as obsolete idols but as "eternal symbols of an eternal, living principle in the world of nature and the spirit."[15] As such they could be deemed worthy of mythic reconciliation with Christianity in an invigorating higher synthesis. In *Balder hin Gode* (Balder the Good), published in 1806, Balder is already seen as prefiguring Christ. In *Hakon Jarl* (1807), which appears to have interested Longfellow, Oehlenschläger also seems to have wanted to synthesize the two religions, thus in a sense repatriating Denmark's Protestant faith. He is quoted as having suggested at the time that "the holy Cross might fuse and become one with Thor's mighty Hammer!"[16] As his work shows, however, this is almost as difficult to achieve in literature as in life.

Oehlenschläger nevertheless continued to produce works on Norse subjects; as late as 1847 he published *Amleth, en Tragedie* and in 1849 (the year before his death) a heroic poem called *Ragnar Lodbrok*.[17] His countryman N. F. S. Grundtvig, on the other hand, also prominent within the neoromantic Norse revival in its early stages and desirous of promoting a Christian heroism (that is, a union of Christian faith and pagan Scandinavian strength and courage), soon saw the impossibility of mythic integration and quit writing in this vein.[18] In Sweden, Geijer, who had also argued for a Norse-Christian synthesis as a young man, suffered a similar disenchantment. Tegnér, after the publication of his saga, withdrew to an aestheticizing classicism. On the whole, you might say, the neoromantic Norse revival in Scandinavia was as short as it was intense. By the time Longfellow visited that part of the world in 1835, the movement was already past its prime. In Copenhagen, he could attend a performance of a play by the indefatigable Oehlenschläger and found Norse philology thriving in the hands of the Rasks and Rafns and Magnússons; but in Sweden, where he arrived in the middle of the summer vacation, the interest in the Norse past was not what he had expected, and there were no signs of a reborn or preserved heroic society. In neither country was there any danger of that part of the national heritage sinking into oblivion once more. It helped define national identity, but it was no longer at the center of creative literary life.[19] This also applies to Norway.

In Germany, the problem of developing a national myth and reconciling it with religious considerations presented itself in a somewhat different light. Having no direct stake in the Eddas and sagas, the Germans at first tended to ignore the Norse and even the Goths. A Renaissance humanist like Ulrich von Hutten was more interested in glorifying a German past in which the symbolic event—symbolic of a *translatio imperii*—was the defeat of Varius' legions by Arminius (Hermann) in the Teutoburger Wald in the year 9 A. D. The task of glorification was facilitated by the discovery and publication of Tacitus' *Germania* toward the end of the fifteenth century. Tacitus paints a flattering picture of the ancient *Germani*, contrasting their way of life with the corrupt manners and customs of imperial Rome. What is more, Tacitus is apparently vague enough on the question of religion to enable the German humanists to argue that their remote forefathers, while undeniably pagans, were basically monotheists.[20] Toward the end of the seventeenth century (1689-90), D. K. von Lohenstein published a (very) long novel called *Arminius*, which detailed this vision. According to Lohenstein, the original monotheistic religion of the Germans was in the custody of the bards but was eventually corrupted by the Druids, who introduced Scandinavian gods such as Tyr and Thor.

However, the Norse gods were rehabilitated during the preromantic period in Germany. The reason was not exactly a more discriminate reading of history; Friedrich G. Klopstock still wanted to present a picture of the Teutonic past centering around Arminius and drawing on Tacitus's *Germania.* He wrote a drama called *Hermanns Tod* (1787). But he was not comfortable with the vague idea of a pagan monotheism. As a poet he felt the need for something more concrete and elaborate in celebrating the German past, something like the Greek mythology so useful to poets. Mallet opened his eyes to what was common in the mythological and legendary heritage of the northern peoples, including the ancestors of the Germans. As Klopstock was also falling in love with *Ossian* at the time, he found it easy to believe Mallet's contention that the Celts as well as the Scandinavians were good Teutons, but Northern mythology did not prove less useful for that reason. He encouraged his circle of poet-friends to draw on it and replaced Greek with Norse myth in some of his own old pieces (Apollo becoming *Braga*, and so forth).[21]

A hundred years later, Richard Wagner was to find the Poetic Edda and the *Volsunga Saga* helpful as a complement to the *Nibelungenlied* in composing the libretto for the *Ring of the Nibelung.*[22] He was better equipped to study the relevant portions of the Poetic Edda than most of his British and American contemporaries thanks to the excellent translations of this work published by the brothers Grimm (1815) and Karl Simrock (1854). Yet these translations did find their way into Longfellow's library, as did J. F. L. Grimm's *Deutsche Mythologie* (1835).[23] Other scholarly German works on Norse subjects were translated and published in America, such as Rudolph Keyser's book about Norse religion.[24] German ideas about the Norse also reached Britain and America through Thomas Carlyle, who quotes Ludwig Uhland on Thor in "The Hero as Divinity."[25] Throughout the period that interests us the Germans took a remarkable interest in the Norse tradition historically intertwined with their own.[26]

The picture changes again as we turn to Britain, the country that concerns us most as background for the Norse revival in America. To the English and Scots, the Norse were pretty much part of the native landscape. British writers did not have to go abroad for Norse topics. There was a Norse presence in the British Isles for centuries; they are frequently the scene of saga literature and some of the poetry may have been written there.[27] The map of northern Britain is replete with Scandinavian place-names, and the Norse language did not disappear before it had made a profound impact on English vocabulary and grammar.[28] Moreover, it appears that it was still spoken in the Orkneys in the days of

Gray. No wonder, then, if Gray planned to include some Norse pieces in his projected "History of English Poetry."[29]

This is not to say that Norse literature and the Norse language were well known in a scholarly sense by Gray or anyone else in Britain toward the middle of the eighteenth century. A sign of the philological and ethnological ignorance of the time was the frequent confusion of the Norse with another retreating ethnic group, the Celts, whose literary monuments were also in need of retrieval.[30] No doubt Mallet must bear part of the blame for this; Klopstock was not the only one he led astray. But the confusion in question can be glimpsed already in 1849 in a poem by William Collins addressed to John Home in which he pleads for an Erse (Scottish Gaelic) revival and prophesies:

> Old runic bards shall seem to rise around,
> With uncouth lyres, in many-colour's vest,
> Their matted hair with boughs fantastic crown'd. . . .[31]

The muddling of the distinction was also very slow to disappear, even after Mallet's equation of Germanic and Celtic was debunked in notes added to *Northern Antiquities*, Bishop Percy's English-language edition of his work.[32] As we shall see, traces of it can still be found in Longfellow and Whittier.

Percy had previously (in 1765) published some prose translations of Norse verse: *Five Pieces of Runic Poetry*. However, he knew little Norse, and what he published were not translations from the originals but from the Latin versions of Bartholin and Worm-Oláfsson, whose mistakes he repeated.

As for Gray, he was genuinely interested in linguistics and philology, and he was certainly able to see the difference between Gaelic and Norse. Yet in spite of the reputation as an expert on these languages that he enjoyed in his own time, his knowledge of the latter language in particular was quite limited. His chief inspiration seems to have been the same as Klopstock's: Macpherson and Mallet. An article of Gray's entitled "Gothi" (The Goths) is among the evidence suggesting that he regarded all the Germanic tongues of northern Europe as Gothic.[33] For the two Norse poems that made him famous throughout Europe and produced whole schools of imitators, he appears to have relied on Latin translations: for "The Fatal Sisters" on Torfaeus's rendering of the original verses from *Njal's Saga* in *Historia Orcadum* and for "The Descent of Odin" on Bartholinus's version of *Vegtamskvidha* in the Poetic (or Elder) Edda.[34]

The fame and influence of these two poems (composed in 1761 and published in 1768) is actually rather puzzling in terms of later standards. "The Fatal Sisters" is a vision of the valkyries at a battle that took place in Scotland in 1014; "The Descent of Odin" tells of Allfadir's visit to Hela, where he asks a dead prophetess about the fate of Balder. Both pieces seem dreary and uninspired today, but I suppose you can say that they are "Gothic" in the romantic sense of the word, and to the Romantics of the time everything "Gothic" was fascinating. However, as Carlyle already notes in "The Hero as Divinity," they will give one no idea of what Norse life and literature were really like—"not any more than Pope will of Homer."[35]

Before turning to Carlyle, something needs to be said about Sir Walter Scott, who took a strong interest in Norse lore not only as a novelist and poet but also as an editor-publisher.[36] One of his Waverley novels, *The Pirate* (1822), is set in Zetland (Shetland) and Orkney about the year 1700. It is replete with ancient Scandinavian lore, often explained and commented on in notes. Scott stresses the point that Norse is still spoken at this time by a population that has preserved many Scandinavian customs and attitudes. He says that when Gray's ode "The Fatal Sisters" found its way to Orkney the old people immediately recognized in it a song that the local fishermen were wont to sing when asked for "a Norse ditty." Gray's other Norse ode, "The Descent of Odin," is said to be in line with the islanders' habit of consulting female fortune-tellers.[37]

In a long poem called *Rokeby* (1813), Scott evokes the days when the Northmen came to Northumberland and "Fixed on each vale a Runic name, / Rear'd high their altar's rugged stone, / And gave their Gods the land they won." He cites *Woden's Croft*, the *Balder*, and *Thorsgill* as examples and generally revels in Norse place-names.[38]

Even more interesting from our present point of view is another long poem by Scott, *Harold the Dauntless* (1817), the topic of which is entirely Norse. Harold is the son of "Count" Witikind, son of Danish King Eric, son of Inguar. Witikind is a Viking who has settled in northern England and in his old age makes peace with the church and receives a land grant in return for his conversion. Harold is furious at this betrayal of their old faith and ideals, breaks off all relations with his father, and goes into an exile in which he is joined by a young page called Gunnar, his foster brother. The two lead a lawless Viking-style life, and Harold is thwarted in love; but on hearing of his father's death Harold returns to claim his land. The church, fearing his rage, leans toward obliging him, but only on condition that he succeeds on a dangerous mission to a mysterious old Celtic castle. Harold does prevail and saves his companion's life by overcoming a demon recognizable as Odin. In the end he is baptized and marries Gunnar, who has turned out to be Eivor, a beautiful—and Christian—Danish maid in disguise who has long been praying for his conversion.

The six cantos in an anapestic meter are not exactly "an experiment in the manner of Norse skalds," as the author suggests in a note. Nor is the story very plausible in historical terms. Pagan Viking life seems to be contemporary with Gothic architecture and Norman-French personal names. The hero is easily larger than life. He is also a berserk who is three times said to foam at the mouth when he goes into battle. He thinks his grandfather Eric may be quaffing "from foeman's skull metheglin draught" in Valhalla—clear evidence of the influence of the Bartholin-Oláfsson translation of *Krákamál*.[39] Yet the poem is significant not only for its exemplariness but as evidence of a homegrown Norse revival in Britain.[40]

Further such evidence is provided by Carlyle, the Victorian writer whose already-cited essay, "The Hero as Divinity," comes close to presenting what Greenway calls a national "myth of origin," although without any whole-hearted attempt to reconcile Norse paganism and Christianity. Lowell, in his "Fable for Critics," suggests that Carlyle is "two-thirds Norse."[41] In his own view he would seem to be considerably more Norse than that: Scandinavian paganism, he says, is more interesting than any other, one reason being that it is "the creed of our forefathers."[42] A little later, he explains that there is no real difference between Norse and Saxon.[43] Most noteworthy is the imperialist note that is added to the suggestions of this type toward the end of the essay: "Nor was it altogether nothing, even that wild sea-roving and battling through so many generations. It needed to be ascertained which race was the *strongest* kind of man; who were to be ruler over whom."[44]

As for Scandinavian paganism, reflected in Norse mythology and literature, Carlyle, following Mallet and Snorri, thinks it was founded by a man called Odin (Odin is even credited with having invented the runes). He emphasizes, perhaps more strongly than necessary, what he views as the "rudeness" and "wildness" of this old culture; but, that done, he feels free to paint a rather flattering picture of it.[45] The "system" developed by the cultural heirs of Odin has its "truth." The account it gives of the powers of nature is more "sincere" than the classical one, although devoid of "Grecian grace." Yggdrasil is an organic symbol of how the world functions and as such vastly supe-

.rior to the mechanical worldview so widespread in the nineteenth century. Yet the Norse myths suggest a basic dualism in the world and nature: the power of sunny Asgard is opposed by the hostile forces of gloomy Jötunheim. Carlyle underlines Thor's positive role as a fighter of these dark forces and follows Uhland in stressing that Thor is the god of "beneficent Summer-heat" as well as of thunder (and, he adds, thunder, to the Norse, was not "mere Electricity"). Balder is another universal symbol: He is the Sun, "the White God, the beautiful, the just and benignant" (whom, says Carlyle, "the early Christian Missionaries found to resemble Christ)."[46]

In 1855, Matthew Arnold published a long poem in blank verse called "Balder Dead" in which he seems to have undertaken to provide Norse mythology with the "Grecian grace" missed by Carlyle. His poem is notable for the comprehensive review of Norse mythology worked into the story centering on Balder's death. It appears that his awareness of it is not only quite recent but thirdhand: He has been studying "The Vision of Gylfe" in *Northern Antiquities*.[47] Arnold's familiarity with Homer, on the other hand, is clearly of a longer date, and he appears to have been preparing himself for his task by rereading the *Iliad* and the *Odyssey* in English translation.[48] "Balder Dead" certainly reads like a translation of Homer. Arnold's Odin is recognizably Zeus, his Frigga (Frea) Hera (although she sometimes reminds one that Snorri says her name was originally Frígída). There are Homeric epithets, repeated phrases, long similes of the kind cultivated by Homer, and imitations of episodes from the ancient Greek epics.

Much of the interest of this poem with its Latinizing title stems from the manner in which the poem suggests that the author felt a need to civilize Norse mythology by adding some traits of another, more prestigious and graceful pagan tradition to his account of it. Yet there may also be a Christian element in the vague prophecy uttered by Balder that he will one day return. It goes somewhat beyond the Norse tradition and may be inspired by the similarities between Balder and Christ pointed out by Carlyle (unless Arnold had also secretly been reading Oehlenschläger and Tegnér).[49] The most impressive part of the poem is the account of Balder's funeral. These lines seem genuinely inspired and are relatively free from Grecian grace. Particularly felicitous is the way in which Arnold plays on the association of Balder with the sun, making the ship carrying Balder's body head for the sunset while growing smaller and smaller to the eyes of the gods assembled on the seashore.

The Norse revival was still going strong in England in the 1870s. There was even another long poem about Balder: Robert Buchanan's "Balder the Beautiful: A Song of Divine Death" (1877). A more important work of that decade was William Morris's long prose poem *Sigurd the Volsung and the Fall of the Niblungs* (1876), based on the *Volsunga Saga* and the Sigurd cycle in the Poetic Edda. Morris also published "The Lovers of Gudrun," a poem based on *Laxdaela Saga* (1870). Artistically, his works are usually considered the high- water mark of the Norse revival in England, and their importance as a point of comparison is enhanced by the fact that their relative excellence may have something to do with the fact that Morris knew Norse.[50] Like Carlyle's *Early Kings of Norway*, they were published too late to influence the American off- shoot of this revival, which had just about run its course by that time; yet the picture of the Norse Revival in England would not be complete without them.[51]

My review of that phenomenon, like those of the Norse revivals in Scandinavia and Germany, has been somewhat summary and even selective as it is only intended as background for the corresponding movement in America. The influence of Norse literature on English literature has been treated in greater detail in a number of scholarly works specifically devoted to the subject.[52] Here I shall only add that nineteenth-century Britain did not prepare the ground for the Americans only or even chiefly through creative writing. It produced works such as Grenville Pigott's *Manual of Scandinavian Mythology*, and the translations in Percy's *Five Pieces of Runic Poetry* and *Northern Antiquities* were followed by William Herbert's two-volume *Select Icelandic Poetry Translated From the Originals* (1804–6), the first translations into English verse done by someone who actually knew Old Norse. Other important English translations appeared as the American discovery of the Norse was just beginning and no doubt accelerated that development, notably Samuel Laing's three-volume rendering of *Heimskringla* with its preliminary dissertation, and G.W. Dasent's translation of the Prose Edda.[53] The latter's translation of *Njal's Saga*, like Benjamin Thorpe's English rendering of the Elder Edda, appeared while the movement was still under way.[54]

THE AMERICAN DISCOVERY OF THE NORSE

Among the first signs of an awakening interest in Norse studies in the United States is an 1829 article in the *North American Review*, "Scandinavian Mythology, Poetry, and History," written by Henry Wheaton, then American chargé d'affaires in Copenhagen.[55] As indicated by the title, it is a very broad sweep, and the contents of the article are fairly elementary. Yet it is noteworthy among other things for the way in which the author salutes Oehlenschläger and Geijer (the historian), representing them as patriots laboring to free their national cultures from the straitjacket of French classicism. The immediate reason for the composition of the article is the publication of the third and final installment of the Copenhagen edition of the Poetic Edda. Among the pieces described are *Vafthrudnismál* (the intellectual duel between Ymir and Odin) and *Vegtamskvidha* (Gray's source for "The Descent of Odin"). Wheaton dwells at particular length on the pieces belonging to the Sigurd cycle, predicting—quite correctly—that they will give rise to many "tragedies and tragic romances." This part of the article must have been particularly useful at the time, considering the absence of an adequate English translation of the Elder Edda.

The description of the Poetic Edda is expanded in Wheaton's 1831 *History of the Northmen*.[56] Oehlenschläger is complimented for his "beautiful imitation" of the *Völundarkvidha*.[57] The emphasis now being on the history, Snorri's *Heimskringla* receives much more attention than in the article. The contributions of Geijer are lauded again along with those of the Copenhagen antiquarian trio: Finnur Magnússon, Rasmus K. Rask, and Carl Christian Rafn. (Longfellow, who was to seek the Danish scholars out in 1835, may first have come across their names here.)

Wheaton's *History of the Northmen* was reviewed by Washington Irving, to whom it appears to have been quite an eye-opener.[58] He expresses astonishment at "the variety of adventurous incidents crowded into these pages" and "the abundance of that poetical material which is chiefly found in early history."[59] Ancient Scandinavia received some further public attention when Longfellow published his review of Tegnér's *Frithiofs Saga* (in 1837). After that the signs of awakening interest came more frequently. Rafn's *Antiquitates Americanae* was reviewed by Edward Everett in 1838.[60] The following year saw the appearance of J. T. Smith's *The Northmen in New England, or America in the Tenth Century*, a book shaped as a dramatic dialogue and aimed at making Rafn's works more accessible to the American public.[61] More impressive from a scholarly point of view was a long article by P. E. Mueller called "The Origin, Progress and Decline of Icelandic Historical Literature" translated from Danish by George Perkins Marsh.[62]

Marsh also endorsed Rafn's ideas about the Norse discovery in *The Goths in New England* (he revived the application of the word *Goths* to all the Germanic ethnicities of northwestern Europe, declaring them "the noblest branch of the Caucasian race").[63]

Creative work of the kind we will be chiefly concerned with began with the forties: "The Skeleton in Armor" first appeared in Longfellow's *Ballads and Other Poems* (1842). The heyday of the creative phase of the American literary discovery of the Norse were the midcentury years; Emerson, Thoreau, Melville, Whittier, Lowell, Taylor, Longfellow, Fuller, and to some extent Whitman used Norse themes in significant ways during that time. A decline set in during and after the Civil War, and this chapter in American literature virtually ended with the seventies.

This is not to say that the Norse were forgotten in America during the waning years of the century. On the contrary, there was to be a proliferation of pedagogically intended retellings of "old Norse tales" such as Augusta Larned's *Tales from the Norse Grandmother (the Elder Edda)* and Mary Elizabeth Litchfield's *The Nine Worlds: Stories from Norse Mythology*.[64] Novels were written on Norse themes, for instance, Robert Leighton's *The Thirsty Sword: A Story of the Norse Invasion of Scotland (1262-1263)*.[65] The interest in the Norse discovery of America remained strong, expressing itself in the publication of a number of articles and books on the subject, including a translation of Torfaeus's *Historia Vinlandiae*.[66] Yet it is clear that we are dealing here with another era and another way of writing. The period of *discovery* was over.

The discovery period is more or less coterminous with the productive years of a fairly small but distinct and surprisingly homogeneous group of writers, both men and women (although mostly men). It wanes with them. The only one of my writers who *begins* her writing career by making a major contribution—at the very end of the period—is Julia Clinton Jones with her long poem *Valhalla* (1878).

A few writers who would fit into the group chronologically seem uninterested in the Norse. This is particularly true of writers of fiction, which is represented only by Melville due to the absence of several celebrated names, notably Poe, Hawthorne, and Stowe. On the other hand, the essay is well represented (Emerson and Thoreau), as is poetry (Melville, Lowell, Whittier, Taylor, Longfellow, and Julia Clinton Jones—plus some short poems by Emerson and Whitman).[67]

By focusing on this group and this period, I hope to fill what must be called a lacuna in American literary history and criticism. If the list of books devoted to the British branch of the phenomenon is already fairly long, a similar list for the American branch would be disconcertingly short. There have been a few articles and stray comments on works by individual authors, but no book devoted to the subject as such. There has, in fact, not been a recognition of its existence as a separate area of literary study. And yet this area is hardly negligible. Nor can the literary harvest of the American literary discovery of the Norse be dismissed as a slavish imitation of the Norse revivals overseas. In many respects it has a distinct character of its own.

In one sense it is not so strange that the American discovery of the Norse should be getting less attention than it deserves in literary history and criticism. At a time when African-Americans, Native Americans, and women are finally being given their due, some other things will necessarily have to take a backseat, including some that have never been overexposed in American literary history, such as works inspired by the Eddas and sagas. In the fourth, revised edition of *Literary History of the United States,* there was still room for a critical comment on Longfellow's "The Skeleton in Armor."[68] The brand-new *Cambridge History of American Literature* does not even mention *The Saga of King Olaf* (while *The Song of Hiawatha* is carefully analyzed).[69]

And yet the themes foregrounded in volumes such as *The Cambridge History of American Literature*—that is, race and gender—must also be prominent in a discussion of the American discovery of the Norse. Indeed, race is perhaps the most pervasive theme in my study. It comes up in one form or another in all of the chapters. It is involved in discussions of empire, the world dominance of Britain and United States, as well in references to the free political institutions of the Anglo-Saxon countries. It cannot be avoided in dealing with the voyaging associated with the Norse "discovery" of America—a favorite topic of the group of authors I will be writing about. As for gender, it is an important matter because of the peculiar position of Norse women and the different ways in which they are dealt with by men and women writers in the age that saw the first Women's Conventions. Another question is why women writers generally speaking seem somewhat less interested in the Norse than the men are.

In other ways, too, it will be seen that the works produced by the American discovery of the Norse are not of merely antiquarian interest but offer a prism through which the American society of the time can be observed. The political use of Norse themes includes what some might call pacifist propaganda. One poem contains an oblique comment on the proper distribution of wealth. Religion is also an important subject: pagan mythology is frequently contrasted—and sometimes merged—with Christian doctrine. In one case, pagan Norse mythology is used in a discussion of the respective merits of (primarily the Christian) religion and the upstart faith in progress associated with modern science.

Fascinating as these aspects of the American discovery of the Norse are, I do not intend to forget that it is a literary and hence an artistic phenomenon. Its place in American literary history needs to be examined in relation to the European and British revivals described in the second section of this chapter: How independent were the Americans in a more technical sense—to what extent did they go back to the original sources and how dependent were they on translations and other materials produced by their predecessors overseas? First and last, there is the critical evaluation of the individual works of art themselves without which an assessment of the American discovery of the Norse cannot be considered complete.

THE CRITICAL CONTEXT

The works that figure in my study are those that make up the harvest of the discovery period of the Norse revival in North America. A few of them are generally considered great (*Moby Dick, Walden*), but for the most part the American writers discussed in the following pages are of interest chiefly because they make use of Norse themes and because of the implications of the ways in which they are used.

The methods I adopt to understand the American discovery of the Norse represent a hybridity, and of necessity so. The Norse materials themselves combine historical fact—or myth and legend—with literariness, and they have their own chronological complexities. What is more, their literariness is as a rule overlaid by another literariness produced by the translations (usually English) on which the American discoverers of the Norse relied. These translations do not only cause some interesting philological problems; they sometimes belong to a relatively early period in the history of English literature (Percy, Gray, Scott, etc.) and reflect the scholarship of that era, as well as its different social and political circumstances. The same thing holds true of the translations of certain works of the British and European revivals that play an important role in the American discovery of the Norse. The task I have set myself is consequently fairly complex. I need to do justice to the varied representations of Norse materials that correspond to a variety of time frames and national identities.

This entails combining literary analysis with attention to the historical context of the Norse originals, that of the period during which they were discovered and translated overseas, as well as that of the American discovery of the Norse itself.

As Myra Jehlen points out in her introduction to *Ideology and Classic American Literature*, the discursive methods of the writers of that period cannot be properly examined without attention to contemporary developments in American literary criticism, namely that "the ideological dimension of literary works has emerged . . . as integral to the entire composition" and, secondly, that "European theories of culture" have benefited American critics.[70] The attention given to race, gender, and class has not only challenged the traditional canon of American literature but has, as Houston Baker noted, shifted "the ordering principle of American historical and American literary-historical discourse."[71] The ideological awareness in recent literary criticism has in fact led to the "discovery" of literatures heretofore ignored. The products of the group of American writers I am studying are not directly comparable to, say, Native American and Chicano literature. As devotees of Norseland, the writers do form a small and distinct group whose achievement has largely been ignored, and they do tend to see themselves as the descendants of a special racial breed; yet they do not exist exclusively as participants in the American discovery of the Norse, and even as such they are a peculiar minority in that they are part of the empowered majority. The use of Norse materials by writers of the American Renaissance fits into the context of current political-literary discourse, but it does so in a different way than minority literature. Race, for instance, appears not in currently political terms but as racism. By a significant coincidence, Emerson's hymn to the superiority of the Northern race and Anglo-Saxon world dominance is the contemporary of *Uncle Tom's Cabin*.

I fully agree with David Levin when he says in *Forms of Uncertainty* that literary form and "issues of historical judgment and interpretation" illuminate one another.[72] The fact that Longfellow's "Tegnér's Drapa" was written during the Mexican War makes it easier to see it as a plea for peace. Conversely, the uncharacteristic ruddiness of *The Saga of King Olaf* may owe as much to the fact that it was written on the eve of the war that was to pit the North against the South as to the content and tenor of Sturluson's text. The literary activity of the participants in the American discovery of the Norse on one level involves a way to comment on current events and recent history, incorporating historiography and ideology.

Charlene Avallone calls for alternatives to the "historical and critical distortions" in the notion of the American Renaissance in "What American Renaissance? The Gendered Genealogy of a Critical Discourse."[73] My study is consistent with Avallone's argument in its attention to Norse references by Louisa May Alcott, Margaret Fuller, and the heretofore wholly neglected Julia Clinton Jones, whose *Valhalla* provides the exclamation point to the ending of the discovery phase of the Norse revival in America.

The formal and cognitive elements of the texts of the American discovery of the Norse are considered in the spirit of poststructuralist methods. This study may not produce examples of falsification of history as spectacular as those unearthed by Michel Foucault in *The History of Sexuality* and other places, but there is no dearth of error and falsification in the American construction of Norseness. Indeed, I shall be focusing on this aspect of the works under consideration so often that I may sometimes seem close to the deconstructionists. In dealing with *English Traits*, for instance, I expose the weakness of the author's pretension to balance the argument by a reference to the mixed ethnic origin of the English before launching into a panegyric of the English "race" in which *English* is frequently equated not only with *Saxon* but with *Scandinavian, Norse, Norman,* and finally *British*. My discussion of *The Conduct of Life* is wholly devoted to the uncovering of discrepancies, illogicisms, gaps, and slippage on which deconstruction relies. It should be mentioned, however, that I am somewhat less pessimistic than Jacques Derrida concerning the nature of language. I proceed to the dismantling of certain texts not so much because of an a priori expectation of incoherence viewed as inherent in verbal discourse, but rather for the reason by which I always try to be guided in my study of the American discovery of the Norse—to focus on the most significant aspects of a given text.

2

Emerson

My reason for beginning with Emerson is not that he initiated the American discovery of the Norse; he was among those who joined the movement in the late 1840s, when it was already under way. But those who were ahead of him were so only by a few years, and it is not possible to trace a line of development from them to him. Basically, the writers I shall be discussing were contemporaneous. In such circumstances the order in which the different authors and works are dealt with becomes a matter of convenience; or, rather, one is free to look for another organizing principle than mere chronology. I have decided to go by genre and begin with two celebrated prose essayists (Thoreau as well as Emerson) before moving on to higher degrees of imaginative intensity (fiction, poetry).

The order obtained in this manner is also on the whole that of the degree of concentration on the Norse. Thus the poetry consists chiefly of texts on entirely Norse subjects. By contrast, in Emerson's essays references to the Norse are scattered over a large number of texts on a variety of subjects none of which are primarily Norse. To deal with all these texts separately would not be practical. A thematic approach is clearly preferable. Fortunately, Emerson's *oeuvre* includes two collections of essays—*English Traits* and *The Conduct of Life*—in which Norse references are used in such a way as to form natural basic foci for discussion in relation to which other texts can be dealt with more briefly. What is more, these foci in both cases are on matters whose significance goes well beyond the study of the Norse revival as such.

ENGLISH TRAITS

The best way to demonstrate that the American phase of the Norse revival is not an entirely innocuous and purely academic affair is to examine what Emerson has to say about race in *English Traits* (1856). In this book he presents what might be called a myth of origin in which the Norse play a central and decisive role in the formation of the English spirit and are extolled at the expense of other "races."

The development of this theme comes as something of a surprise after the suggestions in the opening pages of "Race" that "the best nations are those most widely related" and that the origin of the English nation is particularly mixed.[1] But, as Philip L. Nicoloff has shown, this suggestion is part of Emerson's dialogue with Robert Knox, author of *The Races of Men*.[2] While influenced by Knox in some respects, Emerson is skeptical concerning the part of his doctrine according to which Nature hates hybrids. Having made this clear, he feels free to play down the Celtic and Roman (and indeed the Norman) strains and argue that the English are mainly of Teutonic ("German") and more specifically of Scandinavian stock.[3] As Nicoloff puts it, "he had some wonderful old tales of English racial history to tell."[4]

Emerson's estimate of the Norse role in this history had not always been flattering. In an 1835 lecture called "Traits of the National Character," part of a series on "English literature" and in a sense prefiguring certain chapters in *English Traits*, he says that soon after the Anglo-Saxon invasion of Britain "arrived the new tribes who are commonly known as Danes or Northmen, very little distinguish[ed] unless by an even more beastly ferocity from the Anglo-Saxons." The Vikings were "miscreants . . . without a yard of land," and among them were a "class of fiends," who when combat approached "wrought themselves up to a voluntary madness, howled like wolves, foamed like mad dogs, bit their shields and tore off their clothing, and ran to the combat."[5]

A greater appreciation of the Northern race is reflected in the passage in "Self-Reliance" in which we are invited to "enter into the state of war and wake Thor and Woden, courage and constancy in our Saxon breasts."[6] But the fact that Emerson refers to Woden rather than to Odin suggests that he has not yet "discovered" the Norse per se when this essay was penned in 1840. That discovery is sure to have been furthered by his reading of "The Hero as Divinity" in Carlyle's *On Heroes and Hero-Worship* the following year. Yet his correspondence with the author has nothing to say about the impact of that essay.[7]

Nor do the journals and notebooks, and this comports well with the lack of Norse quotations in the lectures on great men he himself went on to write, in preparation for *Representative Men*. Emerson's more intense interest in the Norse seems to have developed in 1847, when, before going to England (and seeing Carlyle) he borrowed copies of Laing's translation of *Heimskringla* with its preliminary dissertation and Mallet-Percy's *Northern Antiquities* with its translation of the Younger Edda.[8] One of his first acts on arriving in England was to get his own copy of the former text.[9] The first journal reference to Dasent's translation of the Younger Edda also occurs in 1847.[10] Emerson took fairly extensive notes from these works during that year.[11] The long-term change in his view of the Norse brought about by this reading is dramatically reflected not least in *English Traits*.

In this work, the thieves and murderers are no longer the Danes and Norwegians fresh from Scandinavia, but the Normans; and the "bareserk" has become a symbol of enviable strength. In "Race," the author's eagerness to explain the admirable qualities of the English nation in terms of a relatively pure "Norse" heritage causes him to declare *Heimskringla* "the Iliad and Odyssey of English history." Like Laing (and Carlyle before him), Emerson stresses the point that the difference between Saxon and Norse is negligible; they are both Scandinavians.[12] As for the Normans, who also had a Scandinavian background, they are at this point said to have deteriorated during 160 years in France. They have "lost their own language and learned the Romance or barbarous Latin of the Gauls, and . . . acquired with the language, all the vices it had names of. . . . Twenty thousand thieves landed at Hastings."[13]

To be sure, as if to provide credibility for the overall encomium on the Norse there is a paragraph in "Race" conceding that the Scandinavians of the pagan era were no Sunday-school children: "These Norsemen are excellent persons in the main, with good sense, steadiness, wise speech and prompt action. But they have a singular turn for homicide. . . ." There follows a long list of examples from Snorri Sturluson's chronicles.[14] Yet everything is related in a humorous vein, as if this aspect of Norse reality need not be taken seriously; and if Emerson does not like Carlyle grow lyrical speaking of the Viking funeral ships, he does not sound totally unimpressed by King Haki, who, mortally wounded, has himself taken out to sea with his dead comrades and personally sets the ship on fire. Besides, he says, it is only the early sagas that are "sanguinary and piratical"; the later are "of a noble strain."[15]

The suggestions of a volatile and unrestrainedly violent national character are also contradicted by the description of the Norse as "substantial farmers." After reading Laing, Emerson is clearly aware that even in the heyday of the Viking age all Norsemen were not harrying on foreign coasts or carrying out bloody vendettas at home. Moreover, their status as "bonders or land-holders" was bound up with a love of political freedom and a strong individualism.[16] These qualities, it is implied, were passed on to their descendants; the free institutions of England hark back to the Norse.[17]

In speaking of the "strongly individualized" portraits in *Heimskringla*, Emerson also notes that the individuals are often said to be "very handsome." This trait, he says, "only brings the story nearer to the English race." The theme disappears temporarily as he begins to apply what he has said about the Norse, including their less civilized traits, to their modern descendants: He begins by noting that "it took many generations to trim and comb and perfume the first boat-load of Norse pirates into royal highnesses and most noble knights of the Garter" (even though "every sparkle of ornament dates back to the Norse boat"). Indeed, the "traits of Odin" have not yet disappeared completely: "The English uncultured are a brutal nation" (again a series of examples is listed). But very soon Emerson is back on the subject of the appearance of the English: "They are bigger men than the Americans. . . . They are round, ruddy and handsome."[18]

Emerson dwells on this subject at some length. "In all ages," he assures us in one paragraph, "they are a handsome race." Witness the bronze monuments of crusaders in the Worcester and Salisbury cathedrals: although seven hundred years old, they are "of the same type as the best youthful heads of men now in England." It now appears that it did not take so long after all to civilize the Norsemen: the heads of the crusaders "please by beauty of the same character, an expression blending good nature, valor and refinement, and mainly by that uncorrupt youth in the face of manhood, which is daily seen in the streets of London."[19] The next paragraph opens with this sentence: "Both branches of the Scandinavian race are distinguished for beauty." Emerson alludes to the story of Pope Gregory the Great remarking apropos of some young Angles who had been brought captive to Rome: *non Angli sed angeli*. He notes that the Norman chroniclers of the later Middle Ages (when the Norse element had been absorbed into the darker, Romance-speaking population) "wondered at the beauty and long flowing hair of the young English captives." After mentioning once more that "the Heimskringla has frequent occasion to speak of the personal beauty of its heroes," he finally exclaims in a burst of enthusiasm: "When it is considered what humanity, what resources of mental and moral power the traits of the blonde race betoken, its accession to empire marks a new and finer epoch, wherein all the old mineral force shall be subjugated at last by humanity and shall plough in its furrow henceforward."

The mental or intellectual powers of the English are also related to race in "Ability" (the chapter following "Race"), in which Emerson says that the (Saxon-Danish) race was "so intellectual" that "a feudal or military tenure" could not last very long after the Norman conquest.[20] In "Race" he goes on to stress the connection he sees between racial characteristics and moral superiority. The Englishman is characterized by love of truth, sensibility, fine perception, and poetic construction, and all these things flow from the combination of "decision and nerve" with a "fair complexion, blue eyes and open and florid aspect" in his makeup. "The fair Saxon man with open front and honest meaning, domestic, affectionate, is not the wood out of which cannibal, or inquisitor, or assassin is made, but he is moulded for law, lawful trade, civility, marriage, the nurture of children, for colleges, churches, charities and colonies."

Emerson does not have much to say about English women (although he does criticize their shape and note that the French say they have "two left hands").[21] But the affectionate and domestic nature of the English is explained in terms of a "union of qualities . . . fabled in . . . the Greek legend of Hermaphrodite." In other words, "the two sexes are co-present in the English mind," and when there is not a war on, the men "are women in kindness." The prime illustration of this point is Lord Nelson—a good Norse name—but Lord Collingwood, Admiral Rodney, the duke of Buckingham, and Sir John Franklin are also among the alleged androgynes. For some reason, Emerson ends "Race" with a disquisition on English horsemanship. Possibly there is a punning transition from the high-bred quality of the company just listed to the breeding of equine full-bloods. On the other hand, Emerson says the English "came honestly by their horsemanship, with *Hengest* and *Horsa* for their Saxon founders." As for "the other branch of their race," it had been Tartar nomads whose only wealth was the horse, and "the pastures of Tartary were still remembered by the tenacious practice of the Norsemen to eat horse flesh at religious feasts."[22] And "in the Danish invasions the marauders seized upon horses where they landed and were at once converted into a body of expert cavalry."

Emerson's elaboration of a Norse myth of origin in *English Traits* does not really end with "Race." One might say it provides the connecting leitmotif; there is hardly a chapter in the book in which the Norse are not referred to; one might almost say they afford the leitmotif. "Ability" begins with a proposition with which the reader is already quite familiar: "The Saxon and the Northman are both Scandinavians." If there is anything new in the opening paragraph, it is that the portion of the Northmen who had spent 160 years in France, that is, the Normans, get a more favorable review, being regarded as a significant part of the population. At the same time, Emerson warns against exaggerating the difference between Saxon-Norse and Norman. The Normans are usually represented as the aristocratic element, he says, and the Saxons (and pure Norse) as the popular or "democratic" component. But the distinction is "a little mythical"; he is sure "the nobles are of both tribes, and the workers of both." Besides, "what signifies a pedigree of a hundred links, against a cotton-spinner with steam in his mill; or against a company of broad-shouldered Liverpool merchants, for whom Stephenson and Brunel are contriving locomotives and a tubular bridge?"

One notes that if *Stephenson* sounds Teutonic, *Brunel* is clearly Norman-French. However, Emerson goes on to declare, "These Saxons are the hands of mankind. . . . They are the wealth-makers." That *Saxons* is meant to be synonymous with *Norse*—Norwegian Norse—is again obvious when he compares them to trolls: "The Scandinavian fancied himself surrounded by Trolls,—a kind of divine stevedores, carpenters, reapers, smiths and masons, swift to reward every kindness done them, with gifts of gold and silver." Somewhat later in "Ability," Norse matter from the Prose Edda is used apropos of another aspect of English "ability": "When Thor and his companions arrive at Utgard, he is told that 'nobody is permitted to remain there,' unless he understand some art, and excel in it all other men.' The same question is still put to the posterity of Thor."[23] And this posterity is up to the challenge: every man dwelling in England strives to perfect himself "in some art or detail" and is not content unless he feels he has something in which he "surpasses all other men." A few pages later still, Emerson equates Saxon and Norse in yet another way. After noting that the world "is theirs," he says that they have "approved their Saxon blood" not only "by their sea-going," but "by their descent from Odin's smiths" (that is, "by their hereditary skill in working in iron").[24]

Wealth should follow ability. After talking about new inventions such as steam engines and the telegraph in "Wealth," Emerson notes that "the old energy of the Norse race arms itself with these magnificent powers." Once more, the English are the descendants of the great toiler among the Aesir: "Scandinavian Thor, who once forged his bolts in icy Hecla and built galleys by lonely fiords, in England has advanced with the times, has shorn his beard, enters Parliament, sits down at a desk in the India House and lends Miollnir to Birmingham for a steam-hammer."[25]

It is not my intention to trace every suggestion of Norse ancestry in *English Traits*. A few more examples will sufficiently show their pervasiveness. In "Manners," one reads apropos of the overwhelming presence of the English (their "vigor and brawn") that "nothing but the most serious business could give one any counterweight to these Baresarks, though they were only to order eggs and muffins for their breakfast."[26] In "Cockayne," it is stated apropos of an alleged national inclination to blow one's own horn that "the island offers a daily worship to the old Norse god Brage, celebrated among our Scandinavian forefathers for his eloquence and majestic air."[27] In contrast, in "Character" the English are said to "hide virtues under vices, or the semblance of them," and in that respect they are again compared to "the misshapen hairy Scandinavian troll, who lifts the cart out of the mire, 'threshes the corn that ten day-laborers could not end.'"[28] In the same chapter, Emerson quotes a long passage about a certain Halldór in *Heimskringla* and says it "could almost stand as a portrait of the modern Englishman."[29] In "Literature," the English "taste" for "plain strong speech" is traced to Alfred, the Saxon Chronicle, and the Norse sagas. The style of seventeenth-century writing is particularly "hearty and sturdy" and seems to "indicate that the savageness of the Norseman was not all gone."[30] In "Universities," we are told: "The English take culture kindly. . . . It refines the Norseman." Moreover, "the diet and rough exercise" provided by English universities "secure a certain amount of old Norse power."[31] In "Aristocracy," finally, Emerson finds it necessary to go back to the Norwegian Vikings in making the point that "English history is aristocracy with the doors open": "The Norwegian pirate got what he could and held it for his eldest son. The Norman noble, who was the Norwegian pirate baptized, did likewise." So it has been ever since whether you are talking about old established nobility or the nouveaux riches of the Industrial Age: "The foundation of these families lie deep in Norwegian exploits by sea and Saxon sturdiness on land."[32]

Not the least significant aspect of the myth of origin Emerson has elaborated for England is that it is by extension America's. In "Land," the chapter immediately preceding "Race," it is made clear that if

"England is the best of actual nations," "the American is only the continuation of the English genius into new conditions, more or less propitious."[33] I have already cited one reference to "our Scandinavian forefathers" in *English Traits*. The phrase, or some variation of it, pops up fairly frequently, sometimes in surprising contexts, as when Emerson refers to "our Norse ancestors" in "Woman," a lecture read before the Women's Rights Convention in Boston, in September 1855.[34] Nor is this genealogical claim a passing fad with him. As we shall see, he speaks of "the Norse heaven of our forefathers" in *The Conduct of Life* (1860). Again, in the Harvard commemoration speech of 21 July 1865, he says of the "high-bred" alumni commemorated that "they might say with their forefathers the old Vikings, 'We sang the mass of lances from morning until evening.'"[35] Further examples occur in *Society and Solitude* (1870).[36]

The cited passage in the address on "Woman" is also interesting from other points of view. One of them is gender. You might say that it makes explicit the opinion of women implicit in the scant references to them in *English Traits*. The initial statement in the long early paragraph about the oracular and Frigga-like nature of women is that the belief that women have such a nature was a cherished one "in that race which is now predominant over all the races of men." The assembled women are thus given the satisfaction that they share the quality of a goddess and belong to a race that dominates the globe. But the cited statement leads straight to an elaboration of the theme that while woman's intuitive and emotional nature compensates for everything else, including schooling and logic, it also naturally subordinates her to man: "Woman should find in man her guardian."[37]

World dominance is of course also a prominent theme in *English Traits*, and one may note in passing the neat symmetry between the idea of man as the guardian of woman and that of the Anglo-Saxon race as the guardian of inferior races—what Kipling was to call "the white man's burden." But *English Traits* also hints at rivalry between the two branches of the predominant race. Emerson's utterance on the relation between race and world dominance no doubt carries an echo of what Carlyle says on the subject in "The Hero as Divinity," but Emerson and his British friend are not likely to have seen the issue of northern predominance in quite the same way. In "Stonehenge," in which Emerson describes his 1848 visit to the prehistoric monument in the company of Carlyle, he tells Carlyle that he admires the English: "I like the people; they are as good as they are handsome; they have everything and can do everything." But, Emerson says, he knew all the while that when he returned to Massachusetts he would "lapse at once into the feeling, which the geography of America inevitably inspires, that we play the game with immense advantage; that there and not here is the seat and center of the British race; and that no skill or activity can long compete with the prodigious natural advantages of that country, in the hands of the same race. . . ."[38]

THE CONDUCT OF LIFE

America is of course not only a daughter country of Great Britain but also "the heir of all the ages," a fact reflected in the eclectic-anecdotic style characterizing much of Emerson's writing. Whether one views it as another kind of imperialism or as a genuine striving for universality, a book such as *The Conduct of Life* (1860) represents a veritable looting of the international storehouse of quotable language and thinking. Given the prominent role played by the Norse in *English Traits*, it would have been strange if they had been left entirely out of the picture in a book in which no other source of quotations is spurned. A majority of the chapters, which deal with a variety of subjects from a more or less transcendentalist viewpoint, do contain conspicuous assorted references to Norse history and mythology taken from *Heimskringla* or the Prose Edda, and—in one case—from some account of the Norse discovery of America.[39]

However, the use of Norse references in *The Conduct of Life* is quite different from their use in *English Traits*. In the former work it is completely organic; the point that the Norse heritage of England is of the greatest importance could hardly have been made without frequent reference to the Norse themselves. In *The Conduct of Life*, on the other hand, there is no necessary connection between the subject of an essay and the Norse reference(s)—some other international quotation might have done just as well. In this situation my approach must also be different. The unifying theme to be pursued in this case is not one of subject but one of manner. Yet the ad hoc, and in a sense arbitrary manner of quoting the Norse in *The Conduct of Life* is in its way as significant as the persistent and systematic use of the Norse background of Britain to explain the "racial" traits of the English. A critical examination of these quotations will tell us a great deal not only about Emerson's knowledge of Norse lore but also about his method as a thinker and writer toward the end of the 1850s.

I will begin with the chapter on "Power," in which the Norse reference, thrown in between quotations of Bonaparte and Hafiz, has to do with history— the Norse discovery of America—although the introductory part of the paragraph involved is medical in nature. Emerson notes that according to "the old physicians" courage, "or the degree of life," is proportionate to "the degree of circulation of the blood in the arteries." In dangerous or trying moments, these medical authorities are quoted as saying, "blood is collected in the arteries, the maintenance of bodily strength requiring it, and but little is sent into the veins." Moreover, this is the constant condition of "intrepid persons." Emerson is himself mildly skeptical of the physiology of his "old physicians" (making high achievement contingent on high blood pressure) but insists that their "meaning" holds: great performance requires great health. And this is where the Norse example occurs: "If Eric is in good health, and has slept well, and is at the top of his condition, and thirty years old, at his departure from Greenland he will steer west, and his ships will reach Newfoundland. But take out Eric and put in a stronger and bolder man,—Biorn, or Thorfin,—and the ships will, with just as much ease, sail six hundred, one thousand, fifteen hundred miles further, and reach Labrador and New England. There is no chance in results."[40]

To the extent that it simply suggests that good health is an asset in enterprises that require courage and physical strength this statement may be shrugged off as a truism. But the enunciated principle clearly is not meant to be limited to such cases, and the broad equation of courage and health is dubious. The notion that achievement depends entirely on one's degree of physical health and never and in no way on good luck is manifestly false. Even the Northmen knew that; they saw luck and its opposite as quasi-constitutional dispositions that determine one's fate, but they did not tie ill luck to lack of constitutional vigor.[41]

Emerson's use of Norse history also gives rise to some question marks. Beginning with his geography, one may point out that if Eric sails west from Greenland he will hit not Newfoundland but Baffin Island (as some Norse explorers actually did); to reach Newfoundland he would have to sail south, and he would pass Labrador on the way. As for New England, he would have to pass Nova Scotia to get there. Biographically, the passage is just as shaky. To begin with, Eric never reached Newfoundland with his ships. In *Eiriks Saga*, he is said to have reluctantly agreed to join his son Thorstein's expedition to Vinland, but the undertaking was a miserable fiasco; they never got anywhere near Vinland. (According to *Groenlendinga Saga*, Eric fell from his horse on the way down to the ships and returned home.)[42] Possibly Emerson confuses Eric the Red with another son of his, Leif Ericsson.[43] Leif (called "the Lucky") did reach American shores. So did two other Norsemen, Bjarni [Biorn] and Thorfinn [Thorfin], but there is no evidence that they were bolder and healthier at the time than Eric, the settler of Greenland, was at the age of thirty. Bjarni does, in fact, appear to have beheld America first, but only by chance, as he was trying to rejoin his father, who had gone out to Greenland with Eric.

In "Worship," the summary of two passages from "Olaf Tryggvason's Saga" is accurate (except that *Rand* ought to be *Raud*): "Among our Norse forefathers, King Olaf's mode of converting Eyvind to Christianity was to put a pan of glowing coals on his belly, which burst asunder. 'Wilt thou now believe in Christ?' asks Olaf, in excellent faith. Another argument was an adder put into the mouth of the reluctant disciple Rand, who refused to believe."[44] The tone is pleasantly facetious, as in the passage in *English Traits* dealing with the homicidal tendencies of the Norse. It is one of several illustrations of the point that a religion "cannot rise above the state of the votary" ("The god of the cannibal will be a cannibal, of the crusaders a crusader, and of the merchants a merchant"). Now and then an Announcer of "absolute truths" comes along, but even if his message is received reverently, it is "speedily dragged down into a savage interpretation."

The two anecdotes may make the reader smile; they may also distract him or her from worrying about the somewhat one-sided nature of the point they are meant to illustrate. One may feel that the critique of established religion as making too many concessions to time and place is not entirely misplaced. Yet few readers will on reflection agree that religion, Christian or other, never has an elevating effect. Emerson is clearly not out to show us both sides of the coin here. The purpose of the quotations from *Heimskringla*, and indeed of the whole essay, is to ridicule actual religion in preparation for his own announcement of "absolute truths."

The problem again changes as we turn to "Fate," one of the essays in which Norse mythology is pressed into service. "Whatever limits us we call Fate," Emerson notes in one part of the essay. "If we are brute and barbarous, the fate takes a brute and dreadful shape," but "as we refine, our checks become finer," and "if we rise to spiritual culture, the antagonism takes a spiritual form."[45] As a first illustration of this principle, Emerson cites the Hindu fable in which "Vishnu follows Maya through all her ascending changes, from insect and crawfish up to elephant; whatever form she took, he took the male form of that kind, until she became a woman and a goddess, and he a man and a god." (It is intimated that the "antagonism," while very refined at that point, has not ceased to be operative.) The fable out of Snorri's Edda is offered as an alternative illustration of the same principle: "When the gods in the Norse heaven were unable to bind the Fenris Wolf with steel or with weight of mountains,—the one he snapped and the other he spurned with his heel,—they put round his foot a limp band softer than silk or cobweb, and this held him; the more he spurned it the stiffer it drew. So soft and staunch is the ring of Fate."[46]

Fair enough; some kind of point has been made. But is this really an alternative illustration of the general principle previously stated? It would seem that in terms of the earlier analysis the ring of Fate is not always that soft. Nor does the Fenris Wolf's place in the scale of being—he stands for brute and unreasonable violence—appear to entitle him to so ethereal a check. Moreover, it is not really the Wolf's fate that is the main issue in this story but that of the gods. They want to bind him because he is a threat to their very existence, and it is fated that he will one day break loose and swallow the sun as part of a general apocalypse in which the gods of Asgard will perish. Emerson likes to tell this fable, but it does not quite fit the philosophical context.[47]

There is some similar fuzziness in the twin use of Norse mythology in the area of "Culture" where it is argued that culture—personal culture—acts as an antidote to professional malformation and provincial myopia by making people aware of a range of affinities. "In the Norse heaven of our forefathers," says Emerson in the first instance, "Thor's house had five hundred and forty floors; and man's house has five hundred and forty floors. His excellence is facility of adaptation and of transition through many related points, to wide contrasts and extremes."[48] It would appear that the image is intended to help convey the idea that a man should be able to operate on many different levels, and it is not necessarily invalidated because Emerson does not explain this as clearly as one might wish. Nor is the image discredited because the Norse author has nothing of the kind in mind but only wants to impress us with the grandeur of Thor's palace.[49] But the image is simply too grandiose; no one can be expected to relate to other people on five hundred and forty levels. Emerson himself seems to have felt that, because he immediately abandons it, returning to ground level: "We must leave our pets at home when we go out into the street," he adds, "and meet men on broad grounds of good meaning and good sense."

"No performance is worth loss of geniality," says Emerson by way of introducing the other Norse image in this essay: "T'is a cruel price we pay for certain fancy goods called fine arts and philosophy. In the Norse legend, Allfadir did not get a drink of Mimir's spring (the fountain of wisdom) until he left his eye in pledge."[50] Here the analogy is supposed to be with the "pedant" or "scholar" who is positively odious in his community and knows it: "Draw him out of this limbo of irritability. Cleanse with healthy blood his parchment skin. You restore to him his eyes which he left in pledge at Mimir's spring." Note the nimble change of number here: Odin left *one* eye, but Emerson apparently feels that the application of the myth to scholarly pedantic myopia or blindness requires a change to the plural. The application is, however, itself problematic because it deviates too obviously from the Norse myth, which in this case is too well known to be tampered with in this manner: there is no indication that the one-eyed Odin is more morose and pedantic than the original two-eyed one. Nor did he sacrifice one of his eyes in the pursuit of "fine arts and philosophy"; he was chiefly curious to know his fate.

The change of number in "Culture" is a small thing compared with the manipulation of another Norse myth in "Illusion." The source of this myth, the mythology manual in the Prose Edda known in Icelandic as *Gylfaginning*, is mentioned early on in a fine display of universality: "Yoganidra, the goddess of illusion, Proteus, or Momus, or *Gylfi's Mocking* [italics mine],—for the Power has many names,—is stronger than the Titans, stronger than Apollo."[51] "Gylfi's Mocking" is of course itself the story of one long illusion, but Emerson wants to adduce the mockery to which one of the characters in the story, Thor, is subjected in Utgard. Emerson works his way toward it at a leisurely pace, demonstrating the pervasiveness of illusions over a number of pages: "There are deceptions of the senses, deceptions of the passions, and the structural, beneficent illusions of sentiment and of the intellect." Modern science is only making things worse: "And what avails it that science has come to treat space and time as simply forms of thought, and the material world as hypothetical, and withal our pretension of *property* and even of selfhood are fading with the rest, if at last, even our thoughts are not finalities, but . . . each thought which yesterday was a finality, to-day is yielding to a larger generalization?" No wonder if our estimates are "loose and floating," in such a flux. "We must work and affirm, but we have no guess of the value of what we say or do"—and here the Norse myth out of the Prose Edda is worked in: "That story of Thor, who was set to drain the drinking-horn in Asgard and to wrestle with the old woman and to run with the runner Lok [*sic*], and presently found that he had been drinking up the sea, and wrestling with Time, and racing with Thought,—de-scribes us, who are contending, amid these seeming trifles, with the supreme energies of Nature . . . and if we weave a yard of tape in all humility and as well as we can, long hereafter we shall see it was no cotton tape at all but some galaxy which we braided, and the threads were Time and Nature."[52]

Even granting the moral—and that something like it can be read into the Norse story—one may insist that the story takes place in Utgard, the home of the Giants, not in Asgard, the home of the family of Odin. This could be a slip of the pen, not discovered at the time of proofreading.[53] More serious is the fact that Thor does not run against Loki (Thought): His servant Thjálfi (Manual labor) runs against Hugi, later revealed to be the thought of his host, Utgard Loki (not to be confused with the Asgard Loki, who is Thor's companion on this foray into Jötunheim). One also notes that Emerson omits another thing that Thor does do—his attempt to lift the big cat which turns out to be the Midgard serpent. Neither of these changes is likely to be a slip. The first is almost certainly predicated on a desire to streamline the story. As for the Midgard serpent, the author probably felt that part of the fable was too grotesque to fit into his transcendental argument.

The conclusions concerning Emerson's Norse scholarship one must draw based on this examination of some chapters in *The Conduct of Life* are as sad as the light shed on his method of arguing in writing in the late fifties (which again cannot be completely divorced from his method of thinking). The problem is in part that the Norse material is somewhat recalcitrant when it comes to transcendentalist use, in part that Emerson nevertheless insists on using it in pursuit of an anecdotic universality viewed as inseparable from the search for universals. To be perfectly credible, such a way of operating requires careful checking of quotations and rigorous adherence to their actual meaning. But that is a big cat to lift for a universal quoter, and the author of *The Conduct of Life* clearly is not ready to make the effort. Having converted the Norse to small change, he does not seem to care if his coin is genuine or counterfeit as long as he can tell himself that his meaning holds.[54]

3
Thoreau

Thoreau started out as Emerson's disciple and protégé, and it may be more than a coincidence that their interest in the Norse seems to have awakened about the same time. Their use of Norse materials also presents certain similarities of theme suggesting a commonality of inspiration. The references to the Norse are in both cases scattered in prose essays on a variety of subjects that are not in themselves Norse.

However, in spite of these similarities, what strikes one even more in comparing Emerson and Thoreau is their difference. One way of putting it is to say that to Thoreau Norse mythology and history are not primarily useful in fanciful discussions of the characteristics of the Anglo-Saxon "race" or as contributors to universal allusion. As can be seen from the first section of this chapter, he is not a complete stranger to such a use of the Norse. But in *Cape Cod* he proves capable of cool and objective scientific curiosity in discussing whether the Norse explorers made landfall in Massachusetts.

The final section of this chapter focuses on certain passages in *Walden* that also represent a further step in terms of allusive technique. Even in this work we formally remain on the level of the prose essay, but the naturalist's prose sometimes turns into prose poetry, and this is certainly the case in the contexts in which the Norse allusions occur. They are heavy with encoded meaning. My discussion of these instances thus affords a transition to the imaginative potency of the fiction and poetry dealt with in chapter 4.

47

CARLYLE, ETHNICITY, EMPIRE

It is said that Thoreau listened to Longfellow's lectures on "northern" literature as a student at Harvard.[1] But *A Week on the Concord and Merrimack Rivers*, published in 1849 (though based on an 1839 journal) suggests no awareness whatsoever of the Norse tradition. The first evidence of an acquaintance with Norse lore in his writings occurs elsewhere, in "Carlyle and His Works," an article published in 1847, that is, about the time when Emerson was beginning to read in this area in preparation for his visit to Carlyle during his second trip to England.[2] The article shows that the author is well aware of Carlyle's interest in the Norse. "The Hero as Divinity," the lead essay in *On Heroes and Hero-Worship*, is called a "Norse" poem.[3] Carlyle himself is said often to remind one "of the ancient Scald." What is more, the great man—both his essayistic style and his spiritual attitude—are described in terms of Norse mythology also featured in Carlyle's essay. Betraying for the first time his own fascination with Thor, Thoreau twice compares Carlyle to the Norse god of whom the British writer gives so pleasant an account. First, Carlyle is said to answer the question "What is light?" without roundabouts: "He answers like Thor, with a stroke of his hammer, whose dint makes a valley in the earth's surface."[4] A little later, we are told that Carlyle possesses, "though sick and under restraint, the constitutional vigor of one of his Norse heroes, struggling in lurid light, with Jötuns still, striving to lift the big cat—and that was 'the Great World Serpent, which, tail in mouth, girds up the whole world.'"[5] The reference is clearly once more to Snorri's account of Thor's campaign against the Giants. The intended point is also reasonably clear, given the generally favorable tenor of the article. Thoreau does not intend to portray Emerson's friend as a quixotic figure but rather as a titanic laborer in the service of mankind.

In his essay on Carlyle, Thoreau makes no reference to the racial and imperialist side of the former's involvement with the Norse. That does not mean that he missed that part of the message. In *A Yankee in Canada*, a travelogue based on his visit to Quebec in the fall of 1850, Thoreau also reveals an acquaintance with Laing's edition of *Heimskringla*, including the long "preliminary dissertation" on the Norse.[6] In the process he articulates thoughts about the differences between Yankees and Northmen on the one hand and the French on the other that are not unrelated to Carlyle's musings about "the strongest race" in "The

Hero as Divinity" and Emerson's more elaborate racial doctrine in
English Traits. Thoreau's thoughts on this subject may be said to rein-
force their views and demonstrate their representative nature.

The relevant references to the Norse occur in two areas of the
essay. In the first of them, the author describes how he made bold to
approach the red-coated British commandant at the quondam French
citadel. He suggests that there was no Yankee visiting Canada at that
time who was not "more splendidly dressed" than he himself was.[7]
Yet, he says, he enjoyed "some distinction": "I had on my 'bad-weather
clothes,' like Olaf Trygesson [*sic*] the Northman, when he went to
the Thing in England, where, by the way, he won his bride."[8] Thoreau's
identification with the Norse hero is easily the most interesting thing
in this gossipy paragraph (especially as the idea of a personal Norse
affiliation gains a certain prominence in *Cape Cod*). It cannot be separated from his feeling of being in a foreign—French—country, and
three pages later, as he returns to the subject of his cheap "costume,"
he notes that it was "a thoroughly Yankee" one. He seems to be de-
lighted to be abroad, and his account of the Quebec French is by no
means unfavorable in every respect; yet it does reflect something of
the condescending attitude to the nation that lost out in the imperial
struggle for North America that we have already noticed in *English
Traits.*

The difference between the French and the descendants of the
Norse is, however, not considered exclusively in terms of imperialist
success. Thoreau appears to feel that the French would have been
losers, relatively speaking, even if they had been able to keep Canada.
This becomes particularly obvious in the later portion of his essay in
which he notes that Laing derives "the energy and indeed the excellence of the English character" from the Norse rather than the Saxon
strain (a distinction that Emerson, as noted, does not similarly stress).
Thoreau quotes directly from the passage in which the Englishman
relates these qualities to the incomparable freedom and independence of the Scandinavian odalbonde, with this climax: "The individual settler held his land, as his descendants in Norway still express
it, by the same right as the king held his crown,—by udal right, or
adel,—that is, by noble right."[9] At this point Thoreau cannot resist
making a pun at the expense of the original settlers of Canada: "The
French," he adds, "have conquered Canada, not *udally*, or by noble
right, but *feudally*, or by ignoble right. They are a nation of peasants."[10]

Thoreau also has some things to say about race and empire in
"Walking.'"[11] Here, the subject is treated from a rather different point

of view. While not entirely unconnected with contemporary political and social events, the argument is not an ad hoc one predicated on observations made during a particular journey but a more abstract and general outlining of an aspect of the author's philosophy of life— and history—in terms of the controlling image of "walking." There are only two references to the Norse, occurring in one area of the essay, but the important point is that Thoreau does resort to them at a crucial point in his exposition.

"Walking" was completed and published during the early part of the Civil War, at a time when things were not going so well for the North and the loss of the South was a possibility that could not be discounted.[11] In the case of a Secessionist triumph, the future of the North would certainly have lain even more in the West. While the concept of westering is sometimes raised to a metaphysical and metaphorical level in this essay, there can be no doubt about the literalmindedness of the author when he quotes Bishop Berkeley's "Westward the star of empire takes its way." Immediately afterward, New England westering is associated with ancient Norse westering: "Our sympathies in Massachusetts are not confined to New England; though we may be estranged from the South, we sympathize with the West. There is the home of the younger sons; as among the Scandinavians they took to the sea for their inheritance."[12] The reference is clearly to adventurous Vikings sailing west to the Orkneys, Scotland, England, Normandy, Iceland, Greenland, and eventually to Vinland, in search of land and empire. The word *sea* is used metaphorically for the western prairies, likewise open to conquest by those who have inherited no land from their fathers.

Someone else might have elaborated the image a little, comparing the prairie schooners to the Norse dragon ships and *knarrs*. Thoreau goes on to speak of two "panoramas" he has been looking at: one of the Rhine, the other of the Mississippi. The former reminded him of the Crusaders and the medieval past in general, the latter of the future, or rather of a heroic present. But what he really wants to say and has been leading up to, he explains, is that the West he has in mind is "but another name for the Wild." A civilization must not lose touch with the wild if it is to survive. In other words, it is all right if the West is wild, and young men should not hesitate to walk away from the civilized East Coast.

Here the analogy between the young men of Massachusetts and the Vikings obviously does not apply; the westering of the Vikings tended to take them toward civilization rather than away from it. Perhaps Thoreau could have argued with Laing that the invading Northmen brought new vigor to a race that had grown degenerate under the popish and feudal ferules, at the same time using the Anglo-Saxons as an example of what happens when one loses contact with the wild. But he prefers to change the scene and geographical axis, perhaps in the interest of philosophical abstraction. The West is suddenly replaced by the European North as the symbol of the Wild, and the Northern tribes of a somewhat earlier period are painted as invigorating renewers of an effete South: "Our ancestors were savages, and the story of Romulus and Remus being suckled by a wolf is not a meaningless fable . . . It was because the children of the Empire were not suckled by the wolf that they were conquered and displaced by the children of the Northern forests." Here Thoreau can only be alluding to the Capture of Rome by the Goths, an event that, as we have seen, to the representatives of the early "Gothic" revival in Sweden became a symbol of national superiority and a *translatio imperii*.

THE NORSE AND CAPE COD

The work in which Thoreau's interest in *westering* Northmen is most in evidence is *Cape Cod*, a collection of essays based on his visits to the Cape in October 1849; June 1850; and July 1855.[13] In the essays by his hand dealt with so far, his use of the Norse does not really depart from what one might find—or does find—in Emerson. But in *Cape Cod* he goes into territory not visited by his master. Technically, his approach to the Norse exploration of North America could not have provided a greater contrast to Emerson's casual—not to say sloppy—way of touching on the same subject in *The Conduct of Life*. The Norse voyages to Vinland are not the sole or even the principal subject of *Cape Cod*, but they loom large in some areas of this book showing us Thoreau the naturalist and historian at work. At times his involvement with the Norse adventurers assumes a remarkably personal tone, but he is also capable of taking an interest in them for their own sake, not just as a means of illustrating some principle.

In a sense, *Cape Cod* chronicles Thoreau's encounter with the sea. It was an overwhelming experience; his book is the *Thalassa! Thalassa!* of a man long pent up in the womb of the woods. As usual, his account of his experience is a mixture of bookish information and observations made on the spot. Considering his classical background, it is not surprising that there should be a number of quotations from

Homer—in Greek. A bit of philological impressionism is also present, to be sure: "I put in a little Greek now and then," he says, "partly because it sounds so much like the ocean."[14] As a kind of afterthought, he immediately adds, "though I doubt if Homer's *Mediterranean Sea* ever sounded so loud as this." This is where the Northmen come in, the "hardy race, whose younger sons inherited the ocean."[15] Thoreau may not be able to quote freely from Norse literature in the original tongue—as we shall see, he prefers to quote skaldic poetry in Latin translation—but he does say that he was "frequently reminded of the Northmen" at Cape Cod, and the readers of his book are also frequently reminded of them.[16]

An early reminder of this kind provides another example of Thoreauvian impressionism: one summer day, as he came walking along the shore from Boston, the *Datura stramonium* (thornapple), was in bloom, and, he says, "at sight of this Cosmopolite,—this Captain Cook among plants,—carried in ballast all over the world, I felt as if I were on the highway of nations." But he immediately modifies the association: "Say, rather, this Viking, king of the Bays, for it suggests not merely commerce, but its attendant vices, as if its fibres were the stuff of which pirates spin their yarns."[17] Thoreau is wrong in surmising that *Viking* means "king of the Bays," and the comparison may seem far-fetched.[18] Yet its very arbitrariness testifies to his obsession with the Norsemen and their voyaging. He goes on to say that he "heard the voices of men shouting aboard a vessel, half a mile from the shore," but, apparently finding an ironic—and disappointing—contrast with the Vikings, adds that it sounded "as if they were in a barn in the country, they being between the sails." It was a purely rural sound.

Thoreau's suggestion that he was often reminded of the Norse while at the Cape is preceded by the following description of the place: "To the fishermen, the Cape itself is a sort of storeship laden with supplies,—a safer and larger craft which carries the women and children, the old men and the sick, and indeed sea phrases are as common on it as on board a vessel. Thus is it ever with sea-going people. The old Northmen used to speak of the 'keel-ridge' of the country, that is, the ridge of the Doffrafield Mountains, as if the land were a boat turned bottom up."[19] The comparison may seem a bit strained: the step from a storeship laden with supplies and a boat turned bottom up is considerable. Yet the analogy allows Thoreau to take the comparison with the Norse a bit further as he goes on to describe the inhabitants of the area: they "are often at once farmers and sea-rovers; they are more than vikings or kings of the bays, for their sway extends over the open sea also." (He cites a farmer in Wellfleet who had his own schooner and "occasionally ran down the coast a- trading as far as the Capes of Virginia.")

If Thoreau had wanted instead to pursue the keel image and been a little more credulous, he might have adduced a passage in the English-language abstract included in Rafn's *Antiquitates Americanae* in which the Danish professor says that Kjalarness was "so named on account of its resemblance to the keel of a ship, particularly one of the long ships of the ancient Northmen."[20] However, Thoreau does not even mention at this point that Cape Cod may be the Kjalarness figuring in what today is popularly referred to as "the Vinland sagas."[21] This reticence may well be a sign of scientific discrimination. He knew the old Norse accounts of the voyages to North America not only from Rafn's abstract but no doubt also from the Latin translations of the basic texts that the author of the *Antiquitates Americanae* had furnished for those who could neither read Icelandic nor Danish.[22] As a result, he was aware that the Norse texts do not support Rafn's explanation of the name and hence not an analogy with the Norwegian keel.[23] It also becomes clear, when he does mention Kjalarness later, that he is less than certain that the name refers to Cape Cod.

There is, in fact, a note of skepticism in Thoreau's first mention of Thorfinn Karlsefni's expedition to Vinland in "The Sea and the Desert." In this chapter Thoreau does seem to equate the *Straumfjordr* mentioned in the account of this venture with Buzzard's Bay; but after reporting that he and his companion found "one of the principal bones of a whale" washed up on the beach one morning, he adds that "it chanced that this was the most conclusive evidence which we met with to prove what the Copenhagen antiquaries assert, that these shores were the *Furdustrandas* [sic], which Thorhall, the companion of Thorfinn . . . sailed past in disgust."[24] The evidence in question obviously is not very conclusive, and Thoreau is clearly saying this tongue in cheek. What he is really leading up to is a discussion of the poem that Thorhall, who was a skald, composed and recited as he and his men were sailing off on their own. Thoreau does note that Thorhall's disgust with the area they had been exploring was due to the fact that he had found no wine there, but apparently Thoreau is so eager to get to Thorhall's poem that he omits mention of a detail of some importance to a proper understanding of it: that some members of the expedition had gotten sick after eating meat from a stranded whale.

Thoreau is again speaking tongue in cheek when he says he "pre-fers" to quote Thorhall's poem in Latin translation, even though "the antiquaries also give the Icelandic text, because it is the only Latin I know to have been directed at Cape Cod." Here it deserves to be quoted as the only skaldic poetry translated into English by Thoreau from any language:

> Cum parati erant, sublato
> Velo, cecinit Thorhallus:
> Eo redeamus, ubi conterranei
> Sunt nostri! Faciamus alitem,
> Expansi arenosi peritum,
> Lata navis explorare curricula:
> Dum procellam incitantes gladii
> Morae impatientes, qui terram
> Collaudant, Furdustrandas
> Inhabitant et coquunt balaenas.[25]

Thoreau's translation goes like this: "When they were ready and the sail hoisted, Thorhall sang: Let us return thither where our fellow-countrymen are. Let us make a bird skillful to fly through the heaven of sand, to explore the broad track of ships; while warriors who impel to the tempest of swords, who praise the land, inhabit Wonder Strands, *and cook whales*." The Latin version, done by an Icelandic collaborator of Rafn's, can be questioned on some points (this is a difficult text); Thoreau's English translation of it can hardly be faulted (except for the omission of *morae impatientes*). He is of course a very competent Latinist, and in this case he has also penetrated the meaning of at least one word in the Icelandic original: he could hardly have gotten a "heaven of sand" out of the vague *expansi arenosi* if he had not noticed Thorhall's *sandhiminans*.

Thoreau also reveals an interest in skaldic technique as he zealously explains the kennings in three footnotes. One can imagine his delight in noting that "the heaven of sand" is "the sea, which is arched over its sandy bottom like a heaven." In *Walden*, he more than once refers to the transparent water of the pond as a heaven, and in one case, at the beginning of "The Pond in Winter," he even speaks of the "sanded floor" of "the parlor of the fishes," where "a perennial waveless serenity reigns as in the amber twilight sky . . . Heaven is under our feet as well as over our heads."[26]

It must of course be conceded that Thoreau's interest in the Vinland voyages is not primarily of a literary nature. What chiefly preoccupies him is the question of whether Norse adventurers actually reached Cape Cod. His first more explicit comment on this subject, in "The Sea and the Desert," begins with some very levelheaded reasoning. He tells of a "mirage," an optical illusion involving some pools that he and his companion observed as they were crossing "a shallow valley in the desert," and notes that Professor Rafn thinks that the phenomenon in question "had something to do with the name 'Furdustrandas,' i.e., Wonder Strands, given . . . in the old Icelandic account of Thorfinn's expedition to Vinland in the year 1007."[27] Thoreau is skeptical; mirage is "common in all deserts," he says, and these sands are after all "more remarkable for their length than for their mirage." In other words, the explanation of the name given in the Icelandic account (the long time it took to sail past them) is "sufficient and more applicable to these shores." The problem is that you would see a good many sandy beaches if you were to sail "all the way from Greenland to Buzzard's Bay. . . ."[28]

However, no sooner has Thoreau delivered this hard-nosed analysis before he turns the whole matter into a joke: "But whether Thorfinn saw the mirage here or not, Thor-eau, one of the same family, did." Not satisfied with this, he adds that it may have been "because Leif the Lucky had, in a previous voyage, taken Thorer and his people off the rock in the middle of the sea, that Thor-eau was born to see it."[29] Thoreau does not, like Emerson, refer to the Norse as "our forefathers," but he clearly likes to derive his own name from the god Thor, and this is not the only time he associates it with Thorer *(Thorir)*. It is a common, perhaps the most common, Norse name, as he himself points out in his journal as if to make the derivation of his own name from it more certain. In addition to Thorir the Easterner, rescued by Leif Ericsson, he suggests in his journal for 1852 that he might be of the lineage of Thorir the Hound in the *Saga of St. Olaf* and Thorir the Silent in *Harald Fairhair's Saga*.[30]

The tone of Thoreau's etymological-genealogical fantasy in "The Sea and the Desert" is so clearly jocular that it cannot be said to take away from his scholarly stature. Besides, the mirage-in-the-desert theme, and its bearing on Norse voyaging, resurfaces in a strictly scientific vein a little later in the same chapter apropos of the ridge-forming fields of beach grass that Thoreau and his friend described walking across the sand dunes near Provincetown: "Our eyes magnified the patches of beach grass into cornfields, in the horizon, and we probably exaggerated the height of the ridges on account of the mirage."[31] He was "pleased" to learn afterwards from Kalm's *Travels into North America* that the inhabitants of the lower St. Lawrence call this grass *seigle de mer* (sea rye).[32] The reason he was pleased by this bit of information is no doubt that it confirmed not only his own impression but also (and he quotes Kalm on that score, too) that of the Norse voyagers reporting that the grain grew wild in Vinland the Good, thus leaving open the romantic possibility that they were subject to the same mirage on the same spot.[33] However, the question remains unresolved as Kalm also reports that the seigle de mer grows abundantly in Newfoundland and on other North American shores.

The question continues to haunt Thoreau, but when he returns to it in "Provincetown," a chapter that appears to have been written somewhat later, the naturalist has turned historian, and a painstaking one at that. After giving a surprisingly detailed account of the reports of early French explorers of the Cape, he notes that these are the oldest accounts of the area, unless, "as some suppose," Cape Cod is Kjalarness.[34] In that case Thorvald Eiriksson would have been the first to visit these shores (in 1004), unless priority had to be granted Bjarni Herjolfsson, even though he did not step ashore when he got there in 986. Unfortunately, none of the Norse navigators specified the latitude and longitude of the places where they landed in North America, and, he says, with all due respect "we must for he present remain in doubt as to what capes they did see." Indeed, he adds, again agreeing with Laing rather than Rafn, "we think they were considerably further north."[35]

THOR AND VALHALLA IN *WALDEN*

A couple of images in *Walden* have already been cited as hidden parallels to Norse images that come up in *Cape Cod* and perhaps are influenced by them. Overt references to Norse lore are rare in Thoreau's literary masterpiece, whether because he was not yet sufficiently enthralled by it at the time of the experience on which the book is based (the mass of references to Norse literature come in the journals for 1850–51) or because—as Emerson's example would seem to suggest—it does not on the whole lend itself particularly well to transcendentalist adaptation. Still there are two intriguing sets of imagery that deserve to be discussed here, one involving explicit references to Valhalla, the other the God of the Hammer. Properly decoded—everything is not explicit—they show us the author in the uniquely Thoreauvian role of a naturalist who is also a mystic and poet;

indeed, they take us to the very heart of his thought and feeling and together indicate the poles between which his being is swung.

I will begin with the references to Valhalla. In the first of these, at the very beginning of "Baker Farm," Thoreau lists as one of the places to which he was wont to "ramble" the cedar wood beyond Flint's Pond, "where the trees covered with hoary blue berries, spiring higher and higher, are fit to stand before Valhalla." The other reference to the eternal abode of brave men occurs in the passage toward the end of "The Pond in Winter" in which Thoreau describes how the cakes of ice taken out of the pond were stacked up in the open air "in a pile thirty-five feet high on one side and six or seven rods square." "At first" (before they began to tuck meadow grass into the crevices), "it looked like a vast blue fort or Valhalla."[36]

At first sight the two passages may seem disparate. Yet they do have some things in common, notably the reference to the color blue. Thoreau's recourse to this adjective in both contexts is not likely to be coincidental. The color blue is also associated with Valhalla—in yet another manner— in a journal entry from 6 October 1851, that is, from the time when he was still working on *Walden*. In this entry, Thoreau records his thoughts on observing, from a distance, the reach of the Concord River between Bedford and Carlisle: "It is of a light sky-blue, alternating with smoother white streaks, where the surface reflects the light differently, like a milk pan of the milk of Valhalla partially skimmed, more gloriously and heavenly fair and pure than the sky itself. It is something more celestial than the sky above it. I have never seen any water look so celestial. . . . It is such a smooth and shining blue, like a panoply of sky-blue plates," etc.[37] Color symbolism is clearly present in all these cases.[38]

Richard Colyer, in his study of Thoreau's color symbols, notes that blue was Thoreau's "only color for the esthetic, distancing, even mystical atmosphere of meditation"; it is, he says, the color of "sky-water"— that is, water seen at a distance—and of course even more of the cloudless sky itself; it serves to "characterize both the aims of transcendentalism and the sense of the esthetic conditions surrounding the actual activity of perception."[39] Colyer also touches on Thoreau's fascination with the blueness of Concord ice and notes that it stands for purity in a transcendentalist sense. However, this scholar does not mention the blue berries; indeed, he fails to make any reference to Valhalla, thus leaving it for me to try to illuminate the association of the color in question with the Hall of Odin in Thoreau's mind.

It should be noted that the Norse, who were not very transcendentalist-minded, did not associate Valhalla with the color blue. The tree

Laerádr has no blue berries but presumably green needles from which the goat Heidrún nibbles. Eyvind Skaldaspillir, in the section of *Hákonarmál* describing how the valkyries Gondul and Skogul conduct Hákon the Good to Valhalla after he has been killed in battle, has Skogul explain to the surprised champion of Christianity that they are on their way to "the green homes of the godheads."[40] Again, in *Grímnismál,* Grimnir (who should know, being Odin himself in disguise) says the place is "golden shimmering."[41]

Nevertheless, it would not have been so curious that Thoreau should associate Valhalla with the color of pure skies if he had taken the name in the general sense of the abode of the gods, the Norse heaven. Tegnér, who does so in *Frithiofs Saga,* in one passage dresses the gods in skyblue and in another has Frigga braid blue flowers into the hair of King Ring on his arrival in a Norse heaven in which Odin is Allfadir rather than the one-eyed warrior-god presiding over beer drinking. The former Greek professor's Valhalla is an Olympus perched in transcendent blue ether. Thoreau's, on the other hand, appears to be the Hall of Odin, witness the references to trees outside the building and "the milk of Valhalla," not to mention the idea that the place looks like a "blue fort." We are thus faced with the question why he should associate purity in a transcendentalist sense with a place where warriors fallen in battle fight again in the daytime and eat and drink all night. From a transcendentalist point of view, their schedule must seem a poor one in this life and outright pathetic in the next. Yet Thoreau makes Valhalla seem like a very dignified place in the quoted passage from "Baker's Farm," and a connection with transcendence is suggested by the description of the cedars worthy of standing before it as "spiring higher and higher."[42] Nor is the association of Valhalla and its blueness with purity of a transcendental kind in the journal for 1851 in any way belied by the disquisition on ice that follows the paragraph in "The Pond in Winter" comparing the stacked ice to a "vast blue fort or Valhalla."

The latter passage may, in fact, hold the key, or one of the keys, to the question I have posed. The mystery may be at least partially dispelled by looking at some other qualities attributed to ice and by no means unrelated to the beautiful blueness that sometimes characterizes it. The blueness of ice is associated here with the hardness of ice as distinct from the softness of live water, which is more often green.[43] Moreover, the lastingness of ice is dwelled on in the account of what happened to the great pile of blue ice, and it is stressed again in the following paragraph. The crucial point may be the one at which

Thoreau, somewhat inconsequentially,asks: "Why is it that a bucket of water soon becomes putrid, but frozen remains sweet forever?" He answers the question himself, but apparently does not want to take personal credit for the answer: "It is commonly said that this is the difference between the affections and the intellect." It was also commonly said—or written—at the time that the affections pertained to the feminine principle, intellect to the male principle. Emerson in particular liked to emphasize that point.[44] It is permissible to think that the everlasting Transcendentalist purity the misogynous Thoreau associates with Valhalla belongs to the pure and unadulterated male principle.[45]

There are probably those who would rather argue that the belief in the transcendent therapeutic properties of the blue ice associated with Valhalla points to a strong case of the death urge. However, the other theme in *Walden* based on an explicit Norse reference,, while also involving ice, takes us in a rather different direction. It occurs in "Spring," and one may begin the analysis of it with the passage in which Thoreau speaks of his surprise when he struck the ice with the head of his axe and found that it "resounded like a gong for many rods around."[46] On the next page the verb *thunder* is used three times to describe the sound made by the ice of the lake as its breaking up becomes imminent. This theme is followed by a digression on the cryptic ciphers written in thawing sand and clay on the railroad banks: "Thaw with his gentle persuasion," says Thoreau, "is more powerful than Thor with his hammer." The one melts, the other but breaks in pieces.[47] Thor is clearly associated here with the earlier-mentioned thundering and breaking up of the ice. The identification of the Norse god Thor as the opponent of another champion called "Thaw"— note the alliteration—in an ice-demolition contest is likely to appear whimsical at first sight. But the explanation comes as Thoreau proceeds to describe the power of Thaw. He begins by noting that the first signs of a new birth "peep forth" with the stately beauty of the withered vegetation that has withstood the winter, including a plant called "life-everlasting." During his excursions he frequently found these plants "more obvious and interesting . . . than in summer even, as if their beauty was not ripe till then." There are hints of resurrection here, of glorious transfiguration. That theme again is followed up through the introduction of Whitman's favorite symbol of immortality, the grass and its cycle: "So our human life but dies down to its root, and still puts forth its green blade to eternity." If one still does not suspect a cryptic para-religious pattern at this point, it becomes impossible not to when one gets to the next paragraph, which begins with "Walden is melting apace" and ends with "Walden was dead and is alive again." Walden is melting at Easter time, as underlined by the dates furnished by Thoreau. Later, there are overtones of the Bay Psalm Book: ("O Death, where was thy sting?") and a strong emphasis on redemption, a "pardon freely offered to all." "Thaw" thus turns out to have something to do not only with the resurrection but also the redemptory mission of Christ, and the Thaw-Thor opposition rhetorically turns this climactic chapter of *Walden* into an affirmation of the victory of Christ.

The opposition and rivalry of Thor and Christ is a theme that will frequently come up in our study of the American discovery of the Norse. It harks back to Icelandic literature, and there is no reason to think that Thoreau's use of it in *Walden* is entirely unconscious and spontaneous. As Dasent's translation of *Burnt Njal* was not published until 1861, Thoreau may not at the time have been aware of the famous episode involving Thangbrand, the missionary King Olaf sent out to Iceland.[48] But he cannot possibly have missed the passage in Rafn's edition of the story of Karlsefni in which Thorhall, the pagan skald whose verses he cites in *Cape Cod*, argues that it is better to look to Thor for salvation than to Christ.[49]

Thoreau's use of the theme may nevertheless seem surprising in view of his sometimes cavalier attitude to the Christian religion. However, while not a churchgoer, Thoreau is by no means invariably hostile to everything Christ stands for. Besides, the victory accorded the Redeemer in purely rhetorical terms is really that of the vivifying power of spring, the thought of which was as pleasant to him as that of the conservatory power of cerulean ice.

4

Melville

In this chapter we will still be dealing with texts in which the primary subject is not Norse even though they contain significant Norse elements. On the other hand, not one but two new genres—fiction and poetry—are introduced, and one might expect striking differences in terms of allusive technique not only between the essays discussed in the previous chapters and the texts to be dealt with here, but also between the latter works themselves, poetry typically representing a higher degree of imaginative intensity than fiction. However, *Moby Dick* (or, for that matter, *Mardi*) is not a typical novel; nor is *Clarel* a typical poem. *Moby Dick*, the chief piece of fiction to be discussed, contains elements of the prose essay; so does *Clarel*. The poem is not devoid of poetry, but neither is *Moby Dick* (it is, in fact, questionable which of these two texts is more poetic). Not surprisingly, then, the allusive techniques employed in *Moby Dick* and *Clarel* tend to converge. Both the novel and the poem contain hidden or šemi-hidden allusive patterns calling for the decoder's hand.

There are also certain convergencies between the thematic patterns served by the Norse allusions present in *Moby Dick* and *Clarel*. Thus these texts reflect and mutually illuminate each other at a distance of a quarter-century.

As for *Mardi*, the other novel to which I pay considerable attention in this chapter, it supports my demonstration of the presence of partially overt, partially hidden Norse references. The rich patterns of such references in this work, which precedes *Moby Dick* by several years, in a sense makes up for the relative dearth of explicit Norse references in Melville's masterpiece, proving a surprising familiarity with the Norse. Here, too, there are cross-references.

MARDI AND OTHER EARLY NOVELS

Melville's first five books all draw on his own experience as a seaman, as well as (increasingly) on his forced march through the books of the world. In the first of Melville's books, *Typee* (1846), the narrator jumps ship with a comrade and they live a pleasant life in one of the valleys of one of the Marquesas Islands until they discover that their hosts are practicing cannibals, at which point they seize the first chance to escape. *Omoo* (1847), a sequel of sorts, is mainly set in Tahiti. As both these books deal with a seaborne, originally pagan society, one might expect references to the Norse. But there are none in *Typee*. In *Omoo*, one does find a few. A hideous-looking renegade Englishman, who has set himself up as "a war-god" on one of the islands, is compared to Odin. Melville even works in a comparison between the two pagan societies apropos of the obsolete Tahitian custom of making fishhooks and gimlets out of the bones of their enemies: "This," he says, "beats the Scandinavians turning people's skulls into cups and saucers."[1] That statement indicates that he is poorly informed: The suggestion that the Norse habitually used human skulls for banqueting purposes is a startling extension of Worm and Oláfsson's translation error, which only makes the expiring Ragnar Lodbrók say he *hopes* soon to drink mead from his enemies' skulls in Valhalla.

Neither of these references is particularly flattering to the Norse, and the same thing can be said about the ones one finds in *White-Jacket* (1850), a book inspired by the author's year as an ordinary seaman on the frigate *United States*. In one case "the Danish keels of the Vikings" are mentioned, but only in a long list of all the fleets that ever existed, the flagships of which could all come to anchor in the "abounding" Bay of Rio de Janeiro; in other words, the Norse fleets are mentioned only for the sake of completeness, Melville having now caught the bug of universal quotation fever.[2] In a later chapter ("Man-of-War Barbers"), sailors whose hair is ridiculously long are said to "look like Huns or Scandinavians" (the juxtaposition with the Huns proves that *Scandinavians* in this case, as in the example cited above, means *Norse*).[3] As for *Redburn*, the potboiler based on the author's first voyage (published in 1849), there are a remarkable number of references to the classics, the Bible, Islam, and various other traditions, but none to the Norse. It is clear that the sagas are not what awakened Melville's passion for the sea, and taken together these four books might force the conclusion that Melville was not interested in the Norse and knew next to nothing about them at the time.

But wait: there is *Mardi*, the novel Melville managed to produce and publish between *Omoo* and *Redburn* and in which he gives free reins to his imagination in a manner he does not in the other four, more documentary and semiautobiographical books. The story starts out in a familiar way with the narrator abandoning the ship (a whaler) in the company of a comrade, but in this case the defectors entrust themselves to an open boat and the open sea. What is more, the comrade is called Jarl (Norse for *earl*) and hails from the island of Skye in the Hebrides, which was once a Norse colony. He is "the descendant of heroes and kings."[4] His ancestors "were Vikings, who many a time sailed over the salt German sea and the Baltic, married their Brynhildas in Jutland and are now quaffing mead in the halls of Valhalla and beating time with their cans to the hymns of the Scalds."[5] The fact that Jarl is a Viking is underlined rather heavily: thirty-six times he is referred to as "my Viking," This may sound monotonous, but there are many ingenious variations on the theme: Jarl is also called "a Viking," "my good Viking," "the old Viking," "my royal Viking," "my royal old Viking," "my own royal Viking." His royal status, incidentally, is not a mere matter of ancestry. The chapter in which Jarl is introduced is (somewhat incongruously) called "A King for Comrade." His kingship is alluded to again and again. He is said to handle the marlinespike like a scepter.[6] He is repeatedly called "King Jarl."

"Ah! how the old Sagas run through me!" exclaims the narrator as he first introduces Jarl, and his subsequent portrayal of him does suggest some background in Norse lore. It must, however, be said that Jarl's plain-Norse qualities are underlined more forcefully than his regal-Norse ones, and this goes for the outer as well as the inner man. He is big and strong and, although said to be old, has long, yellow hair that streams with the wind. He is "frank as his fathers, although not so much of a buccaneer."[7] As a "descendant of the superstitious old Norsemen," he was "full of old Norse conceits and all manner of Valhalla marvels concerning the land of goblins and goblets."[8] He has one big weakness: "From the sea-monarchs, his ancestors, my Viking had inherited one of their cardinal virtues, a detestation and abhorrence of all vinous and spirituous beverages; insomuch that he never could see any but he instantly quaffed it out of sight."[9]

The big question is: what is the point of this underlining Jarl's being a Viking and a royal one? The passages I have quoted may seem to suggest that Melville, or at least his narrator, does not take Jarl and the Norse quite seriously.[10] Jarl is sometimes made to look less like a king and comrade than an illiterate Sancho Panza, whose function is

to keep a dreaming and impractical master in line. But Jarl's seaman-
ship is never placed in doubt. Nor does the narrator try to conceal
the fact that he would never have reached the Mardi archipelago
without his Viking. It is clearly the close connection between the Viking and the sea that is responsible for his creation. A Norse sea king
is good company if you are "at sea in an open boat, and a thousand
miles from land."[11] The Norse were the first to show how to handle
such a situation, and there are many allusions to Norse seafaring in
the early part of the book. The recurrent reminders that the narrator
and his comrade were sailing in a westerly direction are one example.
Another is the note that there is a rudely carved, open-mouthed
dragon on the prow of their boat.[12] A third is the allusion to the
Midgard Serpent: "How undulated the horizon like a vast serpent
with ten thousand folds coiled all round the globe, yet so nigh apparently that it seemed as if one's hand might touch it."[13] On the next
page, this theme is followed up, as it were, by the following remark:
"The sea serpent is not a fable, and in the sea that snake is but a
garden snake." It hardly makes much sense unless one can assume
that we here have a whimsical pun on the *Midgards[w]orm*.[14]

Jarl is still functional as a symbol of Norse adventure at sea when
he and the narrator board the wreck on which they find Samoa and
Annatoo. He is still prominent as they and Samoa—after Annatoo's
death and their return to their own little boat in the company of
Samoa—rescue Yillah from death at the hands of a pagan priest. But
the Viking begins to fade as they reach Mardi and the novel unex-
pectedly turns into satirical allegory after the disappearance of the
narrator's beloved Yillah and his own apotheosis as the demigod Taji.
In the company of his fellow god, King Media, and the latter's court-
iers (a historian, a poet, and a philosopher), Taji sets out to look for
Yillah—now a symbol of absolute truth—on all the islands, and from
then on the narrative consists chiefly of conversation between these
worthies and others they fall in with during their voyaging. Perhaps
the author had originally had a different, nonallegorical development
in mind in which Jarl would have fitted in as a sea king among sea
kings. One Polynesian ruler is repeatedly called an "old sea king,"
and another is somewhat unrealistically said to have blue eyes and
brown hair—details like these could be related to an original design
of this kind, especially as the Polynesian potentates are also treated
humorously.[15] But Jarl, while as outstanding an emptier of calabashes
as any of the Polynesian sea kings, cannot, however burlesquely, be
transformed into an intellectual and a conversationalist at this point.

After a couple of efforts to make him relevant to the new course of events in the role of an unsophisticated Varangian recruit in Constantinople, Melville allows him to be assassinated by the vindictive henchmen of the priest his narrator killed when rescuing Yillah.

References to the Norse do not disappear completely with Jarl. But they are reduced to stray cases, such as those one finds in *White Jacket*. They do not form any patterns but simply serve the author's craving for a universal allusive framework. If Canute, Norse king of England, is to be mentioned, it has to be in this manner: "Throned on my sea-side like Canute, bearded Ossian smites his hoar harp wreathed with wild-flowers, in which warble my Wallers; blind Milton sings bass to my Petrarchs and Priors, and laureates crown me with bays."[16] By the same token, a description of the magnificent ship of Torf-Egil, "the Danish Sea-king," appears in a long list of magnificent ships sailed by other heroic seamen from Jason on.[17] Perhaps the striving for universal reference goes farthest in the passage in which Woden (Odin) is said to have given suppers: the list of other potentates in history who also gave suppers takes up a whole page.[18] The chief importance of these references, and those in the earlier part of the novel, is that they contribute to the impression that Melville was not really a stranger to the Norse at the time when Emerson and Thoreau were discovering them, even though he did not yet know what to do with this lore.

MOBY DICK

It is now easy to see that the degree of familiarity with Norse lore suggested by *Mardi* is not unimportant as background for my examination of *Moby Dick* (1851), an epic of the sea in which Melville paints another—less humorous—portrait of a sea king who is also a whaleman, using an array of Norse references and allusions for this and related mythologizing purposes. This development is hardly a surprise in the light of what has been said about *Mardi*. What is surprising is the lack of references to the Norse framework in the critical literature on Melville's masterpiece. One must wonder what the reason for this oversight might be. The ability of critics to overlook what they are not specifically looking for, well documented as it is, does not seem a sufficient explanation. Could it be that the references to the Norse have simply gone unnoticed in the universal welter of allusion? That hypothesis also loses credibility when one considers that there is, in addition to a symbolic pattern of "hidden" allusions involving the Norse, a series of obvious references, as explicit as those in the early part of *Mardi,* but less repetitious, more systematic.

The explicit references come first in the novel, and it is convenient to begin with them here. As the reader of *Moby Dick* is well aware, Melville does not introduce Captain Ahab right away. The first reference to the Norse does not apply to him but occurs when Melville after various preambles gets around to describing the ship (in chapter 16). We are told that Captain Peleg, one of the principal owners of the Pequod and once her chief mate, "had built upon her original grotesqueness, and inlaid it, all over, with a quaintness both of material and device, unmatched by anything except it be Thorkill-Hake's carved buckler or bedstead."[19] Although not entirely correct, the reference is ultimately traceable to a passage in *Njal's Saga* in which Thorkel Haki ("the Braggart") is said to have had his exploits "carved above his bed-closet and on a chair in front of his high-seat."[20] Familiar with the passage, Melville could have specified Haki's exploits; however, he prefers immediately to insert another, slightly contradictory but more easily visualized image: "She [the ship] was apparelled like any barbaric Ethiopian emperor, his neck heavy with pendants of polished ivory." This comparison is apt in the sense that the Pequod is also said to be decorated with ivory, albeit "sea ivory." Possibly Melville believed that Thorkel's "buckler or bedstead" was also inlaid with sea-ivory. As for his failure to specify that Thorkel's carved images portray him as having killed a sea monster in Finland and a flying dragon in Estonia, he may have found it inconvenient to work this matter into his description of the Pequod. Yet its suppression surprises since these feats put Haki in line with the captain of the Pequod, whose business it was to kill "Leviathans."

The next Norse reference is already, albeit indirectly, part of the portrait of Ahab. It comes only a few pages later as Melville is drawing his portrait of Captain Bildad, another Quaker and co-owner of the Pequod. Speaking of the Quakers, he notes that some of them are paradoxically "the most sanguinary of all sailors and whale hunters." They do not exactly forget the beliefs and habits formed from childhood, but "still, from the audacious, daring, and boundless adventure of their subsequent lives, strangely blend with these unoutgrown peculiarities, a thousand bold dashes of character, not unworthy of a Scandinavian sea king, or a poetical Pagan Roman." Here the first image is definitely more suggestive than the alternative. It is also the more significant one, as it is really Ahab, not Bildad, who is here—

and not for the last time—compared to a Scandinavian sea king: Melville is about to make a digression in the portrayal of the retired Quaker captain in order to give us a first idea of the character of the hero of the book. "When these things unite in a man of greatly superior natural force," he says, ". . . that man makes one in a whole nation's census—a mighty pageant creature, formed for noble tragedies." (Before reluctantly returning to Bildad, Melville speaks of Ahab's fundamental "morbidness" in an apparent allusion to Hamlet, who was also a Norseman: "Be sure of this, O young ambition, all mortal greatness is but disease.")

Quite logically, then, there is also a reference to the Norse in "Ahab," the chapter in which the protagonist appears in person for the first time. Ahab's failure to materialize during the early days of the voyage creates an uneasy suspense in the narrator, and Ishmael's anxiety is heightened by the heathenish and motley aspect of the crew. He tries to calm his fears by attributing it to "the fierce uniqueness of the very nature of that wild Scandinavian vocation" that he has so recklessly embraced.[21] He is somewhat reassured by the looks of the officers, clearly all fine Americans, and New Englanders at that. But when he finally beholds Ahab on deck, "foreboding shivers" run over him: "Reality outran apprehension." The significance of the reference to whaling as a "wild Scandinavian vocation" with respect to the portrait of Ahab comes from the fact that Melville can hardly have modern Scandinavians in mind but must be using the word in the sense of *Viking* or *Norse*, as we have seen him doing in both *White-Jacket* and *Mardi*. Not only is no officer on the Pequod Scandinavian; there is nothing Scandinavian—in the literal and ordinary sense— about the crew.[22] Nor are any of the several other whalers the Pequod "meets" during her voyage from that part of the world. To be sure, there were Norwegian whalers, but the Norwegians of Melville's time were not particularly wild. On the other hand, wildness is a quality traditionally attributed to the Northmen, many of whom hunted whale. Apparently Melville felt the introduction of his main character required another reference to them. There is supposed to be something wild and "Scandinavian" about *him*.

It should be noted in this context that the next Norse reference in the portrayal of Ahab comes just a few pages later, as Ahab sends a sailor below for his ivory stool: "In old Norse times, the throne of the sea-loving Danish kings were fabricated, saith tradition, of the tusks of the narwhale. How could one look at Ahab then, seated on that tripod of bones, without bethinking him of the royalty it symbolized?

For a Khan of the plank, and a king of the sea, and a great lord of Leviathans was Ahab."[23] Hunting of whales ("Leviathans") is here clearly associated with the Norse. As for Ahab, his status as a sea king is confirmed. He may be many other things, but he is unquestionably that.

The most curious reference to the Norse in the unfolding revelation of Ahab's character and mind, technically speaking, occurs in chapter 41 as Melville reviews the development of Ahab's "morbidness": when the "full lunacy" that struck him after his loss of his leg finally seemed to subside, it did not really do so "but deepeningly contracted; like the unabated Hudson, when that noble Northman flows narrowly, but unfathomably through the Highland gorge." Melville goes on to explain that "as in his narrow-flowing monomania, not one jot of Ahab's broad madness was left behind, so in that broad madness, not one jot of his great natural intellect had perished" (on the contrary, it gains greatly in potency being carried away by and forced to serve his concentrated madness). The Hudson may facetiously be called a "Northman" because it flows from the north to the south, but that geographical note is irrelevant to the context in which it appears. Nor does "noble" strike one as an inevitable attribute of this river. The real, or most important, reason for this comparison is that Melville once more wants to associate Ahab—and his madness—with Norse nobility.

After this chapter there are no more obvious and explicit references to the Norse. But that should not surprise us too much in a book in which even the narrator drops out of sight for long periods of time. One might be tempted to set it down as one of the "discontinuities" in *Moby Dick*, perhaps a change of plan of the kind that follows the insistent portrayal of Jarl as a Viking and sea king in *Mardi*.[24] Yet it can also be argued that the use of explicit references in introducing the ship and her captain has by now achieved its purpose: it has laid the groundwork for a pattern of Norse associations that could not be seen with equal clarity without them. After the preceding demonstration I can only hope that elucidating this pattern will not seem a belaboring of the obvious. It involves, among other things, Ahab's elevation from kingship to godhead.

However, first I want to back up what I am going to say with a few additional notes about Melville's background in Norse lore. I have already noted the uncertainties surrounding the provenance of his references to the furniture of Thorkel the Braggart and sea-ivory thrones, as well as the appearance in *Mardi* of an unidentifiable Torf-

Egil (as mentioned in note 17, the name *may* have something to do
with an earl mentioned in several sagas).[25] On the whole, information about his reading in this area is neither abundant nor precise,
and pinning down his sources is rendered more difficult by the fact
that some of them doubtless are fugitive references culled from works
on a variety of subjects. Yet he did, as mentioned, read *Frithiofs Saga*
in 1848, and in addition to that we know that he borrowed a copy of
Carlyle's *On Heroes and Hero-Worship* from Evert Duyckinck in the summer of 1850, on retiring to Pittsfield to write *Moby Dick*.[26] "The Hero
as Divinity" alone yields all the information about the Norse "system"
posited by my pending argument about a "hidden" pattern of Norse
allusions. The deification of a great man by the people he leads is
one of the main themes in this essay as it is in *Moby Dick*. Finally,
Carlyle speaks of "the old Sea kings" with their "indomitable rugged
energy. . . . Silent, with closed lips . . . defying the wild ocean with its
monsters, and all men and things."[27] Does that sound like Ahab?

Much has been written about Ahab's chase of the White Whale
and its motivation. H. Bruce Franklin has argued that *Moby Dick* "ap-
propriates one of the world's myths—the struggle between Osiris and
Typhon—to arrange its own action and reveal much of what that action means." The identification has its limitations, however; the book
"presents the Egyptian myth of the Savior and the Leviathan he hunts
as a prototype or source of many myths, and suggests itself as a more
accurate version of all these myths." Otherwise put: "Osiris and Typhon
represent a kind of mythical truth transcended only by the mythical
truth which Ahab represents."[28] As for the other less accurate versions of the myth favored in the novel, Franklin says Melville pokes
fun at them—and comparative mythology—in the chapters called
"The Honor and Glory of Whaling" and "Monstrous Pictures of the
Whale." Among those listed by Melville as relevant though inferior,
one notes Perseus and the sea monster (Perseus is jocularly called
"the first whaleman") along with the Christian version of the Greek
myth, St. George and the Dragon. The admission of Hercules, Jonah,
and Vishnu to the club is presented as problematic.

Franklin works out a pretty good case for his theory in the chapter called "Moby Dick: An Egyptian Myth Incarnate." One may note,
however, that he fails to list a Norse myth among the less accurate
versions of the Egyptian myth in the chapters of *Moby Dick* he ad-
duces. (Indeed, no Norse myth is mentioned even among the many
listed as alternative myths he has come upon in his reading of critical
literature: Beowulf's battle with Grendel, Bel-Merodach's struggles

with the dragon Tiamat, and so forth.)[29] And yet there is a highly relevant Norse myth, in line with both Ahab's elevation from sea king to deity and his monster chasing.

As Carlyle, among others, underlines, a basic dualism dichotomizes the universe as conceived by the Norse mind, and it is epitomized by the hostility between Utgard, (the land of the Jötuns) and Asgard (the home of the Aesir). The most prominent champion in the heroic battle against the demonic powers of nature is Thor, and it therefore seems to be a mistake to ignore an apparent identification of Ahab with this Norse divinity in chapter 119 as Starbuck is talking to Stubb about the darkness brought by a violent thunderstorm and associates it with the violent plans of the captain: "The gale that now hammers at us to stave us we can turn it into a fair wind that will drive us towards home" (all they have to do is turn around and sail in the opposite direction, where it is already lightening up). The choice of the verb *hammer* in this context is clearly calculated to prepare the way for the following identification of Ahab with the god of thunder: Starbuck was still speaking when "a voice was heard at his side; and almost at the same instant a volley of thunder peals rolled overhead." The first mate does not know that the voice belongs to his boss and asks, "Who's there?" Ahab reveals his presence by answering, "Old Thunder!"[30]

Thor's long battle with the Midgard serpent is of course a particularly well-known story in Snorri's Edda and one highlighted by Carlyle in "The Hero as Divinity."[31] During his visit to Utgard, Thor fails in his attempt to lift a cat that, he later learns, is the Midgard serpent encircling the earth (Midgard). On a later occasion, he goes on a fishing trip with the giant Hymir, usurps his boat for the purpose of catching the Midgard serpent and almost succeeds. In the end, as Ragnarök is at hand, he finally kills the monster but is himself wounded so badly that he dies. Now Melville goes out of his way to make it clear that the Pequod is all over the place because Moby Dick is all over the place. If one charts the voyage of the Pequod, beginning in New England, one will end up with a line virtually circling the globe (Nantucket, the Azores, La Plata, St. Helena, the Cape of Good Hope, Indonesia, the South Seas to a point south of Hawaii). Moreover, Melville makes Ahab usurp the Pequod to chase Moby Dick just as Thor usurps Hymir's boat to catch the Midgard serpent. The end of the Pequod and Ahab, finally, is as apocalyptic as the end of Asgard and the Aesir.

Most intriguing in the dramatic final pages of *Moby Dick* is the role of Tashtego and his hammer, along with the color red, Thor's color. If Thor goes down fighting and still wielding his hammer, so does Tashtego, and somehow his stance becomes emblematic of Ahab's and the ship's; or let us say that Tashtego (and his hammer) becomes Ahab's final instrument and weapon as he helplessly watches his ship go down. When the captain notices that the flag is gone from the main masthead, he shouts to Tashtego to get a hammer and tack on another. When the whale smites the prow of the boat in which Ahab is sitting, it is noted that Tashtego's masthead hammer can be seen suspended in his hand; "and the red flag, half-wrapping him as with a plaid, then streamed itself straight out from him, as his own forward-flowing heart." At that moment Moby Dick turns on the ship itself, and when it begins to sink, Ahab exclaims in desperation: "What ho, Tashtego! let me hear thy hammer." The last thing that could be seen of the Pequod is Tashtego's red arm still in the act of nailing "Ahab's flag" to the mast.

Even if it had not been for the astonishing series of references to the Norse in the initial portrayal of the Pequod and its captain, the pattern of allusions to Thor's struggles could hardly have been dismissed as peripheral matter on the level of the playful onetime mentions of Perseus and Hercules. Given those initial references, it must be deemed a significant variation on the savior-and-dragon theme, although of course inferior to the author's own "correct" version of this theme.

CLAREL

Written after the Civil War and not published until 1876, *Clarel* comes at the very end of the period to which the American literary discovery of the Norse mainly belongs. The poem was, however, long in the making and is informed by Melville's ongoing struggle for some kind of religious-philosophical certainty. Not only the setting but many of the musings obviously hark back to his visit to the Holy Land in 1856–57, just a few years after the publication of *Moby Dick*. There is a good deal of continuity in the author's associations. With respect to Norse references, there are some curious echoes of *Moby Dick*, including the appearance of a hammer- wielding, monster-chasing Thor. *Clarel* thus also provides some indirect support for my suggestion that such an image is present in Melville's chief novel.

It would not be correct to say that Norse lore is of central importance throughout this Moby Dick of a poem consisting mainly of intellectual conversation between a group of individuals traveling together in Palestine, among whom is a divinity student called Clarel.[32] The author is as much of a universalist as ever and unabashedly makes his omniscient narrator mix the histories and mythologies of all nations and times. Some of the Norse references seem whimsical and inconsequential, not unlike those one sometimes comes across in the shorter poems by the same author.[33] Yet there are also remarkably functional patterns of such references relating to one of the main issues aired in the book: the relation between traditional religion and modern science. The hammer-wielding, monster-chasing Thor appears as this issue is dramatized in a conflict between two of the travel companions, in whose portraits the Norse coloring is as conspicuous as it is diverse.

The first of these two companions to be introduced, and the dominant character of parts 2 and 3, is a Swede who goes by the un-Swedish name of Mortmain ("Dead hand"). Possibly it is supposed to allude to his spiritual bankruptcy. After an unhappy childhood and youth (he is the son of a noblewoman who was not wedded by his father until after his birth) Mortmain leaves the North to become a revolutionary reformer and agitator in Paris during the events culminating in 1848. He gains great personal success and fame, but in the end the experience leaves him disillusioned and despairing of the possibility of doing anything for mankind. It becomes his bitter and monomaniacal conviction that unconquerable evil controls the world. As a result, he decides to drop out of civilization and roves "the gray places of the earth" driven by a desire for extinction.[34] Palestine turns out to be his final destination, and a seemingly travel-guide-style reference to the Norse prince Sigurd's pilgrimage to Jerusalem in 1109 may be considered part of the preparatory portrayal of the Swedish nobleman.[35] Sigurd followed in the wake of a number of prominent Norsemen who had undertaken the same journey after a stormy life. Mortmain (he dies looking at a palm) is definitely to be viewed as a latter-day Viking palmer of noble descent.

Although an aristocrat by birth and an intelligent and educated man, Mortmain is curiously more than once referred to as a "wild Swede."[36] Indeed, both his wildness and his Swedishness are insisted upon in such a way that the concepts tend to become synonymous. This is obviously in keeping with the wildness generally attributed to the "Scandinavians" in *Moby Dick*. More concretely, Melville works in a reference to Iceland as he describes the appearance of Mortmain on a certain occasion: "Like Hecla ice inveined with marl / And frozen cinders showed his face / Rigid and darkened." Apparently the sterile, forbidding landscape of Iceland seemed to him a suitable objective correlative for Mortmain's mental makeup.[37]

However, these lines also support the repeated allusions to the gods celebrated in Icelandic literature, allusions that may be said to prepare the way for the scene setting forth the mentioned ideological conflict between Mortmain and one of his fellow travelers. The first allusion of this kind occurs in the already-quoted canto in which his career is first sketched in what is supposedly a conversation between two of his companions, Rolfe and Derwent: His disenchantment with the course of political events is described in terms of an allusion to Ragnarök and the subsequent, only temporary eclipse of the Aesir:

> What if the kings in Forty-Eight
> Fled like the gods? Even as the gods
> Shall do, return they made, and sate
> And fortified their strong abodes.[38]

This allusion may seem a bit whimsical, and the return of the gods is not in line with the main view of them attributed to Mortmain. That view comes to the fore as he and his companions gaze at the mountains of Moab showing above the valley of Jordan "with cloud-born shadows sweeping through": "The Swede, intent: 'Lo, how they trail / the mortcloths in the funeral of the gods.'"[39] Here the Wagnerian ring cannot but call Norse mythology to mind, even though one realizes that by extension other gods, too, perhaps all gods, are meant. The passing of the gods is symbolic of the fading of modern religious faith, a phenomenon that preoccupies the monomaniacal Swede.

Mortmain's concern about the future of religion becomes particularly obvious in the canto called "The Inscription," in which what one might call the wake of the gods is very much in the foreground. The pattern is more complex in this instance, however. Christ figures very prominently among the gods Mortmain suspects are dead or dying. The gods of the Norse pantheon would implicitly seem to share his fate along with those of other obsolete or obsolescent religions, but the pattern is torn apart when one Norse god—Thor—is suddenly introduced as dangerously alive and well by the other traveler with whom we are chiefly concerned in this section.

The scene of the "Inscription" is the Petraean desert, where the attention of the company is drawn to a rock on which someone has traced in chalk:

> Big there between two scrawls, below
> And over—a cross; three stars in row
> Upright, two more for thwarting limb
> Which dropped oblique. . . ."[40]

It is immediately suspected that the "wild Swede" is the tracer of the cross, which Clarel thinks looks like the Southern Cross. Above the cross they read: "*By one who wails the loss, / This altar to the slanting cross.*" Below is the main part of the inscription, a twenty-one-line elegy confirming that the cross alluded to is the one "set in sky": The beginning goes like this:

> Emblazoned bleak in austral skies—
> A heaven remote, whose starry swarm
> Like Science lights but cannot warm—
> Translated Cross, but hast thou withdrawn,
> Dim paling too at very dawn,
> With symbols vain once counted wise,
> And gods declined to heraldries?

Later, the scribbler asks himself what future nations in the southern hemisphere will think of the cross in their sky: will they class it with Orion's sword "in constellations unadored?"

Derwent, the Anglican priest, is irritated by what he reads; Clarel is intrigued, indeed, "stirred" as he walks away. What he has just experienced ties in with the discussion of science that has been carried on since the company was joined by a geologist called Margoth, according to whom "all is chemistry" and whose special attribute is a hammer. This discussion is resumed in unexpected fashion as Margoth appears on the scene. He lingers for a while in front of the verse traced by the hand of Mortmain, then seizes a piece of chalk left by the scribbler and "rudely scores . . . / A sledge or hammer huge as Thor's," with this legend: *I, Science, I whose gain is your loss / I slanted thee, thou Slanting Cross.*"[41]

The symbolist drama of the "Inscription" is thus found to turn on the opposition of Christ and Thor that we have already had occasion to deal with and will repeatedly come across again. It may perhaps be wondered what Thor has got to do with modern science, but in a sense Melville is following here in the footsteps of Emerson, who associates Thor with the rise of modern industry, which is based on science. The real originality of this particular version of the Thor-Christ story is that the pagan god has not only survived and adjusted to modern times but comes out the winner in the struggle with Christ, if only in the view of the man picked to represent him.

The ethnic affiliation of this man is also worth noting. In spite of the deplorable historical tendency to hold the Jews responsible for Christ's death, one probably should not make too much of the fact that Melville's "slanter" of the cross is a Jew (albeit an "apostate").[42] But it is certainly ironic that the Jewish opponent of Christ should be presented as an incarnation of the Nordic god Thor as well as of an apparently outrageous scientism. Not content with that paradox, Melville has given Margoth a name that, as Walter Bezanson has pointed out, seems to have been put together (rather clumsily from a philological point of view) to evoke the destructive (marring) rage of a Gothic warrior.[43] It will be remembered that the representatives of the first Norse revival in Sweden liked to view the sack of Rome by the Goths (whom they did not clearly distinguish from the Norse) as a symbol of national greatness and that Thoreau refers to that triumph of the people of the North in speaking of the virtues required in the American West. The Rome referred to in those cases is primarily the political entity (the empire), but there is also the Rome of the church, which survived and inherited imperial Roman power. Apparently the Gothic conquest of Rome can also be used as a symbol of a transfer of power from religious faith to science. Margoth's desire to destroy "Rome" is demonstrated at the beginning of the canto called "Of Rome" as the geologist, provoked by the argument of "the Dominican," delivers a scathing rejoinder, from behind a screen but overheard by the scandalized Rolfe and Derwent:

> The broker take your trumpery pix
> Paten and chalice! Turn ye—lo,
> Here's bread, here's wine. In Mexico
> Earthquakes lay flat your crucifix:
> All, all's geology, I trow
> Away to your Pope Joan—go!

Before that, Margoth has, among other things, called Rome "Pounder of the holy hammer"—a clear allusion to the physical similarity between the crucifix and Thor's hammer.[44]

Sometime before this incident, Rolfe, who is not above teasing Derwent himself on occasion, is made to say to the clergyman one morning as "the Israelite" comes into view: "Note, I pray, /. . . / Yon knightly hammer. 'Tis with that / He stuns, and would exterminate / Your creeds as dragons."[45] The Thor symbolism has yet to emerge at this point, but this mythological conflation of the medieval knight killing dragons with his sword and the Norse god falling upon them with his hammer clearly prepares the way for it. Moreover, there is a most remarkable cross-reference to the array of slayers of dragons and other monsters in *Moby Dick* among whom I have included Thor. Rolfe's statement is not a validation of Margoth's point of view; nor can we automatically conclude that the author himself considers this version of the monster-slaying Thor a satisfactory savior figure. But Rolfe's remark must needs color our reading of Melville's subsequent portrayal of Margoth and his cause. It may even cause some of us to go back and ponder again what monster Thor's superior mythological cognate, Ahab, is really out to destroy.

5
Minor Key

So far the subjects of the texts examined have not been specifically and exclusively Norse (although in the case of *English Traits* one might sometimes think it is). In the poems to be discussed in this chapter, the Norse theme is not necessarily treated entirely for its own sake—it may still be used to "illustrate" some point—but it is undeniably the main focus of the discourse in at least four of them (I may stretch the concept just a little bit in the fifth and final selection).

The undividedly Norse focus in combination with the imaginative intensity of poetry may be said to make up for the fact that all the poems, with the exception of *Lars: A Pastoral of Norway,* are relatively short. I suppose they must all be classified as "minor" works. But minor works are not necessarily of minor significance in the conglomerate, especially when there is a general convergence of theme combined with considerable variation in terms of more specific subject matter. Taken together, the subjects chosen touch on most aspects of ancient Scandinavian life. These poems add much to the picture of the American literary discovery of the Norse.

Besides, the authors of these poems were not viewed as minor figures in their day. In fact, Whittier's "Snow-Bound" was long considered a major American poem. Lowell, Longfellow's successor as Smith Professor of Modern Languages at Harvard, was a learned man as well as a poet. In this double capacity he gained international renown and received honorary doctorates from Oxford and Cambridge and from as far away as Bologna. As for Taylor, he was called upon to write the "national ode" for the centennial Fourth of July. His collected poems, like those of Whittier and Lowell, appeared in "household editions."

LOWELL: "THE VOYAGE TO VINLAND"

As a poet, James Russell Lowell was, like so many other American writers of the time, a universalist; when Longfellow suggested that he take a look at Norse literature, he did. The most obvious result of this study was "The Voyage to Vinland," a poem the author himself liked so much that he wrote Norton that he had wanted to make it the title poem of the volume of verse published in 1867 (finally baptized *Under the Willows*).[1]

It is a fairly long piece consisting of three parts. It was also long in the making. In a letter to Charles Briggs of 23 January 1850, Lowell says he is projecting a poem celebrating Leif Ericsson's voyage to Vinland and vows to have his hero sail "straight into Boston Bay, as befits a Bay State poet."[2] Leif is actually the hero of "Hakon's Lay," a poem published a few years later, in which the poet, only slightly less sanguine, celebrates "the brave prow that cut on Vinland's sands / The first rune in the saga of the West."[3] In the end, however, Lowell was to substitute Bjarni (Biörn) Herjolfsson for Leif, and the inspiring minstrel became Thorvald. He says in the already-cited letter to Norton in 1868 that when he finally received the urge to finish the project, he "clapped a beginning upon it, patched it in the middle, and then got to what has always been my favorite part of the plan. . . ."[4] The "beginning" can only be the first part, called "Biörn's Beckoners"; the middle "patched up" presumably refers to the second part, "Thorvald's Lay"; and the poet's "favorite part" is the third and final part, "The Prophecy of Gudrida."[5]

The first part shows us Biörn as a dreamy youth, who yet cannot sleep at night "because the heart within him seethed with blood."[6] His "beckoners," appearing to him in dreams and daydreams, are "yellow-bearded" kings with "grandly compassionless" blue eyes whose fame have reached him and whom he wants to emulate, vaguely conscious of how little time he would have to do so, life being fleeting and dreamlike and even fame lasting only for a while.[7] As the second part opens, Biörn is "still comfortless but for his thought," but things change while he is attending the Yuletide feast for Eric Thurlson. Thorvald, an old bard, is invited to sing, and it so happens that he articulates and puts into words everything that Biörn has vaguely felt: the favorites of Fortune are straight arrows who seek their goal without being diverted by mundane concerns.[8] Biörn (like Leif in the earlier version) is galvanized into deciding then and there that he wants to be a straight arrow:

And then with that resolve his heart was bent,
Which, like a humming shaft, through many a stripe
Of day and night, across unpathwayed seas
Shot the brave prow that cut on Vinland sands
The first rune in the Saga of the West.

However, in the third part, when Biörn and his company after a long voyage behold the shores of America—low, wooded shores—Biörn looks depressed: "Such strange loss there is / Between the dream's fulfillment and the dream, / Such sad abatement in the goal attained." There is no reference to a landing, but Gudrida, the sibyl, is moved to deliver what Lowell in his letter to Norton refers to as "the prophecy of the future America."

"The Voyage to Vinland" is a fantasy, but it is, curiously enough, a fantasy in which historical persons appear in roles that life seems to have denied them. It is true that Bjarni Herjolfsson, sailing from Iceland, came close enough to American shores to see what they looked like, but not because he was an ambitious explorer like Lowell's Biörn—or the historical Leif Ericsson—but rather through incompetence or bad luck: as noted in chapter 2, all he wanted was to rejoin his father in Greenland and spend the winter with him as he was wont to do, and when he saw that the new land had no glaciers, he forced the crew to turn around without going ashore and continued sailing until he reached his intended destination. As for Gudrid, who according to what Lowell tells Norton, "went with them," she did go to Vinland twice (once with Thorstein Eiriksson and once with Thorfinn Karlsefni) but never with Bjarni Herjolfsson. Nor was she a sibyl, even though she once assisted a heathen *spákona* at Herjolfsness in Greenland— reluctantly as she was a Christian—and on that occasion heard her own future foretold.[9]

Such handling of historical data may surprise in a scholar of Lowell's caliber, although perhaps not in a poet of his caliber. On the other hand, only readers familiar with these data are likely to be disturbed by their violation. It is now time to look at "The Voyage to Vinland" in terms of inner coherence and intrinsic poetic merit.

The first part of the poem immediately impresses one with the deft handling of the blank verse, in no way inferior to what one finds in Tennyson's *Idylls of the King*. The use of archaisms and Norse allusions is judicious and restrained. The verbal web is finely woven, with many felicitous phrasings. The overall effect is one of remoteness and at the same time of intimacy. The life-is-a-dream theme is handled very convincingly, and there is a fine empathy with the young man whom ordinary activities do not make tired enough to sleep because he is full of energy and desire to do something big. With goodwill one can view Biörn's situation as a metaphor of the condition of every red-blooded American youth with a measure of personal ambition.

In the second part, the versification has the same Tennysonian ring as in the first part, or almost. The portrait of Thorvald the bard, "white-haired" and "white-bearded," is stereotyped; he is pictured as so old and decrepit that one is surprised when he gets up and delivers his "lay" with force and lucidity. But the image of the "straight arrows" (successful individuals) chosen and dispatched by Fate is worked out very competently, and one is not surprised that Biörn is electrified. One might, perhaps, wish that the word "opportunity" did not appear in this context: "Still o'er the earth hastes Opportunity, / Seeking the hardy soul that seeks for her." Opportunity is not quite the same thing as Fate. Nor does the word sound very Norse but rather calls modern America to mind. On the other hand, America is where Biörn is headed, and perhaps this phrasing can be viewed as part of the transition to Gudrida's prophecy, delivered in sight of the new world.

The third part starts out grandly, and still in blank verse, with a description of the voyage to Vinland (on which Leif Ericsson had not yet conferred this name). It is possibly the most impressive piece of writing in English inspired by Norse seafaring:

> For weeks they sailed, a speck in sky-shut seas,
> Life, where was never life that knew itself,
> But tumbled blubber-like in blowing whales;
> Thought, where the like had never been before
> Since Thought primeval brooded in the abyss;
> Alone as men were never in the world.
> They saw the icy foundlings of the sea,
> White cliffs of silence, beautiful by day,
> Or looming, sudden-perilous, at night
> In monstrous hush; or sometimes in the dark
> The waves broke ominous with paly gleams
> Crushed by the prow in sparkles of cold fire.[10]

Such lines more than make up for the prosiness of the account of Bjarni's voyage in *Groenlendinga Saga*. The problems begin soon after them. The reference to a landfall in Vinland at the end of part 2 having been left standing after the change from Leif to Biörn, some incoherence is caused by the fact that there is no landing in part 3. To reconcile Biörn's failure to land with the ambition attributed to him in the parts written earlier, Lowell generalizes about the gap between dream and reality, but Biörn's disappointment with the shores of America is not really comprehensible if he is not looking for the glaciers of Greenland. Perhaps a disappointed Biörn is more compatible with Gudrida's prophecy than a triumphant Leif would have been; yet there is something singularly anticlimactic about his and his men's dropping out of the story altogether at this point, except as an audience for Gudrida.

About the prophecy itself, Lowell says in his letter to Norton: "I have written [it] in an unrhymed alliterated measure, in very short verse. . . . It does not aim at following the law of Icelandic alliterated stave, but hints at it . . . it runs well and is melodious. . . ." All of this is true, but it is not enough to distract the reader completely from the absurdity of having Gudrida lecture her sea-weary Northmen about "the future America" in terms that would be as incomprehensible to them as they were to her in her sibylline frenzy. One also wishes that she had not been "rapt with strange influences from Atlantis" in doing so.

To be sure, there is an allegorical Norse framework for the prophecy; it is patterned on the final stanzas of *Voluspá* (or Snorri's redaction of this foretelling of the fate of the world). A sympathetic summary interpretation will go something like this: The old gods (sometimes identified as Odin and company) have "shut" the New Land for a long time (presumably because they know its opening will herald the end of their rule). It will, however, open up one day, and when it does, the settlers will within a few generations build a new working world—a world based on equality and opportunity that has everything except "song-craft" and respect for the past. The old gods will have nothing to offer in this situation but will keep drinking "delusion / out of the empty skull of the past."[11] They will hate the settlers, who will hate them in return: "Fateful to Odin, / Here the wolf Fenrir / lieth in wait." Ragnarök will come in the form of an armed conflict engulfing the Old World with its obsolete gods. On its ruins will rise a new and better world sought by "stronger and sweeter" gods, chief among whom will be one who greets all men as godlike: "Is it Thor's hammer / That rays in his right hand? / Weaponless walks he; / It is the White Christ, / Stronger than Thor."[12] Under Christ's aegis, a peaceful but invincible industrial society will flourish, and it will even have singers (although of "birth-carols," not of "swan-songs").

Stated in this way, Gudrida's prophecy sounds optimistic but perhaps not preposterous. Yet there are some further question marks. Perhaps one should not deconstruct an oracle, but if one looks closely at the text, one will see that the phrase "the old world" is used in two senses: in one—vague and general—sense it is a bad and obsolescent old world ruled by bad old gods; on the whole, however, it is the New World already rising in America and hated by the old gods (the one that only lacks "song-craft"), and it is not clear why that world should perish with them (unless, as one fears, "the gods' Twilight" has something to do with the Civil War). The prophecy also contains another, as yet unmentioned theme, a kind of myth of origin that goes two ways: Early on, Gudrida says that the blood of all races and all social strata will go into the making of "The New Man" to rise in America. But, we are repeatedly reminded, she is addressing a group of Northmen, and when she tells them that the new land is theirs to "behold," not to "possess," it is hard to miss the allusion to Moses on Mount Pisgah, and the next stanza does suggest that their descendants are to inherit the land: "Then from your strong loins / Seed shall be scattered, / Men to the marrow, / Wilderness tamers, / Walkers on waves." It will be remembered that there is a similar equivocation in Emerson's account of the origin of the English "race" that according to him is in possession of North America.

WHITTIER: "THE NORSEMEN"

Whittier's poem about Norse explorers in North America has received less than the full attention of scholars and critics. It appears that the last article specifically dealing with "The Norsemen" was published in 1895.[13] The relatively few books that have been written about Whittier, such as those of Albert Mordell and Whitman Bennett, tend to ignore it.[14] Edward Wagenknecht misquotes it in his one fleeting reference to it.[15] Yet it is an interesting poem in more than one way. Quite different in conception from Lowell's "Voyage to Vinland," it also has the distinction of being one of the first "Norse" poems by an American, having been composed in the winter of 1840–41. The author himself appears to have been quite pleased with his feat. "The Norsemen" is among a small number of poems he asked a couple of female-friends to copy for him in August 1841, spurred by a chance of getting published in England.[16] In January 1842, we find him writing to J. T. Fields about publishing it in a volume to be called "Legends of the Merrimack."[17] It was finally printed the following year in *Lays of My Home*.[18]

The title of the volume in which "The Norsemen" was included suggests that we are dealing if not with a myth of origin then certainly with an attempt to domesticate the Norse. So does the title of the mentioned 1895 article defining it as a poem "illustrative of American history." It is clear that Whittier at one time felt his home region was somewhat lacking in historical depth, and while he was by no means uninterested in or disrespectful of the American Indians, it seemed to him that the Norse voyages to Vinland possessed, or could be made to possess, a special significance for Essex County, Massachusetts. The point of departure for "The Norsemen" is a fragment of a rudely chiseled statue found in Bradford, on the Merrimack. In a note appended to the poem, the author concedes that its origin "must be left entirely to conjecture." His conjecture is that it was left behind there by visiting Vikings since "the fact that the ancient Northmen visited the northeast coast of North America and probably New England" is "now generally admitted."[19]

The poem is written in rhymed tetrameters, like a ballad. It is in five sections, the first of which addresses the statue fragment in the style of Keats' "Ode on a Grecian Urn": "Who from its bed of primal rock / First wrenched thy dark, unshapely block?" Next (in the second section), the speaker, referring to himself in the first person, describes the landscape of his "native stream" and the sounds of everyday life in his town that he is so used to—only this time he is distracted by the old gray stone: "My thoughts are with the Past alone!" The daydream begins in the third section: the river valley no longer looks the same; the area is covered by primeval forest; he hears the panther's cry, and the deer are coming down to the water to drink. And then, in the following two sections, the vision: He sees the yellow-haired, blue-eyed Northmen coming up the river in their boats, exploring his home region as at other times they had explored the British Isles and France. However, the vision vanishes as suddenly as it came to him: "The mystic relic seems alone / A broken mass of common stone." It only remains for the poet to draw the philosophical-religious conclusion.

The verse has a somewhat less authoritative ring than the chiseled lines of Lowell's "Voyage to Vinland," and there are a number of factual mistakes suggesting that the author's knowledge of the Norse does not match his familiarity with the part of New England to whose historical background he wants to add them. But even the errors are interesting because of their representative nature. There even seems to be a trace of the widespread confusion of Celtic and Norse for which the Celt Mallet has been blamed. Whittier's statement that "Wild Jutland's wives and Lochlin's daughters" makes one wonder if he knows that Lochlin is synonymous with Jutland.[20] If he does, the juxtaposition of the two names can be regarded as a rhetorical redundancy, and one may assume that the expedition is thought to have left from Denmark (unique as such departure for Vinland would be). But if it did, there is reason to wonder why the poet says, in the final section, that he cannot tell whether the fragment triggering his vision is "A fragment of Valhalla's Thor, / The stormy Viking's god of War, / Or "Praga of the Runic lay, / Or love-awakening Siona" because "no graven line, / Nor Druid mark, nor Runic sign" is left on the fragment of stone to help him determine its origin: this clearly leaves open the possibility that some of the Northmen exploring Essex, Massachusetts, were Celts worshiping Celtic gods. This is not unreasonable in view of the sometimes symbiotic relations between Celts and Scandinavians in Viking times, but the Celtic crew members would have had to be picked up in Ireland or Scotland. Zetland (that is, Shetland, the island off the coast of Scotland) is mentioned in the poem, but only as a place where the Skalds sang "round Odin's mossy stone of power" and in a retrospective account of Viking history stressing the suffering of "the Gael," "the light Frank" and "Iona's black-stoled Culdee."[21]

In keeping with this ambiguity, the description of Scandinavia calls to mind both the gloomy northern landscapes of Celtic Ossian and those in Scott's *The Pirate*, set in "Norse" Zetland: "Their frozen sails the low, pale sun / Of Thule's night has shone upon; / Flapped by the sea-wind's gusty sweep, / Round icy drift and headland steep."[22] It is, however, somewhat incongruous to make it sound as if the Northmen left Jutland in midwinter (in itself an absurdity) but arrived in Massachusetts in midsummer. One might, in fact, think that Jutland is located in the Arctic region and moreover subject to eternal winter as their surprise and delight with the climate change makes them break into saga chanting and Runic rhyming and the poet adds, "The wolf beneath the Arctic moon / Has answered to that startling rune."

The notion that the Northmen on their arrival would be chanting sagas while keeping time beating on their shields is also bizarre,

but not completely out of tune with circulating ideas about the "wildness" of the Norse and misconceptions concerning the nature and
historical background of the Icelandic sagas. Nor is the author of
"The Norsemen" the only bard who thinks that Thor is the Norse
god of war. Perhaps poets are particularly prone to this error because
the name of this god rhymes so nicely with "war" ("Valhalla's Thor, /
The stormy Viking's god of war").[23]

The most original part of "The Norsemen" is the pious philosophical reflection with which the Quaker poet ends the poem,
whether to atone for having fantasized in this manner about a band
of pagan adventurers and their gods or to add significance and valid-
ity to his reconstruction of a chapter in the history of Massachusetts:

> Yet, for this vision of the Past,
> This glance upon its darkness cast,
> My spirit bows in gratitude,
> Before the giver of all good,
> Who fashioned so the human mind
> That, from the Waste of Time behind,
> A simple stone, or mound of earth,
> Can summon the departed forth;
> Quicken the Past to life again,
> The present lose in what hath been,
> And in its primal freshness show
> The buried forms of long ago.

It is, says the poet, as if we were sometimes lent "a portion of that
thought / By which the Eternal will is wrought, / Whose impulse fills
anew with breath / The frozen solitude of death." Moreover, that
powerful thought, whenever we share in it, whispers "of an immortal
origin." It does so "even when it seems / But memory's fantasy of
dreams."

As an intimation of immortality, this is in some ways more like
Proust than Wordsworth, yet not quite like either. The argument in
the latter's famed "Ode" is a Christianized version of Plato's doctrine
of anamnesis according to which adults can still catch a reflection of
the glory of the eternal world by looking at nature with the eyes of
children, who have just come from it. Proust also stresses the incomparable nature of childhood experience, but he does so in a more
secular spirit, attributing to aids such as his celebrated madeleine the
power of conjuring up the past in its primal freshness (this, to him,
means that the past, or his preserved impression of it, is

"extratemporal," and that takes care of the problem of immortality so far as he is concerned). Whittier's statue fragment in a sense has the same effect as Proust's madeleine, but an important difference between him and Proust is that the Frenchman talks about the retrieval and perduration of a past he has actually experienced, whereas the New Englander claims to have resurrected a past that he knows only from hearsay and reading. Such a feat, he feels, requires a sharing in divine power that carries with it the promise of shared immortality.

WHITTIER: "THE DOLE OF JARL THORKELL"

The theme of Whittier's second Norse poem is quite different. He makes it very clear that he disapproves of the pagan Scandinavian religion and the society in which it flourished. It might even be argued that the picture he paints of this society is so dark as to verge on caricature. The sagas certainly have nothing of the kind to tell.

Written at a later time than "The Norsemen," "The Dole of Jarl Thorkell" (ca. 1868) nevertheless gives the impression that the author has been reading up on the Norse. He sees no reason to spare the reader what he has learned. The twenty-eight quatrains of "The Dole of Jarl Thorkell" are sprinkled with Norse names and words: besides relatively well-known ones such as *fiord* and *Yuletime*, one finds *skyr, horg-stone, doom-ring, jokul, jotun, jarl, hersir, vala, fylgja, urdar-moon, Gimli, Hel, Alfheim, Asgard, Aesir, Frey, Njord, Skuld,* and *Frigga.* Perhaps the vocabulary does not render the poem unreadable by the average reader, but it is a learned poem. Learned poems are rarely popular, and I see no sign that "The Dole of Jarl Thorkell" was ever very popular.

The story line is clear and simple enough: There is famine and fever in the land—no fish in the fjord, no grain in the field. Jarl Thorkell slays his cow to Frey (a fertility god) as a gesture of atonement. But the hersir (a district chief reporting to the jarl) says, "The Aesir thirst" and recommends a sacrifice of nursing infants and bedridden old men.[24] The young men loudly approve; the jarl is less happy but does not know what to do. Fortunately, there is a young and beautiful "dream-wife" (that is, vala or sibyl). She is able to convince the jarl that bounteous Frey does not really like bloody sacrifices such as those proposed by the hersir but favors those who like himself are givers of good things. And Jarl Thorkell, who is not a pauper although he slew "his cow" (I suppose the singular is used because it rhymes with "vow" in the previous couplet), breaks three links from his golden neck chain, orders food for the needy to be bought for them, and asks "each man" to make similar sacrifices. Thus the famine and sickness are overcome, and before the year is out Plenty has returned.

It is less clear where the narrated events are supposed to take place; as in certain Edda poems, the evidence is contradictory. The vala is emphatically said to be from "Thingvalla," a name which strongly suggests Iceland, as does the image of "the red torch of the jokul, / Aloft in icy space": Iceland, unlike Norway, is volcano country.[25] Frey had a temple at Thvera in Iceland, a name of which Thorkell's Thevera could be a more easily pronounced and metrically convenient distortion. But the references to jokuls and jotuns fit Norway as well, and the presence of a jarl and a hersir point directly to the social and political organization on the mainland (there were no jarls in Iceland). Rykdal, where Thorkell slew his cow, is otherwise unknown but sounds more like Norwegian than Icelandic. Thevera could be a name created by running together the article and the name of the Vera (valley) in the inner reaches of the Trondheim fjord, which is frequently mentioned in *Heimskringla*. Frey was also worshiped in Trondheim.

One may add that Thorkel[l] is a common name both in *Heimskringla* and the family sagas. The biographical and geographical vagueness suggest that the story of Jarl Thorkell's dole is a made-up one. However, the poet's imagination may have been stimulated by the already-mentioned chapter in *Eiriks Saga* in which Thorkel, the chief farmer at Herjolfsness in Greenland, likewise faced with famine and fever in the land, invites a spákona known as *litil volva* (the little sibyl) to spend a night at his place and tell the people what the future has in store for them. To be sure, Thorbjorg (that is her real name) appears to be a conceited middle-aged woman, noteworthy for her appetite and extravagant apparel rather than for personal beauty.[26] But here Gudrid may have come to Whittier's aid as she does to Lowell's: As noted, this young and beautiful, only recently baptized woman agreed to assist the heathen sibyl on this occasion. The latter's prognostication is as positive as that of Whittier's "dream-wife," and in this case, too, everything prophesied comes true.[27]

Whittier does not say that his sibyl is a Christian, but her message is surely intriguing from a religious point of view. She does not only tell Jarl Thorkell that Frey does not like human sacrifices; she says, "[T]he gods are what you make them." In a different context, this startlingly relativistic-sounding statement would also fit the passage in "Worship" in which Emerson argues that all "absolute" religious truth is adulterated and adapted to prevailing beliefs and circumstances because no religion can rise above the level of its practitioners. Yet the sibyl's message and the outcome of her intervention suggest the opposite: it *is* possible to rise above prevailing beliefs and circumstances to the absolute and ideal (at least if charity can be considered an absolute ideal, something that Emerson denies in "Self-Reliance" and other places). Whittier triumphantly concludes his poem by saying that the "dream-wife" was "wiser than she dreamed" and without knowing it sang of Christ.

This poem is, however, not necessarily just a plea for Christian charity in times of dire distress. There may be a subtext. "The Dole of Jarl Thorkell" tells, after all, about a political dispute the result of which is a levy on the haves for the benefit of the have-nots and the weak and vulnerable in society. The author of "Ichabod" was no stranger to politics, but even if he did not intend it, it is perfectly possible to read a broader suggestion into his text: if redistribution of income by political means works so well in bad times, would it not also be helpful in more normal times?

This could be another reason why "The Dole of Jarl Thorkell" was never a very popular poem.

TAYLOR: "THE NORSEMAN'S RIDE"

"The Norseman's Ride" is a short piece in eight-line stanzas from the early part of Taylor's career as a poet (1846).[28] It was praised by Whittier when it appeared.[29] Today it is of interest as the only American poem of the period entirely focused on Norse eschatology. The Norseman is a dead warrior who rises out of his burial mound and mounts his steed, Surtur, which conveniently surfaces at the same time, and rides off through starry space to Valhalla.[30] That this happens at midnight might make the reader think that he always emerges at that time, like fairies and certain other spirits. But the ride is not a routine one, witness his astonished conversation with himself and his horse: "Far, far around, star-gleams are sparkling / Amid the twilight space/ . . . . / Are those the Nornes that beckon onward / To seats at Odin's board?"

The rider, unlike his horse, is not given a name, and his anonymity confers a certain vagueness and impersonality on the poem, which is largely made up of his observations on encountered phenomena and what awaits him on arrival.[31] The vagueness is increased by the unmarked shifts between observation and expectation, as well as by the fact that some observations seem to come from the author rather than his hero.

One must also say that Surtur is an unfortunate name for a horse on which a Norseman has to ride to see Odin: It is the name of the emperor of the fiery realm of Muspelheim, who is one day utterly to rout the Aesir. Moreover, there is an awkward contrast between the fieriness implied in the name given to the steed and the chilly ghostliness of the beast giving the Norseman a lift in the poem. There is a similar discrepancy between his own alleged reputation as a seasoned warrior-hero celebrated by "the Skalds of old" and the hushed, almost girlish awe that characterizes his reflections during his ride among the stars. From a different point of view, there is not enough contrast between the cold spookiness of the airy path followed by the Norseman on his steed and the banquet hall he is to enter on arrival. The Norse certainly believed in the resurrection of the flesh at least as much as the Christians (Oh Saehrinner!), but the reader of "The Norseman's Ride" cannot feel assured that the mead "poured by the hands of heroes" is real mead, and Skuld's (the youngest Norn's) "star-eye" seems as cold and lifeless as the "star-gleams" surrounding her. It is true that Freya's eyes are said to "outshine in summer / The ever-risen sun," which could be taken as an allusion to her reputedly elevated erotic temperature. But the statement mainly surprises and confuses in the midst of the predominantly nocturnal-hibernal imagery.

Besides, one wonders why the Norseman expects Freya to be dazzling dead warriors in Odin's hall rather than in her own Folkvang (sometimes Taylor, following a well-established tradition, uses the name *Walhalla* [sic] in the general sense of "the abode of the gods," but the mention of Freya follows directly upon a reference to "Oden's [sic] warder" leading heroes "to banquets never done"). On the whole, one might wish the hero's expectations agreed better with manuals of Norse mythology: Where are the Valkyries, who normally carry their chosen slain to Valhalla on their own steeds before waiting on them at Odin's table? Why do the heroes have to help themselves to their own mead?

There are answers to these questions. The general conception of the Norseman's ride and many, perhaps most, of the details are inspired by the account of King Ring's ride to Valhalla in *Frithiofs Saga*. Ring travels to Valhalla on his own horse because he has died quietly attended by his family after committing ritual suicide—*geir-odd*—to gain access to Odin's hall. When he reaches Valhalla in canto 21, Freya (Vanadis) is there (although her bosom is highlighted rather than her eyes and her presence is legitimized by Tegnér's use of *Valhall* in the general sense of "the abode of the gods"). As in "The Norsemen," the Norns are mentioned, but there are no references to the Valkyries—probably because Tegnér in his desire to reconcile Christian faith and Norse mythology plays down the warlike side of the afterlife of the heroes (the gods seem to admire the old king chiefly for his peace-loving qualities).

Canto 21 of *Frithiofs Saga* begins with the old king sitting in his mound with his horse before departing for Valhalla. The horse is impatient and scrapes the floor of the grave with his hoof. Taylor's horse shows his impatience in a similar manner on emerging from the mound. Both horses have hooves of gold. King Ring rides across *Bifrost* (the rainbow), which bends under the weight. Taylor's Norseman says to his horse:

> Not lighter o'er the springing rainbow
> Walhalla's gods repair,
> Than we in sweeping journey over
> The bending bridge of air.

The similarities are interesting as evidence of the impact of *Frithiofs Saga* in America. But the difference between the two texts is also striking. It is remarkable that Taylor was able to recycle so much of Tegnér's material without passing on anything of the joyous sensuousness that characterizes King Ring's arrival in heaven. Compared with "Ring's Drapa," "The Norseman's Ride" seems prim and coy.

LARS: A PASTORAL OF NORWAY

Taylor was not to write any more Norse poems for a while. He, too, was a universalist, and during the next quarter century he favored other cultural traditions; the only sign of an abiding interest in Scandinavia was a book called *Northern Travel* based on a journey to that part of the world in 1856.[32] But in 1872, reportedly during a stay in Gotha, Germany, he produced *Lars: A Pastoral of Norway*.[33] It is a long but fast-paced narrative poem in blank verse dedicated to Whittier. Strictly speaking, the story unfolds in early nineteenth-century Norway, but it is full of references to ancient Norse times, and I am actually not stretching things much if I describe it as a thinly disguised romance of the old Scandinavian North. Taylor, one might say, has simply reversed the anachronism of Tegnér: while the latter updates his Norse original by adding some Christian varnish, the former comes close to repaganizing Norway, or the corner of Norway in which his story is set. *Lars: A Pastoral of Norway* reads like the tale of a pagan Viking who after many misfortunes sees the light and converts to Christianity. The roles played by the women may not be typical of saga womanhood, but they could not be more in keeping with those assigned to their sex in *Frithiofs Saga* or that other Norse-inspired product of the Romantic age: *Harold the Dauntless.* The similarities with Scott's long Viking poem are perhaps particularly striking: Not only does Lars like Frithiof and Harold spend some time in exile; he is also, like Harold, a berserk who, his first amorous engagement having come to ought, gradually mellows under the ennobling influence of another, truly Christian woman.

But Taylor loses no time in alluding to *Frithiofs Saga.* Per, Lars's rival for the hand of Brita, is early on called "That Viking's son, / Whose fathers wore the eagle helm, and stood / With Frithiof at the court of Angantyr, / Or followed fairhaired Harald to the East."[34] Per, a fisherman, seems as steeped in old Norse lore as the fishermen in *The Pirate.* On the next page, in conversation with Brita, he refers to Brynhild. As he challenges his rival to "try knives"with him, his act is associated with the "old Berserker blood"in the veins of the people of Ulvik, his home town or village. The opportunity for single combat comes at the time of the wrestling matches held annually on the shore of Lake Graven "since the days of Olaf." In this uniquely Norse form of wrestling, the participants were hooked together by their belts. Normally it was a relatively innocuous pastime, but with knives involved it is more like the murderous old Norse form of duel called *holmgang.*

The duel ends with Lars, more or less accidentally, killing Per. He is not threatened by prosecution for manslaughter on doing this; such matters, we are given to understand, are settled in the old Norse way in Ulvik, and Per's brother Thorsten vows he will get blood revenge. Nor does Lars fear Thorsten. But Brita, previously undecided between Lars and Per, now wants nothing to do with Lars. Norway is a desert. He decides to go into exile and leaves for the banks of the Delaware, remembering that "his mother's grandsire,"Leif, had sailed to that part of the world with Governor Printz and spent three years in the Swedish colony. In his old age he had praised that country and regretted that "The strong Norse blood could not have stocked it all."[35] *Leif* is of course an allusion to Leif Ericsson; one might say that the Pennsylvanian author views the expedition of Governor Printz as a latter-day voyage to Vinland. The theme is reinforced by the repeated use of the term *Norse* with reference to inhabitants of the region. The people Lars goes to live with are, however, Quakers.[36] He introduces himself to his hosts as "the son of Thorsten"(as Frithiof could have done) and says that his father has told him that "the blood of heathen kings"runs in his family's veins. He underlines that he is nevertheless a Christian, but Abner, his rival for Ruth's hand, takes advantage of his naïve account of his background. Abner shows surprising skill at bringing up the barbarous and homicidal ways of the Norwegians back in pagan times and hinting that nothing good can be expected of a descendant of such people. Lars protests and is supported by Ruth, who says the barbarous old spirit is dead. But alas, it is not dead. One day Abner catches a glimpse of the "rust"-stained knife with which Lars killed Per and tells Lars he is "the proper offspring of the godless tribes, / Who drank from skulls, and gnawed the very bones / Of them they slew."[37] Lars is seized with berserk rage, and Abner escapes with his life only thanks to Ruth's intercession.[38] Fortunately for Lars, he continues to be receptive to her influence. She gradually gets him to adopt the Quaker outlook. He marries her, and for some time the two live peacefully on her father's farm.

However, Lars is lonely for his homeland, and in the final book, after his father-in-law's death, he gets Ruth to embark with him for Norway. On their arrival, Ruth develops misgivings as she sees "the church at Borgum like a dragon sit, / Its roof all horns, its pitchy shingles laid / Like serpent scales, its door a dusky throat": this, she feels, must be a monument of the old abolished worship.[39] Lars tries to allay her fears by saying that he wishes "the dragon in the people's blood" were as harmless as that building.[40] In Ulvik, Thorsten is, in fact, as eager as ever to exact blood vengeance for his brother's death and immediately challenges his brother's slayer to single combat on the shores of Lake Graven. Lars tells him that he abjures "[t]hat murderous law we took from heathen sires," but he is still enough of a Norseman not to want to look like a coward; he accepts. He has, however, no intention of fighting, and when it comes right down to it, Thorsten finds himself unable to kill Lars, who is looking at him with loving Quaker eyes. Ruth steps in with calming words, and Lars chides the spectators who hate to see the fight interrupted with the words, "That God we left, / White Baldur, were more merciful than this."[41] He says that standing there "bared, as though / For runes of death, while red Berserker rage / Kindled in some, in others smouldered out."[42] It is a stark picture, especially for a pastoral, but the story ends as happily as *Frithiofs Saga* or *Harold the Dauntless.* Brita also reappears, is reconciled, and goes off to live with Lars and Ruth in another part of the country.[43]

6

Longfellow

In his *Longfellow and Scandinavia*, as penetrating as it is painstaking, Andrew Hilen underlines that Norse literature was not a major interest of the New England scholar-poet but rather a kind of Romantic sideline.[1] His interest was originally awakened and fed by the "Norse" writings of Gray and Scott. Later, he appears to have read Wheaton's articles on Norse topics in the *North American Review*, and before leaving for Sweden and Denmark in 1835, at age twenty-eight, he may also have been acquainted with *Northern Antiquities*.[2] During his stay in Scandinavia he learned Swedish and Danish well enough to read Tegnér and Oehlenschläger. In Copenhagen, he also gained personal access to scholars such as Carl Christian Rafn, Rasmus Rask, and Finnur Magnússon. Rafn tried to put the American visitor through the Icelandic of "Karlsefne's Saga" (which was about to be published in *Antiquitates Americanae*), and the young professor later acquired a copy of Rask's Icelandic grammar.[3] The latter volume remained partially unopened, however, and Longfellow's knowledge of this language remained rudimentary at best. The only poem of his based on a Norse text is a short piece called "The Broken Oar," inspired by a one-line inscription on an oar washed ashore in Iceland.[4] For his reading of Norse literature he relied, throughout his life, on translations (mainly, but not exclusively, English). Even in translation, his acquaintance with this literature was limited to the Eddas, *Heimskringla*, and a few of the family sagas.[5]

However, his acquaintance with the Poetic as well as the Prose Edda would appear to make Longfellow more well-read in Norse literature than any of the earlier-discussed authors, and if it was not a major interest of his, it certainly inspired one of his major poetic works, and possibly the most successful one: *The Saga of King Olaf.* Before that poem appeared in *Tales from a Wayside Inn* in 1863, he had produced a review with paraphrases and translations of Tegnér's *Frithiofs Saga* (1837), "The Skeleton in Armor," a ballad about a Viking who settled in Rhode Island (1841), and "Tegnér's Drapa" (1847). "The Broken Oar" was published as a kind of coda in 1878. There are also Norse references in works such as *Hyperion* (1848) and *Hiawatha* (1855), the subjects of which are not primarily Norse.[6] His achievement in this domain thus encompasses the whole period I have referred to as the American discovery of the Norse.[7]

This chapter will focus, in chronological order, on the works devoted to entirely Norse topics.[8]

THE REVIEW (AND TRANSLATION-PARAPHRASE) OF *FRITHIOFS SAGA*

In a letter written in Sweden in August 1835, Longfellow told a friend that this country had "*one great* poet, only one," the still-living "bishop of Wexiö," Esaias Tegnér.[9] Swedes will take exception to this verdict and may even accuse Longfellow of ignorance and superficiality in his covering of Swedish culture. But so far as he was concerned, the statement was true and remained true: his relationship with Swedish literature was never to be much more than his relationship with Tegnér. However, that relationship is an important factor in the American discovery of the Norse, and the Swedes will forgive the New Englander his neglect of Bellman in view of what Longfellow did to enhance the international reputation of the author of *Frithiofs Saga* through his "review" of this work.[10]

Not that Longfellow single-handedly revealed this work to the English-speaking world. It had already been reviewed in *Blackwood's Edinburgh Magazine* and the *Foreign Quarterly Review.*[11] As he himself notes in his review, there were two German and three English translations of it. But the English ones in his judgment were so bad that they forced him to make his own translations, and these are likely to have made a difference with respect to Tegnér's American reputation. (One suspects, for instance, that they have something to do with Thomas Wentworth Higginson's desire to produce a verse translation of all of *Frithiofs Saga* and Emerson's telling Longfellow in a letter from 1864 that he had shown him "a new horizon . . . in Sweden.")[12]

Much (eight pages) of the review is taken up by a curiously irrelevant, highly stylized and romanticized description of Swedish nature and country life. However, in the short critical observations that also precede the translations, Longfellow shows good taste when he suggests that *Frithiofs Saga* is too rich in metaphor and other figures of speech. He does reveal a superficial grasp of Norse reality when he excuses this trait on the grounds that the poem was "written in the spirit of the past"—presumably that of the Viking age; as noted in chapter 1, Tegnér's poem is in some respects quite removed from the pagan Norse reality, and a few kennings such as those cited by Longfellow cannot conceal this fact. But this does not prevent the poem from being delightful, and Longfellow does full justice to it as a poet. Although the prose paraphrases tend to contract the original somewhat, he prides himself on being "literal," and he does not omit anything because it might not conform to contemporary New England standards of decency. When Tegnér speaks, in introducing Ingeborg in canto 1, of "*ett silke der det hoppar / ljusalfer två med rosenknoppar,*" Longfellow goes right ahead and translates: "beneath the silken vest of Ingeborg two Elves of Light leap up with rosebuds in their hands."[13] The interspersed verse translations are also remarkably close to the author's intent. Especially the first fragment, the hexameter description of Frithiof's ancestral estate, is uncanny in its ability to evoke the flavor of the original (in spite of the substitution of reindeer for moose). Tegnér himself wrote Longfellow—repeatedly addressing him as *Herr Professorn*—to tell him that he liked his translation better than any other and urging him to complete the job.[14]

One may regret that Longfellow never did produce a complete verse translation of *Frithiofs Saga,* but the reasons for his failure to do so are not difficult to imagine. To begin with, Tegnér, whose mental health was periodically impaired during his later years, did not write his letter until three years after Longfellow sent him a copy of his review, and in the meantime two more English translations of the poem had seen the light of day.[15] Longfellow was a busy man at the time, trying to get on top of his new job at Harvard. *Frithiofs Saga* is a long poem—more than two hundred pages—and what he did translate into English verse is but a small portion of it. Some of the remaining portions are quite difficult because of the baroque wealth of rhetorical figures. What is more, each canto is composed in a different meter, a complication that does not facilitate translation into another language. It was easier, and probably more congenial to the rapidly maturing New Englander, to do the shorter, all-hexameter poem *Nattvardsbarnen* (The Children of the Lord's Supper).

"THE SKELETON IN ARMOR"

Longfellow's own Norse romance, "The Skeleton in Armor," carefully avoids any challenge to developing Victorian morality. The poem, placed first in *Ballads and Other Poems* (1842) contains some echoes of *Frithiofs Saga* but is, on the whole, a product of Longfellow's imagination. Judging by a note affixed by Longfellow, he got the idea while riding on the sea shore at Newport, Rhode Island, and seeing a certain Round Tower there that according to an article by Rafn, was "Pre-Gothic" and hence necessarily from the Viking era.[16] Longfellow associated the tower with a skeleton in armor dug up in the Fall River and believed by some scholars of the time to be that of a Norseman. The result was a tale of a Viking who, like Frithiof, fell in love with a woman of superior social standing, but who unlike Frithiof got his love to agree to run away with him. Sailing west for three weeks, they reach Rhode Island, where they live happily for an unspecified time ("There for my lady's bower / Built I the lofty tower"); the princess, we are told, has the experience of motherhood ("she was a mother"). But one day she suddenly dies and the Viking falls on his sword in despair. A thousand years later his ghost comes to haunt the poet, complaining that no skald has told his story and challenging him to do so or else (the ghost then proceeds to do so himself).

Considering the taste of the time and the level of the public's historical expertise, one is not entirely surprised that this poem, like the volume as a whole, enjoyed great popularity (by 1857 *Ballads and Other Poems* had sold 40,470 copies[17]). Even in relatively recent days it has had its admirers: I find it coupled with "The Wreck of the Hesperus" as a "well-told" tale of the sea in the *Literary History of the United States* and hailed as "a little triumph of seaworthy narrative" by Newton Arvin in *Longfellow: His Life and Work*.[18]

I am not going to discuss literary taste in reviewing "The Skeleton in Armor" even though Poe suggests that one should in the preamble to his review of *Ballads and Other Poems*.[19] However, it must be said that Longfellow did not have a very profound understanding of Norse poetry if he actually believed what he told his father in a letter, that he had succeeded in "giving the whole [of this poem] a Northern air."[20] Choosing the meter of Drayton's "Battle of Agincourt" does not really further that end, and one notes that the wording of the beginning lines (about the "fearful guest" with a "hollow breast") borrows heavily from the end of Longfellow's own translation of a ballad of Uhland's, "Der schwarze Ritter." "The Skeleton in Armor" is

Gothic not in the sense of Nordic but in the sense in which Uhland's poem or "The Fall of the House of Usher" is Gothic.

"The Skeleton in Armor" also reveals the author's insufficient grasp of—or attention to—Norse reality. The problem is not that Rafn's theories about the Round Tower have since been demolished and that nobody today believes that the Fall River skeleton is that of a Viking.[21] (Longfellow himself does not seem to take Rafn's claim entirely seriously, noting as it were tongue-in-cheek that it seems to have been "sufficiently well established for a ballad.")[22] Nor is the idea of a Viking fleeing to the New World with his bride inherently impossible, given the exploits of Leif Ericsson, Karlsefni, and others. But no Norsemen ever sailed to Vinland straight from Denmark, as Longfellow's Viking does; they went there from settlements in Greenland, which is quite close to the North American continent.

Perhaps there is some room for the poetic imagination in this case. But that is not true of Longfellow's description of the part of the Northland from which his hero sets out. If he had been vague about the location of his home, or if he had placed it in Frithiof's Norway, his stylized picture of a dark, cold, wild, and rocky region covered by pine and haunted by wolf and bear would hardly have raised an eyebrow. But his Viking is very specifically said to hail from a spot on the sound between Själland (Zealand) and Skåne, two smiling and well-cultivated provinces. It is the very country that the Reader in Whittier's "Tent on the Beach" correctly describes as "the valleys green / Of the fair island . . . / Lying off the pleasant Swedish [once Danish] shores," but it is hard to recognize in Longfellow's ballad.[23] One is particularly distressed to find the hero hunting not only "the grisly bear" but the "were-wolf" in this part of the world.[24]

This incongruity is not the most serious flaw of the poem. That superlative must be reserved for the ending. It is not unbelievable that the Norse hero would fall on his spear because his wife died.[25] Like regular geir-odd, such an act would render him worthy of Valhalla, and the male companionship of Valhalla is clearly where Longfellow's bereaved hero is headed. The problem is the shocking speed with which the beloved woman fades from the picture as his grieving soul bursts its "prison bars" and ascends to "its native stars." The quoted language, implausible on the lips of a pagan warrior, would fit a widower hoping to rejoin his wife in the Christian heaven, but this Viking is plainly pleased to join the company carousing at Odin's table. The final lines uttered by the skeleton can only be called anticlimactic:

There from the flowing bowl
Deep drinks the warrior's soul,
Skoal! to the Northland! *Skoal!*[26]

It should be added that Longfellow is not alone responsible for this bathos. Tegnér sets a very bad example as he describes the death of King Ring in *Frithiofs Saga*: after committing his oh so discreet geir-odd in the presence of Frithiof and Ingeborg, the old man orders in a horn of mead and, anticipating his own speedy arrival in Valhalla, toasts the wonderful Northland (*du härliga Nord*).

"TEGNER'S DRAPA"

On learning that Tegnér had died, in 1846, Longfellow conceived the idea of writing a "monody" on the bishop the refrain of which would be "Balder the beautiful is dead." In October 1847, he noted in his journal that the poem had been finished and that it had been written "in the spirit of the old Norse Poetry."[27] The name he picked for his poem, "Tegnér's Drapa," is entirely in keeping with this claim. Yet that choice again suggests a somewhat imperfect knowledge of old Norse poetry. True, the skalds deliver "a thundering drapa" at the banquet Tegnér's Frithiof gives in honor of his dead father, and there is a canto called "Ring's Drapa" in which Bragi himself praises the newly arrived king. But as shown by these very examples, *drapa* means encomium (and not necessarily eulogy); Longfellow's poem, or the major part of it, sounds more like a threnody. There are other problems as well if one can assume that not only content but form contributes something to the spirit of a certain national type of poetry. The meter of "Tegnér's Drapa," free verse of irregular length, is certainly more evocative of Pindar than of skaldic poetry. In drawing a parallel between Tegnér and Balder, Longfellow does not follow the precepts in Snorri's Edda (working in kennings as Tegnér does in "Ring's Drapa") but retells the myth of the god's death and funeral in the manner of the ancient Greek poets (carefully leaving out the more grotesque details given in Snorri's account of the event).

This is of course not in itself enough to damn the poem. The problem is that after elaborating the myth of Balder's demise in eight stanzas Longfellow fails to show with any degree of precision how it applies to Tegnér. The connection is by no means immediately clear.

Tegnér may have been a beautiful poet and not bad-looking as a man, but he was not really like Balder. In *Frithiofs Saga*, in which Balder plays so central a role, this god is insistently portrayed as a meek and anemic prefiguration of Christ (he is said to be "pale," "white," "bloodless"); by contrast, the author himself was very much a man of flesh and blood, a lover of feminine beauty and roses and wine, and he could be quite sanguine as a poet, as when he had to be restrained from openly urging the Swedes to reconquer Finland from Russia.[28]

To be sure, Longfellow does not dwell on the paleness of Balder in describing his death and funeral but prefers to highlight his association with the sun:

> They launched the burning ship!
> It floated far away
> Over the misty sea,
> Till like the sun it seemed,
> Sinking beneath the waves.[29]

Longfellow was of course familiar with the idea of dead or dying warriors being set adrift in their burial ships: as noted, Emerson mentions the case of the sea king Haki, and Carlyle waxes lyrical about this "custom" in "The Hero as Divinity."[30] Yet the quoted stanza shows a good deal of originality and power of combination: the Norse account of Balder's funeral has him laid on a ship, but there is no launching, nor any fading into the sunset.[31] Having struck this sublime chord, Longfellow might be expected to add a few stanzas about the sad situation of a nation bereft of its sun, its "*one great* poet." But that is not what happens. After Balder's ship is said to sink like the sun beneath the waves, never to return, the following stanza marks a sudden rift in the narrative texture of the poem:

> So perish the old gods!
> But out of the sea of Time
> Rises a new land of song,
> Fairer than the old.
> Over its meadows green
> Walk the young bards and sing.

This is rather confusing as Longfellow has not described the demise of the old Norse gods, only that of Balder. It is true that the death of the peace-loving Balder is a bad omen for them, but Ragnarök is still far away, and so is the subsequent return of Balder and the emergence of a new set of gods and a set of bards singing "the new Song of Love."[32]

In a following stanza one is surprised to find Longfellow suggesting—at the height of the Mexican War—that the millennium is at hand:

> The law of force is dead!
> The law of love prevails
> Thor, the thunderer,
> Shall rule the earth no more,
> No more, with threats,
> Challenge the meek Christ.

Perhaps this stanza can be explained as a dramatic anticipation of happier times, but the application to Tegnér remains obscure, and one cannot be anything but mystified by the final stanza:

> Sing no more,
> O ye bards of the North,
> Of Vikings and of Jarls!
> Of the days of Eld
> Preserve the freedom only,
> Not the deeds of blood.

Hilen says that "Tegnér's Drapa" is "the key to Longfellow's appreciation of Tegnér": what the Harvard professor admired most in the bishop of Växsjö was "his ability to draw a curtain on the violence of the Norse reality of the ancient legends of the North at the same time that he brought to full poetic bloom the wild freedom, the vigor of life, and the emotions of the heart which were potential in the saga literature."[33] That may well be true. Yet the nonviolent character of *Frithiofs Saga* must not be exaggerated, at least not in relation to the Icelandic original; there may be more violence and "deeds of blood" in this work than in "Frithiof the Bold," and to a considerable extent Tegnér does exactly what Longfellow seems to be telling his successors not to do—sing of "Vikings and Jarls."[34] A less than fully informed reader of "Tegnér's Drapa" might think that Longfellow is criticizing Tegnér for doing so and is calling a halt to the (already moribund) Norse revival.

THE SAGA OF KING OLAF

We are not yet completely done with the Longfellow-Tegnér relationship. Longfellow sings about "Jarls and Kings" himself in *The Saga of
King Olaf*, and while the ruddiness of this work no doubt owes something to the moment of its composition—the eve of the Civil War—
the similarities with *Frithiofs Saga* are too obvious for influence—and
emulation—to be ruled out. In both cases we are basically dealing
with a verse redaction of an old text written in prose (although with a
sprinkling of skaldic verse). As mentioned, *Frithiofs Saga* consists of
twenty-four cantos, each of which is metrically different. In his review
of this work Longfellow suggests that it may "lose something in sober,
epic dignity" in this way, but on balance he thinks it is "a very laud-
able innovation, thus to describe various scenes in various meters,
and not employ the same for a game of chess and a storm at sea."[35]
One notes that while there are twenty-two cantos in *The Saga of King
Olaf*, the stanza pattern is not repeated until the final canto, in which
it is identical with that of the introductory piece.

An important difference between the two poems is that Tegnér's
source for *Frithiofs Saga* is a relatively obscure Icelandic text belonging to the late category of fornaldarsögur but set in legendary time,
whereas the chief source for Longfellow's long Norse poem is the
celebrated *Saga of Olaf Tryggvason*, composed by the most famous writer
of the literary belle époque of Iceland.[36] Olaf Tryggvason, moreover,
is a historical personality, whose life in spite of some legendary additions is largely a given in terms of time, place, and events; one would
therefore expect Longfellow to grant himself less leeway in adapting
the story to his own purposes than Tegnér does. On the other hand,
one notes that he soft-pedals the importance of Snorri's contribution
in the introductory "Interlude" and stresses the idea that *Heimskringla*
represents

> Legends that once were told or sung
> In many a smoky fireside nook
> Of Iceland, in the ancient day,
> By wandering Saga-man or Scald.[37]

One might think Longfellow wants the reader to view his violin-play-
ing fictional narrator ("the blue-eyed Norseman" easily recognized
as Ole Bull) as a continuer of a long oral tradition leaving room for
improvisation and variation.

The question of Longfellow's relation to his given material is not unimportant. We will judge the poem in one way if his intention is to give us a relatively faithful poetic version of Snorri's chronicle; we will judge it in another—in some respects more indulgent—manner if we can conclude that he, like Tegnér in *Frithiofs Saga* or Morris in *Sigurd the Volsung* is out to create a world more or less of his own making, a world that bears a certain relation to an older literary tradition but does not pretend to reconstruct actual history. For this reason, as well as to provide an overview of the contents of this fascinating work, I want to begin by quickly running through it canto by canto, comparing it with Snorri's text.

The introductory canto, "The Challenge of Thor," is meant to state the theme of the poem. It was, however, originally composed in 1849–50 and intended as an introitus to Longfellow's "divine tragedy," *Christus.* It is not based on anything in Snorri's *Heimskringla* history of Olaf Tryggvason but is to be related to the old Norse tradition of making Thor the challenger of Christ, the chief literary manifestation of which is the earlier-cited passage in *Njal's Saga* involving Olaf's emissary Thangbrand. Longfellow does not make use of that passage in any concrete and literal sense, but it appears to be part of his background.[38]

If this canto is introduced rather abruptly and without warning after the "Interlude" in which Ole Bull's violin playing is said to tie everything together, there is a very smooth transition to the second canto, "King Olaf's Return." Standing on his ship on the way back to the country he is to reclaim and redeem, he overhears Thor challenging the Galilean to single combat and loudly accepts it on Christ's behalf. At the same time we are, as it were, thrust *in* medias res. Longfellow picks up the story about fifty chapters into Laing's text, and the major portion of this canto is taken up by the recently baptized prince's going over his life to date in his mind (roughly chapters 1–32, with some added remarks from chapter 92 about the king's character and accomplishments). In his review of Olaf's past, Longfellow omits one seemingly significant event: his marriage to Queen Gyda in England.

After this, Longfellow gives us a selection of episodes from the remainder of Snorri's account of Olaf's career. Canto 3, "Thora of Rimol," tells of how Jarl Hakon, the pagan ruler of Norway Olaf wants to oust, is conveniently assassinated by a thrall in spite of Thora's dramatic attempt to save his life (chapters 53–56). Subsequently, the poet skips half a score of *Heimskringla* chapters: canto 4 takes us straight to chapter 66 and Olaf's wooing of Sigrid the Haughty, which ends with the king insulting the pagan Swedish queen and earning her implacable hatred, which again in due time will lead to his death in a battle involving the king she eventually marries. In canto 5, "The Skerry of Shrieks," which is chiefly based on chapter 70, Longfellow creates an entirely new setting for Olaf's drowning of a band of warlocks and enemies of Christ by binding them to some rocks submerged at high tide. A central role is given to a skald called Alfred (Hallfred Vandraedaskald), whom Snorri does not have introduced to the king until a later chapter. By contrast, Longfellow remains fairly close to Snorri's chapter 71 in canto 6, in which a banqueting Olaf receives a garrulous but entertaining guest whom he later recognizes to have been the wraith of Odin. Canto 7 is a poetic rendering of the story of Iron-Beard, the proud and freedom-loving pagan farmer who is slain by Olaf's men while the king himself is busy vandalizing the temple of Thor and Odin (chapters 75–76). Next, in canto 8 (chapter 78), we get a (somewhat bowdlerized) version of the story of Olaf and Iron-Beard's daughter Gudrun, whom he marries as blood atonement only to find the bride attempting to put a knife in him during their wedding night. Canto 9, "Thangbrand the Priest," deals with the not-so-successful mission of Olaf's clerical emissary to Iceland (chapter 80). Longfellow omits the account of Olaf's torturing the obstinate pagan Eyvind Kinnrifa to death by placing live coals on his belly (one of the episodes Emerson finds so significant in *The Conduct of Life*). But cantos 10 and 11 (chapters 85–87) deal with the campaign against Raud the Strong, the die-hard pagan and sorcerer up north, who is also tortured to death during the attempt to convert him. The following canto, "King Olaf's Christmas," is connected with Laing's chapter 90, in which Hallfred Vandraedaskald meets Olaf in the streets of Trondheim, converts, and becomes "the king's man." But Longfellow, having already introduced Hallfred [Alfred] as Olaf's man in canto 5, develops the story of his conversion in his own way (see below).

In the remainder of *The Saga of King Olaf*, the focus is less single-mindedly on the hero's battle with paganism as events begin to drift toward the denouement. Cantos 13 and 14 (chapters 95 and 102, respectively) deal with the building of the Long Serpent and the hiring of a crew for the biggest of all warships. Cantos 15 and 16, based on chapter 100, take care of some of the complicated events that lead up to King Olaf's last battle: "A Little Bird in the Air" tells of how Queen Thyri, the pretty sister of King Svein (Svend) of Denmark, has been forced to marry old King Burizlaf of Vendland but flees the realm and comes to Norway, where she is promptly married to Olaf; in "Queen Thyri and the Angelica Stalks," the queen chides her spouse for bringing her worthless weeds and challenges him to retrieve her possessions in Vendland—unless he is too afraid of her brother. "King Svend of the Forked Beard" (Canto 17) is a straightforward summary of the events in chapters 108–9: how the Danish king, who has married Sigrid the Haughty, is prodded by his bride to assemble a large fleet in order to punish Olaf Tryggvason and allies himself for this purpose with King Olaf of Sweden, "Eric the Norseman" (Hakon Jarl's son), and Earl Sigvald. The next canto is a free rendering of Snorri's account of the treachery of Earl Sigvald, who after pretending to be Olaf's friend and gaining his confidence leads him and his ships to a place where they are confronted with an overwhelming force (chapter 110). Canto 19, under the umbrella theme of "King Olaf's War-Horns," covers the early events of the battle as described in Chapters 112–16. Canto 30 elaborates the episode involving Einar Tamberskelver so laconically reported in chapter 118. Canto 21, "King Olaf's Death-Drink," deals with the climactic moments of the battle when the king and his comrade-in-arms, Kolbiorn, jump into the sea and are never seen again (chapters 120–22).

The final piece, "The Nun of Nidaros," is a kind of epilogue for the content of which Longfellow alone is responsible: at an unspecified time after Olaf's death, an abbess in Trondheim called Astrid hears a voice speaking in the distance. She cannot identify it, but it is St. John speaking not to her but to Thor:

> It is accepted,
> The angry defiance,
> The challenge of battle!
> But not with the weapons
> Of war that thou wieldest!

From now on, it is going to be "Cross against corselet, / Love against hatred." Love, says the voice, is stronger than anger and conquers all, Christ is eternal. Thor, by contrast, is informed that he is but a "brumal" shape that will disperse with a not distant dawn.

I suppose an epilogue of this kind was needed. Having deviated from Snorri's script by making Olaf's challenge of Thor the leitmotif of his version of the saga, he could not very well end it in the same way as the Icelandic historian: it might have looked too much as if Thor got the better of the king in the end. Having St. John, "the beloved disciple," come in and pick up where Olaf left off is a way of covering this up. Perhaps the cited stanza can also be said to contain an implicit recognition of the ironic discrepancy between the teaching of the gospel and the weapons wielded by Olaf during his tenure as Christ's champion. But I must begin my more critical examination of *The Saga of King Olaf* by noting that the suggestion that Christ's victory is near—as a conclusion to the story just told—looks like a non sequitur. If anything, *The Saga of King Olaf* appears to demonstrate that might is right and that it is indeed still Thor's day.

On the whole, the Thor-Christ opposition, loosely imposed on Snorri's story, is not handled particularly well. In canto 1, Longfellow has Thor introduce himself to Christ before issuing his challenge:

> I am the God Thor,
> I am the War God,
> I am the Thunderer!

One must not chastise Longfellow too severely for thinking that Thor is the war god when everybody else in his time seems to have done so. But it does look like a mistake on Longfellow's part—if he wants to demonize Thor as the challenger of Christ—to have him produce his hammer and say that he uses it to subdue "giants and sorcerers." After all, giants are viewed as demonic powers in Norse mythology, and the sorcerers are depicted as the most obstinate enemies of Christ in Longfellow's own poem. Slaying warlocks, Thor is only doing what Christ's champion Olaf Tryggvason is doing.

Longfellow's use of the Christ-Thor theme is only one aspect of a tension between his "saga" and the text of Snorri, our chief source of information about the events narrated. As we have seen, the New England poet in many respects stays quite close to Snorri, thereby suggesting that he wants to conform to known historical facts, including those concerning the Christianization of Norway and Iceland. On the other hand, there is much that suggests that he is bent upon creating a world of his own that is not always in keeping with Snorri's story or, for that matter, history as we know it from other sources.

The reason is that Longfellow, like Tegnér before him, finds the historical truth and the letter of the Viking age a bit too crude for the sensibilities of a modern audience. One result is a number of anachronisms that in his work are more disturbing than the anachronisms in *Frithiofs Saga* because of the greater historicity of the story he tells. The suggestion that the warlocks killed by Olaf were as awful "as the Witch of Endor" (in Samuel 1:28) and the comparison of Einar Tamberskelver to St. Michael would seem to fit a much more Christian environment than Norway at the end of the tenth century. By the same token one wishes that Thangbrand when arriving in Iceland just before the year 1000 had not found the people poring "day and night" over "their books."[39]

Longfellow's desire to slightly update history and bring it a little closer to a more polite and polished age is also reflected in his versification. He does favor falling rhythms as more Teutonic sounding than iambs and anapests, and his line is sometimes short enough to pass for an allusion to Norse poetry. But there is no serious attempt to reproduce the effect of skaldic verse, so generously quoted by Snorri—no kennings, no alliteration. Instead, rhyme is *de rigueur*, except in "The Challenge of Thor" and "The Nun of Nidaros." Varying the rhyme pattern is one of Longfellow's chief means of varying the stanzaic structure.

In this context one must note the influence of Danish and Swedish folk ballads, of which Longfellow was excessively fond.[40] As mentioned in the introduction, these are not strictly Norse texts, being written in "modern" forms of Scandinavian. Longfellow may have been as capable of overlooking this fact as Emerson.[41] In any case, he imitates the Scandinavian ballads—meter, rhyme, and refrains—in *The Saga of King Olaf*.[42] Perhaps that is not in itself absurd in terms of his purpose: to envelop the inevitably rough surface of Norse life with a gentler wrapping; it is anachronistic, but only in the sense in which a production of *Hamlet* in nineteenth-century costumes is anachronistic. However, the borrowed refrains do not always seem to fit the context in the strict sense. Particularly curious is the insistent use of the refrain "Dead rides Sir Morten of Fogelsong" in the canto in which Olaf is visited by the wraith of Odin.[43] To be sure, Sir Morten is also a wraith, but there his relevance ends. It is a rather early anticipation of the allusive technique used in "The Waste Land."

Almost as surprising is the refrain from a Danish folk ballad used in canto 4 to characterize Queen Sigrid the Haughty:

> Queen Sigrid the Haughty sat proud
> and aloft
> In her chamber, that looked over meadow
> and croft.
> Heart's dearest,
> Why dost thou sorrow so?

Nothing in the queen's situation as described by Longfellow really calls for such a refrain.[44] Nor does this suggestion of tenderhearted melancholy fit what is known about the queen's character. It seems completely out of place when the wooing comes to an abrupt end as the king slaps the queen in the face and utters some very unchivalrous words on being told that she has no intention of converting to Christianity:

> Queen Sigrid the Haughty said under
> her breath,
> "This insult, King Olaf, shall be thy
> death!"
> Heart's dearest,
> Why dost thou sorrow so?

This canto also illustrates a certain tendency on Longfellow's part to retouch Snorri's portraits of Norse women to bring them in line with the ideas about womanhood cherished by many in his own day. A pretty clear instance of what Foucault calls the Victorian "hysterization" of women occurs in the previous canto.[45] Longfellow clearly falsifies the character of the resourceful and determined Thora when he portrays her as weeping while she keeps Jarl Hakon hidden under her pig sty and swooning when he has been betrayed and decapitated by his attendant thrall. There is no support in Snorri's text for this.

The omission of the episode in Olaf's early life involving the young, pretty, and widowed Queen Gyda in England also seems significant in this context. It will be remembered that Thoreau says Olaf "won his bride there." Actually, she picked him out as the most eligible bachelor in a crowd of men lined up for her inspection. No doubt she was taking advantage of her royal rank in doing this, but basically she was merely exercising her right as a Norse widow to pick her own husband. Longfellow is likely to have viewed her as unspeakably aggressive.

It is true that in Gudrun's attempt to assassinate Olaf, her father's slayer, during their wedding night one may recognize the grit of true saga women.[46] But then, as already noted, Longfellow gives a somewhat bowdlerized account of other activities that night. In "Thora of Rimol," Longfellow deliberately changes historical fact—as given by Snorri—for apparently prudish reasons. Jarl Hakon is not fleeing from the Christian pretender and his "men in mail," as Longfellow suggests, but from the farmers who have finally lost patience with his habit of sending for their daughters and wives so that he could sleep with them for a week or two. Longfellow says nothing about the jarl's libertinage.[47]

The New England poet plainly seems more comfortable joining the two sexes in androgynous terms. In canto 14, his tone is rapt as he portrays the youngest man on the Long Serpent:

> Einar Tamberskelver, bare
> To the winds his golden hair,
>   By the mainmast stood;
> Graceful was his form, and slender,
> And his eyes were deep and tender
> As a woman's, in the splendor
>   Of her maidenhood.

He does not leave the matter there but gives Einar a ballad of his own in the account of the battle of Svald. Instead of Snorri's laconic words we get this final stanza:

> Then, with smile of joy defiant
>   On his beardless lip,
> Scaled he, light and self-reliant,
>   Eric's dragon ship.
> Loose his golden locks were flowing,
>   Bright his armor gleamed;
> Like Saint Michael overthrowing
>   Lucifer he seemed.

Such stanzas seem to appeal to a peculiar kind of Victorian sensibility. So does the description of the inseparable companionship of Olaf and Kolbiorn during the same battle: Longfellow stresses the similar appearances of the two. As the deck of the Long Serpent is being cleared and Earl Eric is looking for Olaf, he suddenly sees "two kingly figures arise":

> Two shields raised high in the air,
> Two flashes of golden hair,
> Two scarlet meteors' glare,
>   And both have leaped from the ship.

In spite of his early triumph in England, King Olaf does not come through as a ladies' man. The first two marriages he attempts after his return to the Northland are political and end badly. Yet romance, as noted, comes to him in the end in the form of the young and pretty Queen Thyri. "A Little bird in the Air," the ballad in which the two get together, is exceedingly charming, and so is the following one, in which Olaf redeems the faux pas of presenting the fugitive queen with a pretty but from a business standpoint worthless angelica stalk by mounting a naval expedition for the express purpose of recovering her property in Vendland. As Olaf returns, triumphant, he reveals a gallant and *courtois* side of which Snorri seems to have been unaware:

> Then said Olaf, laughing,
> "Not ten yoke of oxen
>   Have the power to draw us
>   Like a woman's hair!
> "Now will I confess it,
>   Better things are jewels
> Than angelica stalks are
>   For a Queen to wear."

Whether true to the historical Olaf or not, this episode adds to the portrait of Longfellow's protagonist, and other ballads in which he handles Snorri's matter freely, yet skillfully, add further traits to the picture. Considerations of space only allow me to deal with one more example, "King Olaf's Christmas," remarkable for the manner in which the central theme of the poem is integrated with the portrayal of the king's character: Olaf is reveling with his berserks and bishops. The berserks (Longfellow seems to think that all the king's men are berserks) are making "the sign of the Hammer of Thor" over their drinking horns. In the meantime the king places his sword in front of his skald (Alfred) and says he is to have it if he sings a song "with a sword in every line." As the skald is acquitting himself of this task, the berserks shout "Long live the Sword, / And the King!" He has hardly fulfilled this condition, however, before the king adds another one, raising the "cross-shaped" hilt of the sword and telling him to choose carefully between Thor's hammer and Christ's cross. The skald then kisses the cross-shaped sword hilt in sign of submission to Christ. At that very point the sun rises outside, with a miraculous result:

> On the shining wall a vast
> And shadowy cross was cast
>   From the hilt of the lifted sword,

> And in foaming cups of ale
> The Berserks drank "Was-Hael!
> To the Lord!"

It is all very clever, the sword and the cross being pretty much the same thing to the king.

This canto is further evidence that Longfellow was not blind to the ironic discrepancy between the gospel of Christ and Olaf's way of Christianizing Norway. Perhaps it can also be argued that he sees the battle between Thor and Christ as raging in the king's heart as well as in the Northland. But if it does, Christ cannot be said to make much headway; unlike the pagan hero of *Frithiofs Saga* and Scott's *Harold the Dauntless*, Olaf does not grow noticeably meeker and milder in the course of the story. Nor is this something to be deplored. It simply means that when it comes to the crucial matter of his hero's character, Longfellow puts his retouching brush aside. In a sense, he has no choice but to do so: Snorri's Olaf is not easily "emasculated." But Longfellow ought to be given some credit for the manner in which he handles the least ingratiating side of his hero. He may leave out the episode involving Eyvind Kinnrifa and fail to mention that the report Thangbrand brought back from Iceland caused the king to order all Icelanders in Norway to be rounded up. But he leaves in the torture killing of Raud and the slaying of the old Iron-Beard; he exposes Olaf's chilling insensitivity to the shrieks of the drowning wizards. The result of this balancing act is a very credible portrait of the central character. King Olaf lives in these ballads.

7

The Women Writers

The prominent women writers to be dealt with in the first section of this chapter, with the exception of Harriet Beecher Stowe, are somewhat marginal to the period with which we are mainly concerned, roughly 1840–65. Alcott was born in 1832 and did not publish anything in the forties; *Moods*, her first novel, was not published until 1865. Dickinson (born in 1830) did not really get going writing poetry until the late fifties, even though the first item in *Complete Poems* is dated Valentine's Day, 1850.[1] Fuller was already writing and publishing in the forties, but she did not live beyond that decade and was not involved in the full bloom of the American discovery of the Norse.

It must also be said that none of the prominent women writers of the time shows sufficient interest in things Norse to make it possible to write chapters about them like those I have written about Emerson, Thoreau, Melville, and Longfellow. It therefore seems fitting to group them together in a final chapter. To omit them altogether would be to omit an opportunity to touch on some of the ways in which gender may have affected the use of Norse themes at the time. Moreover, demonstrating the inexistent or scant interest in the Norse on the part of the most celebrated women writers of the time helps buttress the point that the American literary discovery of the Norse was basically the achievement of a relatively small group of male writers during a well-defined time period.

I will not end my chapter about the women writers on a negative note. Margaret Fuller has a fair number of references to Norseland, such as they are. Besides, in the second section of this chapter I will break open the canon and introduce a not-so-well-known woman writer who did indeed care about the Norse: Julia Clinton Jones. In purely chronological terms she, too, is somewhat marginal. *Valhalla*, her first publication, which is the one that interests us here, did not appear until 1878, that is, the same year as Longfellow's last "Norse" poem, "The Broken Oar." It is, however, a kind of throwback to the romantic heyday of the Norse revival in Europe and America, and as such it undoubtedly deserves to be included here. It is also one of those unique creations that tend to shatter established patterns. Its length and scope makes it the only American poem of its kind fit to stand beside Longfellow's *Saga of King Olaf.*

FOUR FAMOUS WOMEN WRITERS

As one peruses the works of Harriet Beecher Stowe, one is faced with an absence of Norse references as absolute as in those of Hawthorne: nothing in her antislavery novels, *Uncle Tom's Cabin* and the interminable *Dred*; nothing in the books devoted to the New England past, such as *The Minister's Wooing, The Pearl of Orr's Island,* and *Oldtown Folks*; nothing in her "Italian" novel, *Agnes of Sorrento.*[2]

Faced with such an attitude on the part of a woman writer, one might be tempted to attribute it to her sex. Norseland was after all on the whole a masculinist society. Its originally heroic character, favoring military bravery and intrepid exploration might a priori be expected to be less attractive to women then to men. Yet the idea that the discovery of the Norse is in itself gendered only takes us so far: as shown by the example of Hawthorne, lack of interest in the Norse is not a specifically feminine trait.

If there were some evidence—even external—that Stowe was somewhat familiar with the Norse, it might be worthwhile to go beyond the notion of a gender-based lack of affinity and attribute her ignoring them in her writing to reasons of a kind that might also apply to Hawthorne. One might suspect that Stowe avoided bringing the Norse up in *Uncle Tom's Cabin* and *Dred* because she knew they kept slaves and reserved freedom for themselves. One might think that she left them out of her New England novels because the New England past she wrote about was still entirely ignorant of the exploits of Leif Ericsson and the Norse generally, so that a reference to them would have been as anachronistic as it would have been in Hawthorne's *The Scarlet Letter.* One might even have thought that as a writer still at home in eighteenth-century New England Puritanism she was disgusted by Norse paganism. But there is no evidence of any kind of an awareness of ancient Scandinavia in her work. Stowe was well-read in areas in which every educated person of the day was eager to display their learning, such as the classics and the Bible. But she was not a chaser of new horizons. She never discovered the North.

It is hard to think of an oeuvre more different from that of Stowe than Emily Dickinson's. Yet the difference is quite small from our present point of view. Jay Leyda's *The Years and Hours of Emily Dickinson* reveals that she went to hear Jenny Lind in 1851, but other than that the nine hundred pages of that work yield no signs of exposure to Scandinavia, let alone ancient Scandinavia.[3] There are no references to the Eddas and Sagas, nor to the "Norse" works of writers such as Gray, Scott, Arnold, Morris, and Longfellow, nor, for that matter, to her friend Thomas Wentworth Higginson's interest in Norseland. The same thing must be said about the nine hundred pages of *The Letters of Emily Dickinson*.[4]

Dickinson's poetry suggests a somewhat greater awareness of *modern* Scandinavia. There is a reference to reindeer and Finland in one poem. In another "the dialect of Danes" is used as an image of incomprehensibility. In a third we are told, "The Hemlock's nature thrives—on cold— / The Gnash of Northern winds / Is sweetest nutriment—to him— / His best Norwegian Wines."[5] The only reference that might be viewed as specifically Norse occurs in an argument that one's response to the song of an oriole has less to do with the bird in the tree than with the listener's ear and imagination: ". . . whether it be Rune, / Or whether it be none / Is of within."[6] However, the word *rune* had long been used in Britain and America in the sense of *poetry* or *song* with reference to the Celts as well as to the Norse, with whom, as mentioned in the introduction, they were often confused. Even giving her the benefit of the doubt in this case, one may say with confidence that Norseland did not figure prominently in Dickinson's otherwise large frame of reference.

Turning to Louisa May Alcott, one cannot say that she utterly ignored the Norse, but she certainly makes scant use of them as a writer. Perhaps this daughter of a destitute transcendentalist dreamer could not be expected to refer to them in the genteel fantasies published anonymously in the fifties and collected by Madeleine Stern in *Behind a Mask: The Unknown Thrillers of Louisa May Alcott*.[7] But given that the male heroes of *Moods* are said to have been modeled on Emerson and Thoreau, in whose immediate neighborhood she grew up, one might have expected some of their interest in the Norse to be reflected in the novel.[8] However, the only thing in her "divorce novel" that calls ancient Scandinavia to mind is the heroine's family name, which for some reason is Yule. Alcott appears to have decided early on that Norse themes, to the extent that they should be used at all, belonged in children's books, more specifically in books written primarily about and for boys. There are none in *Little Women*, the genteel-sounding, thinly veiled autobiography published in 1868.[9] *Little Men*, published three years later, is primarily about children of the "common" sort and primarily about boys.[10] This book does contain an allusion to the Norse. One of the boys in the orphanage is introduced as "quick-tempered, restless, and enterprising, bent on going to sea, for the blood of the old Vikings stirred in his veins, and could not be tamed."[11] That is a good description of certain heroes of the sagas, but the theme is never followed up in the portrayal of this character, nor are the Vikings referred to again in any other context in this book.

The next time Alcott makes a reference to the Norse is in 1886, also in a book primarily about and for boys—*Jo's Boys*.[12] The penultimate chapter of this work is called "Aslauga's Knight," also the title of a "German" story by Fouqué cherished by one of Jo's boys, who identifies with the knight in his love for a local girl.[13] Aslaug is the name of the daughter of Sigurd and Brunhild raised by her grandfather. In the pagan Norse saga this extraordinarily attractive young woman becomes the wife of Ragnar Lodbrók and hence queen of Denmark, but in the bizarre German story a Christian knight, "a friend of the Skalds" and avid collector of "Runic writings," is so taken with the image of the pagan beauty that he becomes her knight and lover even though she is long dead. In the end he is—rather surprisingly—united with her in paradise. In other words, Alcott is quoting Norse mythology at one remove and in a "purified" form in *Jo's Boys*. The other, more gender-neutral books she wrote contain innumerable geographical and historical references. Greece and Rome, classical mythology, and the study of Greek and Latin come up quite regularly, the Norse never.[14]

In view of the primarily male concerns that seem to have fed the interest in the Norse shown by the male writers discussed in earlier chapters, it is perhaps not surprising that the "androgynous" Margaret Fuller should be the one who—to some extent—breaks the pattern of apparent indifference to the Norse among the more celebrated women writers (I am not using the term *androgynous* in the sense in which Bonaparte referred to Madame de Staël as "that miserable androgyne," but in the sense in which Fuller herself recommends this quality as an ideal for both sexes in *Woman in the Nineteenth Century*). As already noted, premature death put an early end to her writing career. How much she actually knew about the Norse is debatable. But what she did qua feminist with what she did know permits us to think that she might have done more, had she lived.

Fuller's first book, *Summer on the Lakes*, published in 1844, is not a feminist work.[15] It is a short travelogue based on a cruise on the Great Lakes undertaken in the summer of 1843. The prose is laced with poetry written by the author herself, and the first reference to the Norse comes in an epigraph in which Fuller apologizes for the slim fare provided by her book:

> I give you what I can, not what I would
> If my small drinking-cup would hold a flood,
> As Scandinavia sung those must retain
> With which the giant gods must entertain;
> In our dwarf day we drain few drops and soon must thirst again.

Besides the curious syntax, one notes the vagueness of the allusion. It appears to be to the story of Thor's visit to the land of the giants, told in Snorri's Edda.

It would not be correct to say that these verses set the stage for frequent references to the Norse in the book itself. The inland seas of what was then very much the American West might conceivably have inspired such references in a nineteenth-century author steeped in Norse lore. But Fuller is steeped in classical lore and more likely to associate the western landscapes with Greco-Roman art and literature. Thus her visit to a tall bluff called "the Eagle's Nest" on the Fourth of July helped her understand what "the Greek expresses under the form of Jove's darling, Ganymede."[16] The Norse-sounding name of a famous Danish sculptor, Thorvaldsen, is brought into the picture in this context but only as the inspirer of a poem called "Ganymede to His Eagle" composed that very morning (as a neoclassicist, he took no stock in Norse themes).

The western woods suggest to Fuller "little romances of love and sorrow," specifically one called "Gunhilda."[17] She also refers to this poem as a "ballad," and in spite of the Norse name of the heroine it has more in common with medieval-Christian Scandinavian balladry than with Icelandic literature. The virginal moral angst it tells of has nothing at all to do with the only Norse Gunhild(a) Fuller is somewhat likely to have heard of, a tenth-century Norwegian queen portrayed both in Sturluson's Chronicles and the sagas (Njal's, Egil's) as beautiful and intelligent, but cruel, power-hungry, sensual, and well versed in witchcraft.

So far the result of this discussion has been to expose Fuller's conventional side. But the most interesting aspects of *Summer on the Lakes* from our point of view are her comments on the people she meets, and they are somewhat less commonplace. She pays much attention to the Indians, but she also has a good deal to say about Swedish and Norwegian immigrants, and dealing with them she seems somewhat preoccupied with the question of ethnicity and race. On one Wisconsin farm, she was deeply impressed by "the master of the house," who was seated "in the inner room" and "had been sitting there long, for he had injured his foot on ship-board, and his farming had to be done by proxy." "He was," says Fuller, "of Northern blood, with clear, full blue eyes, calm features, a tempering of the soldier, scholar, and man of the world in his aspect." A man of kingly demeanor, he had a queenlike wife whose looks were equally remarkable, although contrastingly dark like those of a princess won in a southern land. Fuller does not think foreigners like these can be expected to bring up their children the way she requires "Americans" to do—to be fit for hard work and any vicissitudes: "The Arab horse will not plow well."[18]

The statement is noteworthy as Fuller is otherwise all in favor of democracy and the melting pot. On an earlier page she claims to have seen "Norwegian peasants at work in their national dress." Beautiful children were straying nearby, and the mother, who was also beautiful, was of Welsh descent.[19] Later, after mentioning the Germans, Norwegians, Swedes, and Swiss she saw disembarking in Milwaukee, she produces a strikingly inclusive image of the future fusion of races in America: "Who knows how much of old legendary lore, of modern wonder, they have already planted amid the Wisconsin forests? Soon, their tales of the origins of things, and the Providence which rules them, will be so mingled with those of the Indian, that the very oak-tree will not know them apart,—will not know whether itself be a Runic, a Druid, or a Winnebago oak."[20] (Conceptually, Norse and Celtic are kept well apart in this instance!)

Fuller's famous feminist tract, *Woman in the Nineteenth Century,* was first published in 1845 (although a primitive version of it was published in the *Dial* in 1843).[21] As one sets about reading it, one is bound to feel confirmed in the impression that the author's imagination is dominated by Greco-Roman and biblical themes. Greek and Roman goddesses, along with the women of classical antiquity, fictional and historical, furnish the illustrations of what womanhood can and has been almost to the point of crowding out the modern examples. Norse goddesses, as well as Norse women, no matter how powerful and heroic, are conspicuously absent. As Fuller is not the kind of author who places her light under a bushel—she quotes in Greek, Latin, Italian, Spanish, and German—one is tempted to conclude, with some astonishment in view of her obvious universalist aspiration, that she was ignorant of Norse mythology and literature.

But then, as one begins to approach the end of the work, one is suddenly confronted with a version of the story of Idun, the keeper of the golden apples that keep the gods forever young.[22] The situation of the gods becomes critical when Idun is abducted to the land of the giants through the treachery of Loke. But Loke is compelled to bring her back, which he does in the guise of a falcon (pursued all the way to Asgard by the king of the giants, who has transformed himself into an eagle). The salient point of the tale is that Idun returns in the shape of a swallow. "We must welcome her form as the speck on the sky that assures the glad blue of Summer," adds Fuller somewhat whimsically. "Yet one swallow does not make a summer. Let us solicit them in flights and flocks!"

The story of Idun thus serves simply as a way of introducing a section of the book dealing with some women viewed as harbingers of the future. In herself Idun obviously is not much of a feminist heroine. However, just a few pages later, there is another reference to Norse myth more significant in feminist terms. It brings the question of race to bear on the attitude Fuller would like to see in young American women: "As to this living so entirely for men, I should think when it was proposed to women they would feel, at least, some spark of the old spirit of races allied to our own. 'If he is to be my bridegroom *and lord,*' cries Brunhilda, 'he must first be able to pass through fire and water.' 'I will serve at the banquet,' says the Walkyrie, 'but only him who, in the trial of deadly combat, has shown himself a hero.'"[23] Fuller is intimating that if American girls had more of the spirit of their racial forebears in them, they would not be in such a haste to "get married."

It is, however, not clear precisely what forebears Fuller has in mind. The vague use of the plural ("races allied to our own") corresponds to a certain ambiguity in the use of names. *Brunhilda* is a Latinized form of the Norse *Brunhild* (the equivalent German form is *Brünhild*). But *Walkyrie* is not a Norse form (nor, for that matter, German—Wagner has *Walküre*). A footnote to Brunhilda says "see the Nibelungen Lays," but the pagan valkyries do not appear in the medieval-Christian *Nibelungenlied*, although they do in Wagner's opera, in which the libretto has been supplemented with Norse materials. What is more, in the old German poem Siegfried does not pass through fire and water to get to Brünhild as in the Edda but wins her hand—for Gunther—by defeating her in single combat disguised as his friend.[24] The possibility that the author of *Woman in the Nineteenth Century* was more familiar with the Edda than with Wagner's libretto is virtually nullified because in introducing the story of Idun she attributes it not to the Edda but to "the Scandinavian Saga."

The Norse references do not appear in the 1843 *Dial* article later expanded into *Woman in the Nineteenth Century*.[25] It may therefore be significant that the use of the story of Idun is followed by the note that "a crowd of books" was sent to the author when her friends learned that she was writing about "Woman's 'Sphere,' Woman's 'Mission,' and Woman's 'Destiny.'"[26] It is just possible that one of these books was a Norse mythology.

It must, however, be said that there are no signs that Fuller developed a stronger interest in the Norse before heading for England and the Continent the following year.[27] In a "letter" to the *New York Tribune* dated November 1846, she does attribute to Carlyle "the heroic arrogance of some old Scandinavian conqueror" and compares him to "the powerful smith, the Siegfried melting all the old iron till it glows to a sunset red, and burns you if you senselessly go too near."[28] By a curious coincidence, Thoreau resorts to somewhat similar Norse imagery in the previously mentioned lecture about Carlyle read before the Concord Lyceum in 1846 and published in *Graham's Magazine* the following year (if you ask Carlyle what light is, says Thoreau, "he answers like Thor with a stroke of his hammer"). The difference is that while Thoreau's portrayal of Carlyle is clearly predicated on an interest in Norse lore that he shared with the Scotsman, Fuller's use of the German name Siegfried again points us to Wagner's libretto. At the time when Thoreau and Emerson, Fuller's collaborators on the *Dial*, were "discovering" the Norse, her own explorations were taking her in a very different direction. In Italy she got involved with

Mazzini and the Roman Revolution. On her way back to the United States in 1850, she died in a shipwreck off Fire Island.

JULIA CLINTON JONES' *VALHALLA*

Valhalla: a Saga in Twelve Parts is not the only work published by Jones. Other themes also tempted the pen of this granddaughter of DeWitt Clinton, who ran for president of the United States against Madison in 1812 and later served as governor of New York. In 1887 she published *Cleopatra*, a glowing, Shakespeare-based account of the Egyptian queen's relationship with Mark Antony, told in the first person singular.[29] This work was followed in 1894 by *Our Roll of Honor, or, Poems of the Revolution*, which shows an involvement with the Daughters of the American Revolution.[30] But *Valhalla*, first published in San Francisco in 1878 and reissued in New York two years later, is not only her first but her magnum opus.[31]

The text of the poem is preceded by a fairly long preface that is not the least fascinating part of the book. Like the poem itself, it stands in intertextual relations to a remarkable number of writers and texts mentioned in the course of this study, so much so that it may almost be said to sum things up and for that reason, too, deserves to be examined as the symbolic end product of the Norse revival in America.

Echoes from overseas are particularly common (although it is hard to tell to what extent they have reached Jones indirectly via the long introduction to R. B. Anderson's *Norse Mythology; or, the Religion of Our Forefathers*, which was first published in 1875).[32] One is struck by the manner in which Jones establishes a direct blood link between the Norse and her American readers via Britain, the motherland once colonized by people from the European North: "It is much to be deplored," she says, "that so slight a knowledge of Scandinavian Mythology prevails, popularly, with those who boast descent from Hengist and Horsa, and whose pride it is that in their veins flows the blood that long ago thrilled through the bold hearts of the Vikings, descendants of the old Norse Gods."[33] On the one hand, Jones tends to equate the Anglo-Saxons and the Norse; on the other, she states that England—and by extension the United States—would not have amounted to much if "the sons of Thor and Odin" had not taken over when the Anglo-Saxons (like their Teutonic forebears) faltered and turned complacent and effete.[34] Here one recognizes some of the ideas propounded by Carlyle and Laing (and recycled by Emerson in *English Traits*).

In explaining why the Vikings deserve to be better known, Jones paints a picture of their historical role in which they are hard to recognize: "Planting wherever they trod, the germs of a glorious freedom, they were the revolutionists of that age, and all succeeding ages owe them a lasting debt of gratitude for the noble harvest that has sprung up from the seeds and liberty and truth by them sown."[35] This noble harvest is the Anglo-Saxon world, and in making that point Jones heavily underscores the moral superiority of the "Gothic" race: "To their scorn of luxurious feebleness,—to their unswerving love of temperance and morality, do we to-day that which has led us on from height to height,—the principles which have placed England in the foremost rank of the nations, and which are blazoned forth on the glorious flag of her daughter, our own United States."

In dealing with the alleged superiority of the Northern faith that is part of this picture, Jones stresses the role of the climate in the spirit of Montesquieu: "Lost in the contemplation of the ice-bound peaks of his native land . . . the Norseman's hardy spirit was lifted up from earth to the thought of a higher existence; thus did his nature become nobler and more aspiring through contact with his grander, bolder surroundings, and so gave birth to a purer Mythology."[36] By contrast, the climate of the South makes its inhabitants "effeminate and sensuous."

The suggestion that Norse mythology was purer than that of the Greeks also calls Schlegel's "On the Poetry of the North" to mind. But what is most intriguing is the distorted echo of Scandinavian writers such as Tegnér and Geijer, Grundtvig and Oehlenschläger, who at one time, driven by patriotic pride, dreamed of reconciling Christianity and Norse paganism. Jones closes her preface with a series of analogies between the two religions (Balder is compared to Christ; Heimdall to Gabriel; "Ragnarock" to the Day of Doom; Gimli to New Jerusalem; the Trinity of Odin, Vili and Ve to the trinity of the Father, Son, and Holy Spirit). Jones wishes to "show the very close similitude between what we are taught by the Church to regard as her peculiar doctrines, and the Mythology of the North, whose origin is involved in the obscurity of past ages."[37]

The point is so exaggerated that it may well cause one to question the depth of Jones' knowledge and understanding of pagan Scandinavia. The text of the poem itself suggests some limitations of the kind we have already found in other writers. She is not likely to have possessed a firsthand acquaintance with the Norse language. One of the plurals of *valkyrie* she repeatedly uses is *valkyriar*, that is, she uses the masculine Norse plural ending that more correctly appears in *einheriar* (the fallen heroes in Valhalla). One may also doubt that Jones knew much about Norse literature as distinct from mythology. We are inured to seeing the word *saga* used in any imaginable sense today and not likely to be astonished to find her calling her long poem a saga. Yet usage was more strict in her day, not least when Norse lore was involved; the word could refer to the Icelandic sagas as distinct from the Eddas, or to the goddess of history, one of Odin's wives. Based on the Eddas, *Valhalla* should not really be called a saga. As a construction of the history of the Aesirs and their struggle with the Jötuns, it is more like an epic with Miltonic overtones. One notes that Jones also uses the word in other curious ways, as when she says that "the old Skalds and Sagas" strove to "evolve the truth dimly shining before them."[38]

Jones refers to the Elder Edda in a footnote near the beginning of her poem, and if she has a specific translation in mind, one that she herself has read, it must be that of Benjamin Thorpe, as mentioned the first authoritative English translation, first published in 1866. For the Younger Edda, she may have used Dasent's well-established translation. But Anderson's mythology is likely to have supplied Jones with Edda myths as well as with ideological background.

Among famous creative writers whose influence may easily be traced in the text of *Valhalla* is—not entirely surprisingly—Longfellow. Jones's frequent use of the word *skoal* is certainly inspired by the last stanza of "The Skeleton in Armor," in which Longfellow introduces it and explains his spelling.[39] The equally frequent references to *Ragnarock*, another dubious spelling from a philological point of view, hark back to *The Saga of King Olaf*, in which it is also used because it yields easy English rhymes. In yet another case, Longfellow's influence seems to fuse with that of Tegnér. Like *Frithiof's Saga*, *Valhalla* features a "Bragi's Song," and its sensual character is not the only thing that calls the Swedish bishop to mind.[40] It will be remembered that Tegnér in describing Ingeborg's physical charms uses what Longfellow in his translation refers to as "Elves of Light." Tegnér's term is *ljusalfer*, and a footnote to Longfellow's translation suggests that this is the Norse term, when in reality it is the Swedish term. The appearance of *Ljus-Alfers* (the Swedish word with an English plural ending added) in a description of Odin's retinue is inexplicable unless one may assume that Jones has read Longfellow's *Frithiof's Saga* translation, footnotes and all.[41]

Jones's dependence on secondary sources and the limitations of her first-hand knowledge of the Norse do not mean that she is not an original poet. Her originality occasionally turns into oddity, as when she lists the titles of her twelve "parts" in alphabetical order in the table of contents (so that, for instance, the introductory description of Valhalla comes after "Ragnarock" and "Regeneration"). But the oddness in this case masks true originality in the handling of the Norse myths. *Valhalla* is not a loosely organized collection of "old Norse tales." The myths have been carefully selected and ordered—on occasion reinvented—to fit the author's poetic temperament and the vision of world history she strives to convey.

In her attempt to bridge biblical and pagan Scandinavian mythology, Jones gives her poetic imagination a good deal of latitude. Stories from the Eddas are assembled and manipulated into a kind of universal history with the emphasis on the fate of the gods. We learn, with some surprise, that Valhalla was not always the kind of place described in the Eddas:

> Love is the rule of all
> In Valhalla's high hall!
> Love is the Lord! Love never fails!
> Meekness and strength,
> Mingled at length,
> By love poised in Odin's just scales.[42]

Until Loki's fall, compared to Lucifer's.[43] After that momentous event, the story of the Aesir is the story of the war between good and evil. "Ragnarock" is mentioned in every one of the twelve parts of *Valhalla*; no matter what the Aesir are doing, we are reminded of their coming doom. On the other hand, the final part, "Regeneration," is longer than the actual account of "Ragnarock." The author needs room for her final fusion of the two mythologies. The Aesir are brought back, but in Gimli-New Jerusalem the power is no longer with the "Aesir trinity" in which Odin had functioned as "the Soul of the Universe"; it now belongs to the triumphantly appearing "High and Mighty One," also referred to as "the Judge Supreme" easily recognized as the Judeo-Christian Lord.[44]

With humanity—including the "Goths"—taking a backseat in this grand cosmic drama, race does not play the same role as in Jones's preface. The theme appears only in references to the white arms and bosoms of the goddesses, the golden hair of the valkyries, Freya's blue eyes, and so forth. (Although Jones hardly deviates from the Edda texts in this respect, such references take on a different significance in her work.)

On the other hand, gender, a subject not touched upon at all in the preface, looms fairly large in the poem. This is all the more striking as the overall scenario does not seem to call for such an emphasis. Using a slightly anachronistic, yet hackneyed phrase, one might say that Jones reveals an interest in sexual politics.

In this context, factual mistakes are not always easy to tell from the free play of the poetic imagination. Vingolf (the goddesses' hall, where fallen heroes were also welcomed) is separate from Valhalla, but in "Bragi's Song" the two places seem to have been conflated. What is more, the einheriar drink wine as well as mead, and the valkyries provide sex as well as drink: While the heroes are being greeted by the gods,

> Radiant couches for them are preparing,
>> Banquets that strengthen the warrior-soul;
> Maidens alluring full beakers are bearing,—
>> Love mingling with love in o'erflowing bowl.
> Softly recline they on warm bosoms, thrilling
>> Every quick pulse of the swift throbbing heart;
> Fulla for Friga their mead cups high filling,—
>> Joy is imperfect where love hath no part.
> Safely surrounded by Passion's sweet longing,
>> Feast they and rest they till dawning of light.[45]

It is hard to see who the "maidens" are if they are not the valkyries. The term means that Jones cannot be referring to the joys of faithful and chaste wives who have joined their dead husbands in Folkvang, the hall of Freya. In fact, Folkvang is a name that does not appear in *Valhalla* (although it would seem from the ending of the preceding section of Part Third, "Einheriars' Song," that Bragi is doing his singing in that joyful place). What is clear is that bacchanalian orgies are here described in terms as bold as those used by any French novelist of the time. Jones seems to celebrate free love. A line such as "Joy is imperfect where love hath no part" is best viewed as a critique and correction of the traditional Edda myth, which only has the valkyries waiting at table after bringing their chosen heroes to the banquet hall.

Part seventh, "Thor and the Daughters of Aegir" (the waves) is another place where the narrative takes on an erotic coloring somewhat at odds with the stated aim of her poem—to demonstrate the purity of her forefather's faith—and at the same time appears to tell us something about the author's views on sex. Jones seems to have composed this part of the poem virtually from scratch as if to replace Thor's fishing, an episode for which one looks in vain in *Valhalla*: she dwells on the physical attractions of the daughters of the seagod with obvious pleasure:

> On their azure pillows lying,
> . . . .
> From Asgard, Midgard, Jötunheim,
> Gently rocking to and fro,
> Aegir's daughters ceaseless go;
> Mantles blue the maidens wear,
> Snow white bosoms gleaming bare
> . . . .
> . . . .

But the story is really about male lust:

> Hither comes Thor,
> The Thunderer.
> To sport with those maids at rest,
> Sleepily lies each maiden calm,
> Gently drifting, with snow-white arm
> Folded on billowy breast.
> . . . .
> . . . .
>
> Clinging, clasping in caresses,
> To his breast the great God presses
> Each soft maid, while floating tresses
> Wrap him in embraces cold.
>
> Burning Thor, with kisses fierce
> Will their frozen bosoms pierce,
> Seizes in enfolding arms;
> Filled with passion, strong desire,
> Lustful flames e'er mounting higher,
> Pressing wildly yielding forms,
> Riots on the sparkling charms.

Not realizing what he is up to, the Daughters of Aegir are at first receptive to Thor's advances:

> Strange regrets and vague alarms
> Wake too late! now filled with storms
> Of wild wrath, they vainly try
> From his mighty arms to fly.

Alas, they are no match for Thor. Part seventh ends with the god of the hammer raping and generally manhandling the daughters of Aegir before returning to Bilskirnir muttering in his red beard and laughing contemptuously. One may of course wonder why Jones would go out of her way to make one of the Aesirs look as bad as Apollo and Zeus in what she sees as the less pure Greek mythology. It looks like a political statement.

The didactic purpose of *Valhalla*, as stated in the preface, is twofold. First of all, the author wants to show "the close similitude" of the Edda story and the doctrine of the church. But she also wants to instruct a readership that she feels is scandalously unaware of its Norse heritage. To be sure, the completely uninitiated reader may get somewhat confused or get the wrong impression of the Norse pantheon because of the distortions due to her overriding first purpose and the obtrusion of a personal political agenda. One may also remark upon the ruthlessness with which Jones sometimes introduces a host of sometimes obscure Norse names, as, for instance, in the third section of "Creation." She expects the neophyte to consult the "alphabetical index of notes" at the end of her volume. Possibly such a reader is better served by one of the prose compilations constructed on more neutral principles, such as, for instance, the earlier-mentioned *Tales from the Norse Grandmother (the Elder Edda)*, published about the same time (in 1880). Having said that, however, one can only salute Jones's achievement. A lover of verse somewhat familiar with Edda literature can still read *Valhalla* as a twice-told tale and find it a pleasurable experience. Jones does not only have an excellent command of the poetic language of the time and the metrics of Longfellow; she has a lively poetic imagination, especially when she finds the topic congenial, as in "Thor and the Daughters of Aegir." She is an interesting acquaintance to make.

8

Summary and Conclusion

As one surveys the dates of the texts concentrated on in the preceding chapters, one finds that virtually all of them were published in the forties, fifties, and sixties. There is a certain tendency for them to cluster around the midcentury mark, and one may look at the original phase of the American literary discovery of the Norse as primarily a prewar event. *The Saga of King Olaf,* while published in *Tales of a Wayside Inn* in 1863, was, in fact, finished on the eve of the war; indeed, the first canto, "The Challenge of Thor," was written in 1849. The history of Lowell's "The Voyage to Vinland" goes back to the same year. *Clarel* was published in 1876, but its inspiration dates back to a trip to the Holy Land in 1856–57 and Melville spent a long time working on this gigantic poem. Wholly postbellum works such as Whittier's "The Dole of Jarl Thorkell" (ca. 1868), Taylor's *Lars: a Pastoral of Norway* (1873), and Longfellow's "The Broken Oar" (1878) reflect the lingering involvement with the Norse of aging pioneers. Only in one case, Julia Clinton Jones, author of *Valhalla* (1878), are we dealing with someone who joins the group when the discovery phase of the Norse revival in America is practically over.

One result of this concentration of the movement to a relatively short period is that there are no clear lines of development (such as would force a strictly chronological treatment of authors and works). Whittier's second Norse poem reflects a more somber view of the Norse than his first one, but that is hardly enough to set a trend. As for the formal use of Norse elements, *Society and Solitude* is not different from *The Conduct of Life;* the imagery of *Clarel* sometimes recalls that of *Moby Dick,* published twenty-five years earlier. Jones's *Valhalla* may have appeared late, but in many respects it represents a summary of the themes and influences that make up the American discovery of the Norse.

The intensity of involvement with the Norse in the individual texts tends to vary with the genre. It is relatively low in the essays, which are never primarily about a Norse topic. The same thing holds true of the fiction, although whaling, the most obvious subject of *Moby Dick*, is referred to by the author himself as a "wild Scandinavian vocation," and the chief whaleman, Ahab, is repeatedly compared to a Scandinavian "sea-king." The involvement with the Norse is definitely most intense in the poems, which are all devoted to entirely Norse topics with the exception of *Clarel* and *Lars: A Pastoral of Norway* (a work formally set in nineteenth-century Norway).

Virtually all the texts examined may be characterized as original American creative writing. I have not had occasion to discuss any American translations from the Norse, the reason being that there are none during the time period to which the American discovery of the Norse belongs. The chief translation attributable to the Norse revival in America is Longfellow's rendition into English of Tegnér's *Frithiofs Saga*, a modern Swedish work although based on an Icelandic romance.

This hiatus again has to do with the fact that there is no indication that any of the writers discussed yielded to the temptation of learning Old Norse, although Longfellow is on record as having nibbled at the hook. That also means that the firsthand acquaintance of American literati with Icelandic literature is almost exclusively through translations, mainly English (although Longfellow appears to have known a Swedish translation of *Heimskringla*, as well as Mueller's Danish *Sagabibliothek* and some German Edda translations).

Even within these limits, the range of reading seems to have been fairly narrow, at least judging by the use to which the reading was put (which is what chiefly concerns us here). The Elder, or Poetic, Edda clearly was not studied much by our authors, with the possible exception of Jones. Part of the explanation may be that no complete modern English translation of this work appeared until well into the sixties. Yet one is surprised at the quasi completeness of the neglect of the content of this work. It was, after all, drawn upon in modern manuals of mythology, and Henry Wheaton gives a fairly detailed account of it both in his 1829 article in the *North American Review* and in his *History of the Northmen,* and yet Emerson says in a journal entry that only three of the poems contained in it are extant. In his essays he sometimes refers to "the Edda" as if there were only one—Snorri's.

Longfellow is supposed to have been better informed; he is said to have consulted Rhüs's and Simrock's German translations of the Poetic Edda on occasion. But the limit of even his interest is indicated by the fact that he left unopened the pages of his copy of the excellent translation of the same work done by the Brothers Grimm. The chief reference to Saemund's Edda in Longfellow's own poetical works appears to be the suggestion that one of the weaving maidens of Sigrid the Haughty sang "Of Brynhilda's love and the wrath of Gudrun." As evidence of an acquaintance with the Sigurd cycle this is slightly superior to the casual use of the word *Brynhildas* in the generic sense of *Norse brides* in Melville's *Mardi*.

The Prose Edda, notably the manual of Norse mythology contained in *Gylfaginning* ("The Beguiling of Gylfi") was accessible both in the second volume of *Northern Antiquities* and in Dasent's 1842 translation. Emerson and Longfellow owned both works, and they have clearly played an important role in the American discovery of the Norse. The references to Ragnarök and the return of Balder in a number of poems are derived not from the prophetic end of *Voluspá* in the Elder Edda but from Snorri's retelling of the prophecy in *Gylfaginning*. Thoreau's references to Thor's struggles against the Jötuns in his essay on Carlyle, like Emerson's references to the Fenris Wolf in *English Traits* and *The Conduct of Life*, come from the same text.

The impact of the Younger Edda was limited, however, to the mythological part. Snorri's poetics, as given in the part of his Edda known as *Skáldskaparmál*, was not only less popular with translators but clearly ignored by our American poets. None of them attempts to write skaldic verse in their "Norse" pieces. Lowell says he "alludes" to the alliterative Norse *stave* in "The Voyage to Vinland" by writing "The Prophecy of Gudrida" in an "unrhymed alliterated measure." But neither he nor Longfellow nor Jones experiments with kennings the way Tegnér does in *Frithiofs Saga*. Indeed, the interest in kennings in the texts I have examined is limited to the analysis of some verses by Thorhall to which Thoreau proceeds in *Cape Cod*. Yet even he does not speak of them as *kennings*, and if his reading of Thorhall influenced his writing in any way it was only in the prose of *Walden*.

This lack of skaldic emulation on the part of the American poets who took an interest in Norse lore is in keeping with the image of the skald projected in their works. Jones' Bragi is a god and consequently in his best years, but both Lowell and Longfellow depict their Norse entertainers as "hoary" old men reminiscent of Demodokos and other

Homeric bards, not to mention Homer himself. It is clear that the skalds were not real to them.

The family sagas, with their generous quotations of skaldic verse, were also pretty much unknown during the period that concerns us. It is uncertain how much Longfellow actually used his copy of Mueller's *Sagabibliothek*. We know that he did not cut the pages of Hagen's translation of *Volsunga Saga*. Emerson pontificates about "the sagas" in some of his later essays, but he seems to have only the chronicles of *Heimskringla* in mind. Melville's narrator enthuses about them in *Mardi* without seeming to have anything in particular in mind. There appears to be an overt reference to a passage in *Njal's Saga* in *Moby Dick*, yet one wonders what the actual source is as even this text was not translated into English until 1861. Most widely known were what is now popularly referred as the "Vinland sagas," materials accessible at the time to those who (like Thoreau) could read Latin in Rafn's *Antiquitates Americanae*, and to those who could not in digested form in Rafn's abstract or the accounts of Norse voyaging given in the first volume of *Northern Antiquities* and Laing's preliminary dissertation.

Laing's translation of *Heimskringla* came at a time when it could help accelerate the American discovery of the Norse (1843). It was apparently read very carefully by several of our authors. Emerson calls Snorri's royal chronicles "the Iliad and Odyssey of English history" and quotes from not a few of them in *English Traits*. Thoreau went to the trouble of locating all the references to individuals called Thorir and copied the information into his journal. Longfellow, who at least indirectly identified with Harald Fairhair in a novel of his youth, in middle age used the *Saga of Olaf Tryggvason* as his chief source in writing *The Saga of King Olaf*.

The English facilitation of the Norse studies of their American brethren was not limited to translations of Icelandic literary texts. The influence of the account of the Norse given in the first volume of *Northern Antiquities* (the "history of Denmark") can be seen in various ways, including a certain tendency to confuse Norse and Celtic (notably in Whittier's "The Norsemen"). Laing's preliminary dissertation on the Norse was a strong influence on Emerson and Thoreau. Among creative writers, Gray may be held responsible, along with Scott, for the Gothic traits found in certain American poems on Norse topics, as, for instance, in Longfellow's "The Skeleton in Armor." Scott's *The Pirate* is probably, along with *Ossian*, among the sources of the arctic weather and rocky gloominess with which American

Romantic poets (Longfellow, Whittier) love to imbue their Danish landscapes. Carlyle's "The Hero as Divinity," which was published before Laing's translation of *Heimskringla* with its preliminary dissertation, seems to have been instrumental in getting Emerson and Thoreau involved with the Norse. It is, apart from *Frithiofs Saga*, the only text of the Norse revival that we know Melville was familiar with at the time of the composition of *Moby Dick*.

When one speaks of the influence of Carlyle, one is to a certain extent speaking about the influence of Germany. He is with respect to the American discovery of the Norse what Coleridge is to the American discovery of German Romantic philosophy. "The Hero as Divinity" is replete with German lore: the author cites Jean-Paul, Novalis, Schiller, and—specifically on the subject of the ancient Scandinavians—"Grimm, the German antiquary" (on the etymology of *Odin*) and Uhland (on the place of Thor in the Norse pantheon).

Schlegel's influence—his remarks on the superior purity of Norse mythology as compared with that of the Greeks—is probably also largely indirect; it may, for instance, have affected Jones through the mediation of Anderson. It is, however, hard to say anything concrete and precise about this indirect kind of German influence on the American discovery of the Norse. Nor are we in a much better position when it comes to direct German influence. Hilen's list of the titles in Longfellow's Scandinavian library includes, besides the mentioned translations, books such as J. K. L. Grimm's *Deutsche Mythologie* and Rudolph Keyser's *The Religion of the Northmen*. It appears that they were not left unopened. But no specific passages in Longfellow's "Norse" works are directly traceable to them. The source of some of Fuller's Norse references seem to be Wagner, but we do not really know how she came by them. The most clear-cut instance of direct German influence is Alcott's use of Fouqué's "Auslaga's Knight" in *Jo's Boys*, a work published in 1886 and hence strictly speaking posterior to the discovery period of the Norse revival in America.

We are on somewhat firmer ground with respect to the modern Scandinavian connection. I have not been able to pinpoint any direct debts to those early Danish and Icelandic representatives of the Norse revival: Bartholinus, Wormius, and Torfaeus; although strong, their influence is indirect and through others (as in the case of the unfortunate references to skull drinking traceable to Wormius). But Copenhagen continued to be a center of Norse studies, and the American exposure to nineteenth-century Danish scholarship was more direct. After the pioneering work of Wheaton, Longfellow visited

Copenhagen, where he met the chief "Northern antiquaries": Rask, Rafn, and Magnússon. He refers to an article of Rafn's in a note appended to "The Skeleton in Armor." Thoreau keeps up a spirited dialogue with "Professor Rafn of Copenhagen" in *Cape Cod.*

With respect to more belletristic Scandinavian influences, one notes that Longfellow acquired copies of Oehlenschläger's *Hakon Jarl* both in Danish and German in preparation for a never-completed poem of his own on the ill-fated jarl. He translated Oehlenschläger's "Thor's Fishing" and "The Dwarfs" and published them in *Poetry and Poets of Europe.* He also did one of several translations of Tegnér's *Frithiofs Saga.* This translation was read by Jones and probably also by Taylor. The impact of this work is visible throughout Taylor's "The Norseman's Ride" and is still strong enough twenty-six years later for the name of Tegnér's hero to be dropped in *Lars: A Pastoral of Norway,* a work that topically has more than one thing in common with the Swedish romance. Longfellow himself is strongly influenced by it both in "The Skeleton in Armor" and in *The Saga of King Olaf.* The latter work is also marked by the influence of Danish and Swedish folk ballads, which the author knew through editions published by some of the foreground figures of the Norse revival in Scandinavia and did not rigorously distinguish from genuinely Norse texts.

There is also likely to have been a certain amount of communication and mutual influence within the group of American writers involved in the literary discovery of the Norse, especially as several of them knew each other and some lived in the same town. Thus the fact that Emerson's and Thoreau's interest in ancient Scandinavian lore seems to have been awakened at the same time, along with the impact Laing's preliminary dissertation had on them both, suggests that the former may have passed his discovery on to his younger neighbor as happened in the case of their orientalism. Fuller's collaboration with Emerson and Thoreau on the *Dial* may have come too early for them to have spent much time talking about the Norse. Alcott, on the other hand, was a permanent inhabitant of Concord, Massachusetts, and her father an associate of Emerson and Thoreau; it is therefore hard to believe that she would not have heard the Norse mentioned, although obviously not often enough to make her a devotee of Norseland. Again, it is hard to imagine what Emerson could have had in mind besides Longfellow's review of *Frithiofs Saga* when he told him that he had made him aware of "a new horizon . . . in Sweden." We know that Longfellow encouraged Lowell to pay attention to the Norse. Whittier praised Taylor's "The Norseman's Ride," and the latter in due time dedicated *Lars: A Pastoral of Norway* to his friend and mentor.

Vague and limited in significance as the ascertainable exchanges within the group may be, there can be no doubt but that the group existed and did its work during a well-defined period in American literary history. Nor can it be denied that the American discovery of the Norse, while heavily indebted to work done on the other side of the Atlantic, assumes a character of its own in part because of the passing of time (the Americans getting a late start), in part also because of the different social and political conditions in the New World.

As a first illustration of this point one may mention the American attitude to Norse paganism, in a sense the defining element of ancient Scandinavian civilization. In this case the different historical circumstances generally speaking make for a sharp difference between the literature generated by the American discovery of the Norse and the works belonging to the heyday of the Norse revival in Scandinavia. As mentioned in chapter 1, the Scandinavians found their very national origins—as well as what they saw as the greatness of their early history—inextricably bound up with the pagan religion. Writers such as Geijer and Grundtvig originally hoped to be able to bring about a synthesis of heathen and Christian ideals. By contrast, the corresponding American movement was more detached, and the basic incompatibility of the two religions is more or less a foregone conclusion—with one striking exception: Jones not only refurbishes the old "Gothic" myth of origin in *Valhalla* (more about that theme later) but labors to demonstrate the similarities between pagan Norse mythology and the doctrine of the church. There are some other attempts to manage if not a reconciliation then at least a rapprochement between the two religions, but shorn of national fervor and nostalgia they are different in spirit even when seemingly paralleling themes are found in the Scandinavian writers.

In one case the rapprochement is rather twisted and provocative: Emerson, in his essay on "Worship," supports his denunciation of what he sees as the ineffectiveness of Christianity—and any high-aiming but institutionalized religion—by gleefully relating how the recently converted Olaf Tryggvason tortures and murders compatriots who refuse to abandon the old faith. What matters in Emerson's view is not whether you are a pagan or a Christian but the level of the culture in which you are immersed and that determines your behavior in either case.

Whittier's way of narrowing the gap between the pagan and Christian religions in "The Dole of Jarl Thorkell," while not without a boldness of its own, is more generally acceptable and also more in line with the nineteenth-century Scandinavian approach to this task: A young and beautiful sibyl declares that the gods are "what you make them" and proceeds to remake the image of Frey (supposed to be asking for human blood) in terms that, we are told, are really prophetic of Christ.

Even closer to a Scandinavian—and in this case also British—tradition is the presentation of Bálder as the forerunner of Christ. This theme had already been used both in Oehlenschläger's *Balder hin Gode* and Tegnér's *Frithiofs Saga*. Indeed, it can be glimpsed in Carlyle's "The Hero as Divinity." Thus Longfellow is following a well-established overseas pattern when he makes this rapprochement between the two religions in "Tegnér's Drapa." So is Taylor in *Lars: A Pastoral of Norway* and Jones in *Valhalla* (both works written after Matthew Arnold had further reinforced the connection in "Balder Dead").

As mentioned, the Americans stress the incompatibility of the Norse and Christian religions more often than their similarities. Particularly common is the opposition of Christ and Thor, which itself harks back to Norse times. It is the leitmotif in *The Saga of King Olaf*, in which it is prophesied in the final canto that Christ will win in the end. It crops up in "The Voyage to Vinland" in the form of a promise that Christ will one day reign in the land descried by Biörn and his crew. More subtle, as well as more original, is the chapter "Spring" in *Walden*, in which the effect of Thor's hammer is poetically contrasted with that of an agent called Thaw, coyly but unmistakably associated with Christ rising from the dead at Easter time.

Longfellow produces a sophisticated variation on the theme in "King Olaf's Christmas," one of the cantos in *The Saga of King Olaf*, in which—in the midst of "berserks" making the sign of the hammer—he has his as yet unconverted skald kiss the cross-shaped hilt of the sword in sign of submission to Christ. The irony of a champion of Christ converting with the aid of the sword comes out very well in this way and contributes to the reader's growing uncertainty as to who is really getting the upper hand: Christ or Thor. But the only case in which Thor is brazenly—if sardonically—awarded the victory is the section in *Clarel* in which the hammer-wielding geologist representing modern science claims to have "slanted," that is, caused to decline, the cross of Christ.

Thor's role as the chief opponent of Christ obviously has something to do with the mostly modern tradition that insists on making him the god of war. This function was hardly what made Thor the most popular god among the Norse during the later part of the pagan era. While not unpopular with warriors, he was much revered by farmers as a provider of cleansing thunder and rain and a protector of crops who fought off giants and trolls and other evil spirits bedeviling them. Some American writers, perhaps following Carlyle, have given Thor his due as a fighter of giants and other demonic monsters. Thoreau compares Carlyle to him in that role—that of a divine drudge. Longfellow does so somewhat imprudently in *The Saga of King Olaf*, in which the God of the Hammer is otherwise himself demonized not only as the War God but as the enemy of Christ. The cryptic Thor symbolism in *Moby Dick* is based on a conception of the god as a slayer of monsters.

A rehabilitation of this deity in socioeconomic terms, perhaps owing something to Carlyle's portrayal of him as "the god of peaceable industry," occurs in *English Traits*, in which Emerson claims that the carrier of the thunderbolt has "lent Miollnir to Birmingham for a steam-hammer." On the whole, Norse mythology proves surprisingly useful to the debate of the great issues of the day. It is hard to separate the pacifist ending of "Tegnér's Drapa"—the vision of a post-Ragnarök world—from the fact that the poem was composed in 1847, that is, during the Mexican War. Norse eschatology is also pressed into service in "The Voyage to Vinland," in which the prophecy delivered by the young and beautiful sibyl Gudrida reflects the author's wish for a prosperous and above all peaceful future for the United States after the destruction wrought by the Civil War. In "The Dole of Jarl Thorkell," the young and beautiful sibyl is in essence telling the authorities that the haves should share with the have-nots. Occasionally, to be sure, the letter of the myth is sacrificed in the process, as when Jones introduces something like gender equity in the halls of the gods and makes Thor the villain in a denunciation of rape ("The Daughters of Aegir").

The prominence of beautiful young sibyls in some of the "Norse" poems, on the other hand, has to do with a certain limitation affecting the use of Norse history in the service of social and political activism, a limitation that again may not be totally unrelated to the fact that the users are mostly male. It is closely connected with the male attitude reflected in the lecture Emerson read before the Women's Rights Convention in Boston in 1855—the one in which he speaks about the Frigga-like quality of woman and says that it was "a cherished belief" among "that race which is now predominant over all the races of men" that women had "an oracular nature" (fitting in with what he sees as their predominantly intuitive, emotional, and religious nature). Other than that, Emerson shows little interest in Norse women, and apart from their appearances as sibyls they do not loom very large in the male writing inspired by the American discovery of the Norse. The princess in "The Skeleton in Armor" is granted only a shadowy existence and ultimately seems irrelevant as the hero heads for the beer hall of Valhalla (a symbol of transcendence to the inveterate bachelor Thoreau). Even in *The Saga of King Olaf*, in which he is following a Norse script, Longfellow, to the extent that this is at all possible, tends to confine women to less aggressive roles than those given them by Snorri. He leaves out the episode in which Queen Gyda picks Olaf Tryggvasson as her husband out of a large number of men brought together for her inspection. He makes Thora of Rimol swoon in genuinely Victorian fashion. He gives us a Sigrid the Haughty who when we first meet her is romantically lovelorn and depressed. Neither he nor his American colleagues attempt to make political hay with the fact that ancient Icelandic women, unlike American women, could own property and declare themselves divorced from a man they did not like. Nor is there, with the exception of Gudrun in *The Saga of King Olaf*, any attempt to present them as they often appear in the sagas and Eddas—as tough and independent schemers and instigators of blood revenge and other killings, which make some of them look like true valkyries or "choosers of the dead."

What could have been done with the images of women presented in Icelandic literature can be glimpsed in Fuller's 1845 pamphlet *Woman in the Nineteenth Century*, where she suggests that American girls would do well to follow the example of Brynhilda, the valkyrie, who expected great things from any man who presumed to become her lord and master. (Young American girls are into much of a hurry to get married, according to Fuller.)

The beauty of Norse women, not seldom dwelt on in Icelandic literature, is also a somewhat neglected theme in the American literary works that concern us here. Emerson says "both branches of the Scandinavian race" are handsome, but he is critical of the physical shape of Englishwomen, who doubtless belong to one of these branches. Whittier's and Lowell's sibyls are abstractly said to be beautiful and a refrain in *The Saga of King Olaf* insistently declares Thora of Rimol "fairest of women." (Jones might be said to break this pattern: She dwells quite concretely on the physical attractions of Freya, Frigga and the daughters of Aegir. But none of these divinities is strictly speaking a *woman*.)

Concretely, the male writers actually show a greater interest in the looks of men, and they do so in a manner that again ties the matter of race to the matter of gender, setting up a kind of racial ideal. Blue eyes and yellow (or "golden") hair are referred to in Whittier's "The Norsemen," Lowell's "The Voyage to Vinland," *The Saga of King Olaf,* and the chapter "Race" in *English Traits.* In the two latter texts, there is clearly a connection between these traits and good looks. "The Heimskringla has frequent occasion to speak of the personal beauty of its heroes," Emerson notes, and Longfellow's golden-haired Olaf is repeatedly said to be handsome.

Jones seems to adhere to the same racial ideal in portraying her goddesses, mentioning the golden hair of the valkyries, the blue eyes of Freya, the white skin of the daughters of Aegir, and so forth. But only Emerson and Longfellow make androgynous qualities part of the pattern. The former speaks of the astonishment "the beauty and long flowing hair" of young English captives and their angelic appearance caused in observers in more southern lands. According to *The Saga of King Olaf,* Einar Tamberskelver had a "beardless lip" as well as "golden locks" and looks like the angel Michael.

When it comes to traditional male ideals such as courage and strength, one notes that they are not celebrated as enthusiastically as in the Eddas and sagas. This phenomenon may have something to do with the religious or ideological bias of many of the authors involved: Quakerish (Whittier, Taylor) and pacifist (Lowell, Longfellow). Strength and courage are no doubt often needed in peaceful enterprises; in "Power," Emerson attributes various degrees of these qualities to the Norse explorers of North America. But in ancient Norse literature, courage and strength tend to be the companions of violence and gore. Such things cannot be avoided entirely if one is following a Norse source featuring some memorable battles, as Longfellow does in *The Saga of King Olaf,* but the American literary discovery of the Norse gave birth to no fresh tales of carnage of the kind found in Scott's *Harold the Dauntless.*

This is not to say that the American writers universally avoid touching on the less pleasant aspects of Norse life. These may even be exaggerated, as when Melville suggests in *Omoo* that the ancient Scandinavians drank mead out of the skulls of their enemies—that is, a reckless extension of the widespread misconception that they hoped to do so in Valhalla. But he is less wide of the mark in attributing a lack of sobriety to the Norse and charging them with superstition in *Mardi.* Emerson justly speaks of their "singular turn for homicide" (*English Traits*), and Whittier does not hesitate to exploit the fact that human sacrifice was known in pagan times ("The Dole of Jarl Thorkell").

But the positive side of Norse culture also gets its due. Even the wildness Melville imputes to the inhabitants of the ancient North has its admirers. Emerson clearly thinks it supplied a valuable element in the composite character of the English "race," and Thoreau alludes to the warlike vigor of the tribes of the northern forests in arguing that a civilization must find room for the wild if it is to survive. Slightly paradoxically, perhaps, both Emerson and Thoreau also celebrate the settled society of independent farmers and the institution of the *Allthing*, as described in Laing's preliminary dissertation and in the text of *Heimskringla* on which his discussion is based. Virtually everybody pays homage to the more enterprising and outgoing spirit of the Norse reflected in their shipbuilding and seafaring.

Norse seafaring cannot be separated entirely from the violent side of Norse life, as its purpose often enough was plunder and murder in foreign—and sometimes not so foreign—lands. But in this case, too, our writers do find a more inspiring, adventurous, and not in every respect unproductive side to it: trade and colonization. Emerson stresses the importance of transplanting Norse individualism and love of freedom to English soil. He even has a good word for the historical effect of "the pirates" in "Aristocracy." As for the purely adventurous side of the Viking Age, it is significantly what Whitman seizes upon (and gives a transcendentalist twist) in section 7 of "Salut au Monde." Melville alludes to it both in *Mardi* and *Moby Dick*. Thoreau touches on it in *Cape Cod*. Lowell adds lines about the competitive spirit, the quasi-Greek desire to do great things, and connects it with the Norse exploration of North America in "The Voyage to Vinland."

The interest in the Norse discovery of America quite naturally was greater in the United States than in Britain: the thought of Leif Ericsson sailing into Massachusetts Bay some six hundred years before the Mayflower could not hold the same romantic appeal for British writers as it did for Lowell and his fellow New Englanders. None of the British authors introduced in chapter 1 seem to have cared enough about the subject to do anything with it. In the New World, on the other hand, virtually all the authors involved touch upon it in one way or other.

The treatment of the subject is usually characterized by a determination not to be circumscribed by known historical facts. The attitude of the American discoverers of the Norse with respect to these is sometimes quite disarming. Whittier's "The Norsemen" is admittedly a fantasy: the poem is based on the "generally accepted" fact that the Norse reached American shores and what looks like a sculpture fragment of stone found near his hometown. The origin of the piece of rock is anyone's guess, says Whittier, and *his* guess is that it was left behind by a band of Norsemen whom he envisions coming up the Merrimack. Longfellow is equally charming in justifying the story told in "The Skeleton in Armor," which is based on the combination of the report of a skeleton in armor unearthed in the Fall River and an old tower in Newport that Professor Rafn insisted must have been built in Norse times: the case is "sufficiently established for a ballad," says the poet. In other cases, the manner in which facts are disregarded cannot but raise an eyebrow: "The Voyage to Vinland" mingles historical data and pure fantasy in a bewildering way: Bjarni ("Biörn") Herjolfsson may have reached American shores in 986 but not out of ambition and not in the company of a beautiful young sibyl called Gudrida, as suggested in the poem. It is not clear to what extent, if any, these discrepancies are due to ignorance on Lowell's part, but the author of *The Conduct of Life* definitely thinks that Eric the Red, the settler of Greenland, sailed to Vinland. Thoreau alone maintains— on the whole—a scrupulously scholarly posture in dealing with these historical events. His judgment is superior to Rafn's when it comes to the question of where the Norse explorers made landfall in North America.

Whatever the answer to that question, it remains an acquired fact that the Norse expeditions to Vinland—including that of Thorfinn Karlsefni, which lasted four years—did not lead to permanent settlement. Nor do the American poets celebrating the transatlantic ventures of the Norse contest that fact. But they sometimes have a funny way of acknowledging it. Lowell leaves Biörn and his ships sitting in view of the American East Coast, and we have to infer from Gudrida's prophecy that they hoisted sail and went back to the Old World as soon as she had finished speaking. The progress of Whittier's Norse crew up the Merrimack is cut short as his vision fades, and we cannot even speculate about what happened after that. Longfellow leaves us ignorant of the fate of the children of his suicidal Rhode Island Viking and the crew that must have assisted him in fleeing beyond the ocean with his princess.

This kind of reticence is not in itself to be construed as gestures in the direction of creating something like a myth of national origin. But Whittier is clearly out to domesticate the Norse adventurers and add depth to the historical background of his home region. Lowell, with admirable fidelity to historical fact, has his sibyl tell Biörn and his crew that the population of the new continent is to be diverse both racially and socially, but at another point she tells them that strong settlers of the American wilderness will in due time issue from their "strong loins." Lowell is not likely to be alluding to the relatively few Scandinavian immigrants who had come to the United States at the time; what he has in mind must be a more pervasive penetration, something like what he has read about in *English Traits*, in which Emerson labors so hard to absorb the Anglo-Saxon element into the Scandinavian strain and maintains that the strength and hardiness of the Norse who conquered England is still at work in America, which is "in the hands of the same race."

Lowell may also have been influenced by the theories of his fellow New Englander Marsh, who expanded the "Gothic race" to include all the Caucasian inhabitants of northwestern Europe and attributes to it whatever is best in Western civilization. The preface to Jones's *Valhalla* demonstrates the lingering influence of these ideas (possibly filtered through the introduction to Anderson's *Norse Mythology; or the Religion of Our Forefathers*).

In Thoreau's *Cape Cod*, the Nordic myth of origin receives a special, more personal coloring based on the assumption that his name is derived from *Thor*. Thoreau clearly likes to think that this means that his family is of Norse origin. But unlike Emerson he is not content to think so only in the general sense that America is a land in the hands of the same Scandinavian race as the mother country. He goes a step further and plays with the idea that he is a descendant of the shipwrecked Thorir rescued by Leif Ericsson.

Both in Thoreau and Emerson one finds traces of a peculiarly Anglo-Saxon racial pride directed at the French. Emerson does not hesitate to suggest in *English Traits* that the Normans invading Britain in 1066 were morally inferior to the Norse invading northern France under Ganger-Hrolf *because* of their long residence in France and their adoption of the French language "with all the vices it has names for." He shares the contempt for France as an unstable and garrulous loser nation harbored by many Englishmen of his time. Thoreau's handling of this issue in *A Yankee in Canada* is less outspoken and less directly tied to the question of power. Yet one notes that he identifies with Olaf Tryggvason while in Quebec. From a different point of view, he extols the love of freedom characteristic of Norwegian farmers nobly standing on their *udall* rights, contrasting it with the "ignoble" and "feudal" situation of a (French Canadian) "nation of peasants."

We are here touching upon some of the reasons why the American literary discovery of the Norse is chiefly a New England affair (even Melville was a resident of Massachusetts at the time of the composition of *Moby Dick*). No doubt the cultural hegemony of New England during the period involved is in part responsible for this limitation: New England is where the authors were, and to a considerable extent the publishers. But the fact that the Vinland sagas could be thought to suggest that Norsemen made land in New England and in one case spent years there must have stimulated not only the incorporation of the Norse experience into local history but also identification through blood ties stretching back to Anglo-Norse times. In *The Northmen in New England,* J. T. Smith stresses the point that New England has a special interest in the Norse explorations of North America. It is possessive feelings of this kind that led to the erection of the statue of Leif Ericsson on Commonwealth Avenue in Boston.

The prevailing economic and social conditions in the northern and maritime section of the eastern seaboard must also have played a role. There was seafaring as well as farming, and it is not surprising that Thoreau was frequently reminded of the Norse while at the Cape. The area in which he himself lived was still largely agricultural and populated by independent farmers descended from the freeholders who confronted the troops of King George just as the Norwegian bönder had done when the unpopular Olaf the Stout tried to regain his kingdom (one of the latter's slayers was Thorir the Hound, with whom Thoreau also liked to identify).

The predominant role of New England helps explain why the original literary phase of the American discovery of the Norse, in spite of a modest spillover into the seventies, is on the whole a thing of the past after the Civil War. The war brought about or accelerated change in the United States. New England was beginning to lose its cultural hegemony to New York. As if that were not enough, the demographic center of gravity was shifting westward, away from the eastern seaboard. Thoreau may have observed (in "Walking") that the young men of Massachusetts, like their Norse counterparts, "took to the sea for their inheritance," that is, went west across the Great Plains; but the similarity between the Viking ships and the prairie schooners apparently was not strong enough to yield sustained literary inspiration.

The fact that the American discovery of the Norse was basically a romantic development may also have contributed to its demise. The romantic movement came relatively late to the United States. If the United States was to catch up, the romantic movement had to come to an end. The Civil War may also have been helpful in bringing about

that event. In any case, the leading writers of the postwar genera-
tion—Howells, Twain, James—could not be expected to continue a
trend so thoroughly associated with an obsolescent literary posture.

The early decline, like the late beginning, is one thing that distin-
guishes the American phase of the Norse revival from its British coun-
terpart. Great Britain did not suffer upheavals such as the American
Civil War, and the break between romanticism and realism appears
to have been less abrupt. In the United States the Norse revival pe-
tered out in the seventies with Taylor's *Lars: A Pastoral of Norway* and
Jones's *Valhalla.* In Britain, that decade, as noted, may be viewed as
the climax of the Norse revival in that country.

The American discovery of the Norse had always been different
from both the Scandinavian and the British revival in that it was
marked by a certain distraction. The writers involved are interested
in the Norse, to be sure, but only as they are also interested in a lot of
other things. With the exception of Jones—but not Fuller—they all
seem to be universalists. Such a diversity of inspiration is no doubt
very fine in a way, but being the heir of all the ages comes at a price:
the larger the surface one covers, the less likely one is to penetrate to
any depth. I do not know if this means that the aspiration to universality is necessarily synonymous with sloppy scholarship, and one can
certainly be guilty of scholarly sloppiness without being a universalist, but there are plenty of errors in the works belonging to the American phase of the Norse revival. They assume scandalous proportions in
The Conduct of Life, and even Thoreau is not entirely free from them.

Produced during a relatively short period of time, the American
body of "Norse" writing through the seventies is also characterized by
a relative dearth of original works of any length on Norse subjects. It
may seem less prepossessing than the corresponding British body aes-
thetically as well as quantitatively. Some of the poems wholly devoted
to Norse topics, such as Taylor's "The Norseman's Ride," must be
called slight. Even the longer ones are not examples of sustained excellence. The two first sections of Lowell's "Voyage to Vinland," for
instance, are promising enough, but in the third and final section,
Gudrida's prophecy, interesting as it is in itself, artistically strikes one
as an anticlimactic nonsequitur. In Longfellow's *Saga of King Olaf,*
again, the selection of episodes from *Heimskringla* is judicious, and a
variety of stanzaic forms are handled with admirable skill, but there
are jarring and ill-advised notes, such as the introduction of specific
refrains from Danish folk ballads that do not always fit their new contexts. Jones's epic of the gods, finally, contains parts written with both

gusto and verve, but it is somewhat uneven and marred by exaggerated zeal in the attempt to reconcile Norse paganism and Christianity, as well as by its proximity to the extravagant claims made for the Gothic race in the preface.

It would be a mistake, however, to dismiss the American phase of the literary rediscovery of the Norse as insignificant. It is true that it is dwarfed in some respects against the background of the partially preceding, partially contemporaneous European revivals, but it also gains in significance from being part of a vast international movement, just as it gains in significance from serving as prelude to the tide of educational literature and creative writing on Norse themes that was to rise in subsequent decades and has yet to recede.

The discovery phase of the Norse revival in America was brief, but it was intense: while it lasted, a majority of writers got involved in one way or another (notable exceptions: Poe, Hawthorne, Stowe, Dickinson). It was not entirely limited to New England; as noted, even Whitman, down in New York, felt the need to include the Norse in saluting the world, and Taylor was a native of Pennsylvania who moved to New York on coming of age; Melville was no longer living in Massachusetts when he wrote *Clarel.* The lack of personal involvement must not be overemphasized: if the scholarship sometimes seems superficial and the attention accorded the Norse less than concentrated and sustained, some writers—Longfellow and Thoreau—were affected deeply enough by their reading to identify with specific heroes in saga literature. One may, in fact, turn the argument around and say that at least some American authors spent a very respectable amount of time on Norse studies considering the great number of other literary traditions they felt duty-bound to pay attention to. Nor is the result of their creative efforts in this particular domain entirely negligible. *The Saga of King Olaf,* in spite of its flaws, is an impressive piece of work and—a mark of the true classic—gains by repeated reading. It deserves more attention than it is receiving, and the same thing can certainly be said about Lowell's "Voyage to Vinland" and Jones's *Valhalla.* The presence of Norse references and allusions in literary masterpieces such as *Walden* and *Moby Dick* must be called significant. The influence and representative nature of *English Traits,* bizarre as some of its theses may seem today, can hardly be doubted. And one must perforce admire the versatility and true Yankee ingenuity shown in adapting Norse history and mythology—such as the voyages to Vinland and the hammer of Thor—to discussions of the distinctly American issues of the day.

Notes

CHAPTER 1. INTRODUCTION

1. The Scandinavian ballad tradition doubtless is historically connected with the older Edda poetry. It appears to have originated in Norway about 1300, but the oldest manuscripts are from the sixteenth century.

2. Example: Peter C. Asbjornsen, *Popular Tales from the Norse* (New York: Appleton, 1859).

3. *Heimskringla* means "circle of the world." It is the first prominent word in the Icelandic text and was apparently first used by scribes as a convenient short title for the work (unwittingly following the lead of the early Jewish scribes who named the books of the Torah in the same way). The title *Edda* is of uncertain origin.

4. In spite of the ambiguities affecting the past and present use of the word *Norse*, it is better suited to our purposes than any other. British scholars sometimes speak of the "Scandinavian revival" in Britain, but the term *Scandinavian* is in my opinion too indefinite with respect to time and besides could be taken to imply that Norse civilization is the essence of Scandinavian civilization (which is very far from being the case). This drawback also adheres to *Nordic*. It is probably a lost cause to insist that *Viking* is not a synonym of *Norse* since all Norse were not Vikings and all Vikings not Norse: *Viking* remains the sexier term.

5. The use of the term *Gothic* as synonymous with *Norse* was, in fact, quite common, and for a long time. In a sense it is sanctioned by the Poetic Edda, in which the term is sometimes applied to Norsemen as a kind of badge of honor.

6. This phase of the movement is covered in C. F. Barnason, "The Revival of Norse Literature," (Ph.D. diss., Harvard University, 1936).

7. The Silver Bible, like the De la Gardie manuscript collection, is kept in the Uppsala University Library, visited by Longfellow in 1835.

8. Here Mallet acknowledges his indebtedness to Danish scholars, including Wormius. His debt to the latter (for the preservation of *Krákamál*) is particularly interesting, as Wormius, or rather his Icelandic collaborator, Magnús Oláfsson, misconstrued a passage (kenning) in Ragnar Lodbrók's death song in his Latin translation, giving rise to the misconception that Norse warriors could not wait to get to Valhalla and drink mead out of the skulls of the enemies they had killed (rather than from "curved branches of skulls," that is, drinking horns). Through Mallet and other translations of Oláfsson's Latin, the erroneous notion of Norse skull drinking spread and thrived. We shall find traces of it in the works of the Norse revival in America.

145

9. *Gothic* in this context is a pis aller English translation of *götisk*. Alrik Gustafson consistently uses it in his *History of Swedish Literature* (Minneapolis: University of Minnesota Press, 1963). The term *götisk* alludes to the glory of the Goths, to be sure, but it needs to be noted that it has a special, native Swedish connotation because of the ancient "tribal" division of the country into *svear* and *götar* (Beowulf's Geats). Thus "Gothic" architecture, abhorred by the French Classicists, could never have been referred to as *götisk*.

10. Unfortunately, English translations of Geijer's poems are hard to come by. In Swedish, they are easily accessible in *Dikter* (Stockholm: P. A. Nordstedt, 1926, and subsequent printings).

11. Tegnér knew this saga from E. J. Björner's *Nordiska kämpadater* (Stockholm, 1737), but "Frithiof the Bold" is conveniently accessible to English-speaking readers in William Morris and Eiríkr Magnússon's translation in *Three Northern Love Stories* (1875; reprint, London: Longmans, Green, and Co., 1901). The most recent English translation of Tegnér's own work appears to be *Frithiof's Saga* (New York: Exposer Press, 1960).

12. This is not quite the way it goes in the original: The Norse text makes no mention of romantic *amours enfantines*. As an adult, Ingebjorg is somewhat less chaste and high-minded than Tegnér makes her out to be. Her main topic of conversation, while Frithiof is wooing her, is a golden arm ring that he has. There is no suggestion that she is an ennobling influence on Frithiof. The latter does not rebuild the temple of Balder; her brother Halfdan, who is as evil and treacherous as Helge, does. Nor does Helge die in a confrontation with Jumala (the Finnish god); he is killed by Frithiof in a final showdown. There is no reconciliation between Frithiof and Halfdan in the name of a Balder presented as a forerunner of Christ.

13. The "loss" of Norway in 1814, when this country was forced into union with Sweden, was another such jolt.

14. English translation: *The Gold Horns* (London: Thomas Wise, 1913).

15. John L. Greenway, *The Golden Horns* (Athens: University of Georgia Press, 1977), 159.

16. Greenway, *Golden Horns*, 153–54.

17. *Amleth* is based on the third and fourth books of the *History of the Danes*, written in Latin by Saxo Grammaticus, an older contemporary of Snorri Sturluson.

18. Besides poetry, the "Norse" chapter in Grundtvig's bibliography includes translations of Snorri and *Nordens mytologi* (1808).

19. The most complete bibliographical study of the Scandinavian "dream of the saga times" (including twentieth-century developments) is Jöran Mjöberg's *Drömmen om sagatiden*, 2 vols. (Stockholm: Natur och Kultur, 1969–70).

20. Chapter 9 of *Germania* is of particular interest in this respect.

21. The first "Norse" poem by a German preromantic poet was "Gedicht eines Skalden" by Klopstock's friend H. W. von Gerstenberg (1766).

22. The *Nibelungenlied* is roughly contemporary (thirteenth-century) with the *Volsunga Saga*. But Siegfrid's early exploits—his killing of Fafne and so forth—are only referred to vaguely and in passing. What is more, the whole story has been updated to fit the age of chivalry; there is no mention of the pagan gods of the North. For an up-to-date discussion of the relation between the Norse and German traditions, see the section on *der Stoffkreis* in the introduction to *Das Nibelungenlied*, edited by Helmut de Boor, 22d ed. (Mannheim, Germany: F. A. Brockhaus, 1988).

23. Appendix D in Andrew Hilen's *Longfellow and Scandinavia* (New Haven: Yale University Press, 1947).

24. Rudolph Keyser, *The Religion of the Northmen* (New York: C. B. Norton, 1854).

25. Thomas Carlyle, *On Heroes and Hero-Worship* (1841; reprint, London: Oxford University Press, 1959), 46.

26. For a painstaking survey, see P. M. Mitchell, "Old Norse-Icelandic Literature in Germany 1789-1849, with a Critical Bibliography" (Ph.D. diss., University of Illinois, 1942). For the earlier years, there is Margrethe Schioler Micek's "Scandinavian Antiquity in German Literature from 1745 to 1773" (Ph.D. diss., University of California, 1962).

27. E. V. Gordon, *Introduction to Old Norse*, 2d ed. rev. A. R. Taylor (Oxford, England: Clarendon Press, 1957), xxxviii.

28. Among place-names, one notes York (*Jorvik*) and Grimsby. As for vocabulary, some of the most common English words—such as *sister, egg, sky, Thursday*—are Norse. So are the personal and possessive pronouns *they, them, their*.

29. The last decade in particular has seen a veritable explosion of interest in this aspect of the history of the British Isles, witness works such as J. D. Richards, *Viking Age England* (London: B.T. Batsford, 1991), A. Ritchie, *Viking Scotland* (London and Edinburgh, Scotland: B. T. Batsford, 1993), and Richard A. Hall, *Viking Age Archeology in Britain and Ireland* (Princes Risborough, England: Shire, 1990)—to mention just a few.

30. Gray also translated some pieces of Welsh poetry and intended to include them in his "History of English Poetry."

31. *The Works of William Collins,* edited by Richard Wendorf and Charles Ryskamp (Oxford, England: Clarendon Press, 1979), 57.

32. Thomas Percy, *Northern Antiquities*, 2 vols. (London: T. Carnan and Co., 1770), 1.ii and 2.v–vi. Among other things added by Percy is a supplement giving, for comparison with Mallet's Frenchified translation, J. Göransson's Latin version of Snorri's Edda (Uppsala, Sweden, 1746). On the whole the work has been thoroughly adapted for British consumption, as can be gathered already from the title page, on which it is introduced as "A Description of the ancient Danes, and other Northern Nations, including those of our own Saxon Ancestors, with a translation of the Edda, or system of Runic mythology, and other pieces from the ancient Islandic Tongue."

33. William Powell Jones, *Thomas Gray, Scholar* (New York: Russell and Russell, 1965), 100–105.

34. William Powell Jones, *Thomas Gray, Scholar,* 101, 106. D. C. Tovey, *Gray's English Poems* (Cambridge: Cambridge University Press, 1898), 239.

35. Carlyle, *On Heroes and Hero-Worship*, 45.

36. Percy's *Northern Antiquities* was republished as *Illustrations of Northern Antiquities* with additions by Scott, coeditor of the volume along with H. W. Weber and Robert Jamieson (Edinburgh, Scotland, and London: Longman, Hurst, Rees, Orme, and Brown, 1814).

37. Beginnings of chapters 15 and 21.

38. *Rokeby*, canto 5, line 1. I am quoting Scott's poetry from the *Complete Poetical Works of Sir Walter Scott* (Boston and New York: Houghton Mifflin, 1924).

39. *Harold the Dauntless*, canto 3, line 5.

40. For a more detailed account of Scott's interest in the Norse, see P. R. Lieder, "Scott and Scandinavian Literature," in *Smith College Studies in Modern Languages* 2, no. 1 (1920): 8–57.

41. Carlyle's *Early Kings of Norway* (London: Chapman and Hall, 1875) testifies to his continued fascination with the Norse, but it is too late a work to have much relevance to the Norse revival in America.

42. Carlyle, *On Heroes and Hero-Worship*, 20.

43. Ibid., 24.

44. Ibid., 42–43.

45. There is no indication that Carlyle clearly sees the difference between the remote times from which the old mythology comes to us and the relatively sophisticated day of Snorri Sturluson.

46. Carlyle, *On Heroes and Hero-Worship*, 23–24.

47. Judging by the reference to skull drinking, Arnold also read the Bartholin-Oláfsson translation of Ragnar Lodbrók's death song in the same volume.

48. For Arnold's reading preparatory to the composition of the poem, see *The Poems of Matthew Arnold*, 2d ed. by Miriam Allott (London and New York: Longman, 1979), 376–77.

49. For Carlyle's treatment of the Balder theme, see *On Heroes and Hero-Worship*, 45–46.

50. Morris also published a translation of the *Volsunga Saga* (London: Longman, Green and Co., 1870) (as well as the already-mentioned translations in *Three Northern Love Stories* done in cooperation with Eiríkr Magnússon).

51. For a full discussion of William Morris's "Norse" work, see J. N. Swannell, *William Morris and Old Norse Literature* (London: William Morris Society, 1962).

52. Here are some titles, listed in the order in which they were first published: C. H. Nordby, *The Influence of Old Norse Literature Upon English Literature* (1901; reprint, New York: AMS Press, 1966); Frank E. Farley, *Scandinavian Influences in the English Romantic Movement* (1903; reprint, Boston: Ginn, 1980); C. H. Herford, *Norse Myth in English Poetry* (Manchester, Enlgand: Manchester University Press, 1919); R. B. Allen, *Old Icelandic Sources in the English Novel* (1933; reprint, Folcroft, Pennsylvania: Folcroft Library Editions, 1977); Karl Litzenberg, *The Victorians and the Vikings: A Bibliographical Essay on Anglo-Norse Literary Relations* (Ann Arbor: University of Michigan Press, 1947).

53. *The Heimskringla, or, Chronicle of the Norse Kings*, translated by Samuel Laing, 3 vols. (London: Longman, Brown, Green, and Longmans, 1844). *The Prose or Younger Edda Commonly Assigned to Snorri Sturluson*, translated by George W. Dasent (Stockholm and London: W. Pickering, 1842).

54. *The Story of Burnt Njal, or Life in Iceland at the end of the Tenth Century*, translated by George W. Dasent, 2 vols. (Edinburgh, Scotland: G. Richards, 1861). *The Edda of Saemund the Learned* translated by George W. Dasent (London: Trubner, 1866).

55. Henry Wheaton, "Scandinavian Mythology, Poetry, and History," *North American Review* 38 (January, 1829), 18–37.

56. Henry Wheaton, *History of the Northmen, or Danes and Normans, from the Earliest Times to the Conquest of England by William of Normandy* (London: Mussan, 1831). (The complete title is curious in that it appears to suggest that all Northmen are either Danes or Normans.)

57. Wheaton, *History of the Northmen*, 81.

58. Washington Irving, "Wheaton's History of the Northmen," review, *The North American Review* 35 (1832): 342–71.

59. Ibid., 344. Possessing no personal expertise in the field, Irving does not deliver an in-depth critical analysis of Wheaton's work but is, on the whole, content to summarize and cite. Occasionally, he adds materials from other sources.

60. *The North American Review* 46 (1838): 161–203.

61. This work (Boston: Hilliard, Gray, and Co., 1839) came on the heels of Carl Christian Rafn's pamphlet "America Discovered in the Tenth Century" (New York: W. Jackson, 1838), and it is dedicated to "his Excellency Edward Everett."

62. The translation was published in two installments in *The American Eclectic* 1 (May 1841): 446–66 and 2 (July 1841): 131–46.

63. George Perkins Marsh, *The Goths in New England* (Middlebury, Vermont: Philomathesian Society of Middlebury College, 1843).

64. New York: Phillips and Hunt, 1881, and Boston: Ginn, 1890.

65. New York: Scribner's Sons, 1892.

66. R. B. Anderson's *America Not Discovered by Columbus*, first published in 1874 (Chicago: S.C. Griggs and Co.), went through a surprising number of editions. Thomas Wentworth Higginson documented his interest in "The Visit of the Vikings," *Harper's* 65 (September 1882), 515–27, and Ernest Fales followed with *History of the Northmen's Visits to Rhode Island and Massachusetts in the Tenth Century* (Providence: F. N. Shaw, 1888). Torfaeus's work was published as *The History of Ancient Vinland* (New York: John G. Shea, 1891).

67. There was also a lively American drama during the period I am concerned with. But I know of no play that needs to be taken into account in the context of the American discovery of the Norse. When an American playwright of the time looked for an exotic theme, he tended to look south, not north. Thus N. P. Willis composed *Bianca Visconti* (1837), set in fourteenth-century Milan, and *Tortesa the Usurer* (1839), set in medieval Florence; Robert Montgomery Ward penned *The Gladiator*, a play frequently performed from the thirties on; George Henry Boker wrote *Lenore de Guzman*, produced in 1853–54 and *Francesca da Rimini* (1855); and so forth.

68. *Literary History of the United States*, edited by Robert Spiller et al. (New York: Macmillan, 1974).

69. *The Cambridge History of American Literature*, edited by Sacvan Bercovitch (Cambridge, England: Cambridge University Press, 1995).

70. Myra Jehlen, "Introduction: Beyond Transcendence," in *Ideology and Classic American Literature*, edited by Sacvan Bercovitch and Myra Jehlen (Cambridge: Cambridge University Press, 1986), 1.

71. Houston Baker, "Figurations for a New American Literary History," in *Ideology and Classic American Literature*, 169.

72. David Levin, *Forms of Uncertainty* (Charlottesville: University Press of Virginia, 1994), 10.

73. Charles Avallone, "What American Renaissance? The Gendered Genealogy of a Critical Discourse," *PMLA* 112 (October 1997): 1115.

CHAPTER 2. EMERSON

1. *The Complete Works of Ralph Waldo Emerson*, edited by E. W. Emerson, 12 vols. (Boston and New York: Houghton, Mifflin and Co., 1903), 5:50.

2. The subtitle of Knox's book (London: H. Renshaw, 1850) is "A Philosophical Enquiry into the Influence of Race over the Destinies of Nations."

3. *Works*, 5:55.

4. Philip L. Nicoloff, *Emerson on Race and History: An Examination of English Traits* (New York: Columbia University Press, 1961), 152.

5. *The Early Lectures of Ralph Waldo Emerson*, edited by Stephen E. Whicher and Robert E. Spiller, 3 vols. (Cambridge: Harvard University Press, Belkap Press, 1959), 1:241–42. As noted by the editors, the passage is informed by Sharon Turner's account of the Norse in her *History of the Anglo-Saxons*, 6th ed., 4 vols. (London: Longman, Rees, Orme, Browne, and Green, 1836), 1:205–12.

6. *Works*, 2:72.

7. The correspondence invariably deals with the business aspects of the book, Emerson wanting to help his friend get out an American edition of it (a project thwarted by Appleton's publication of a pirated edition). See *The Correspondence of Emerson and Carlyle*, edited by Joseph Slater (New York: Columbia University Press, 1964).

8. *The Journals and Miscellaneous Notebooks of Ralph Waldo Emerson*, 16 vols. (Cambridge: Harvard University Press, Belknap Press, 1960–82), *Works*, 10:17 and 10:131n.

9. *Journals and Miscellaneous Notebooks*, 10:336.

10. Ibid., 10:17.

11. The attention thus accorded the Prose Edda and *Heimskringla* provides a stark contrast with the absence of quotations from the Poetic Edda and the family sagas, English translations of which were not available. At the time when Emerson was working on *English Traits*, he seems to have thought that only three fragments of the Poetic Edda ("Voluspá," "Hávamál," and "Magic") were extant (*Journals and Miscellaneous Notebooks*, 11:65). In later essays there are references to "The Norse Edda" and "the Edda," as if there were only one (*Works*, 7:287 and 8:13).

12. Like Carlyle, Laing frequently refers to the Norse as "our ancestors" (e.g., *Heimskringla*, 1:114), and uses phrases like "this northern branch of the one great race" and "the one great Northern race" (1:11, and 29). He differs from Emerson only in his insistence that what is great about England (and indeed about North America) is due to the Norse, not to the Saxon strain, which is said to have been tamed by feudal and ecclesiastical overlords (1:7–8). Emerson is more even-handed.

13. *Works*, 5:60.

14. *Heimskringla*, 1:232–49.

15. *Works*, 5:59–60.

16. Ibid., 5:57. The word *bonders*, picked up in Laing's preliminary dissertation, is strictly speaking an impossibility. Laing apologizes for it, noting that *bönder*, the correct plural of Norse *bondi*, "does not suit the English ear" (1:100)

17. Emerson does not seem to have any use in this essay for Mallet's Montesquieu-inspired association of free institutions and the climate of the North. He may, in fact, never have adopted this view. In a Civil War poem called "Voluntaries," he notes that Freedom had traditionally been associated with the North: "Long she loved the Northman well." But "Now the iron age is done, / She will not refuse to dwell / With the offspring of the Sun" (*Works*, 9:206).

18. *Works*, 5: 65.

19. Ibid., 5:66.

20. Ibid., 5:75. Howard Mumford Jones, in a note to this passage in his edition of *English Traits* (Cambridge: Harvard University Press, 1966), remarks that Emerson could be "clearer" here and explains that what the author means is that the Anglo-Saxons were "too intelligent" to permanently accept a feudal way of life (218). But the lack of clarity is likely to be due to the fact that Emerson's use of the word "intellectual" in this context echoes Laing's preliminary dissertation. Laing likes to stress the "intellectuality" (not just the intelligence!) of the Norse, but he does so at the expense of the Saxons, who, he says, had lost their spiritual independence along with their courage, were easily defeated by their Scandinavian cousins, and unlike them possessed no great literature (e.g. 1:9–11, 87). As mentioned in an earlier note, Emerson did not share this distinction between Norse and Saxon, and he therefore could not be expected to echo Laing more fully and clearly.

21. *Works*, 4:66.

22. The notion that the Scandinavians (or "Goths") were immigrants from Asia harks back to the introductory pages of *Heimskringla*. It is promoted by Mallet (cf. *Journals and Miscellaneous Notebooks*, 10:131).

23. The Younger Edda is quoted from *Northern Antiquities*, 2:123 (cf. *Journals and Miscellaneous Notebooks*, 10:138).

24. *Works*, 5:92.

25. Ibid., 5:162.

26. Ibid., 5:104. This personal note foreshadows Emerson's complaint about what he sees as the decline of his genetic heritage in "Terminus" (*Works* 9:251):

> Curse, if thou wilt, thy sires,
> Bad husbands of their fires,
> Who, when they gave thee breath,
> Failed to bequeath
> The needful sinew stark as once,
> The Baresark marrow to thy bones. . . .

27. *Works*, 5:147.

28. Norse mythology is here fused with English popular superstition from Milton's time: The quoted phrase is from "L'Allegro," 2:109–10.

29. *Works*, 5:134–35, 139–40.

30. Ibid., 233–36.

31. Ibid., 207, 210.

32. Ibid., 174.

33. Ibid., 36.

34. Ibid., 11:406.

35. Ibid., 344.

36. Ibid., 7:22, 175–76.

37. Ibid., 11:426.

38. Ibid., 5:275. We are here touching on the subject of Manifest Destiny. For a broad picture of the relation between race and American imperialism, see Reginald Horsman, *Manifest Destiny* (Cambridge: Harvard University Press, 1981).

39. Emerson's interest in the voyages to Vinland seems to have been curiously limited compared with, say, Thoreau's; Emerson betrays no awareness of Carl Christian Rafn's *Antiquitates Americanae* (Copenhagen, 1837) or even of J. T. Smith's 1838 *The Northmen in New England*, printed in Boston. However, there is an abridged version of the "facts" in part 5 of Laing's preliminary dissertation and a lengthy account of this chapter in Norse history in *Northern Antiquities* (1:279–305). The latter text may be particularly relevant in that it mentions that the Norse were the first to sail across open oceans (rather than along the coasts) and suggests that they cannot have made their landfalls far from Labrador and Newfoundland (see Emerson's text below).

40. *Works*, 6:55.

41. A quatrain called "Northman" appears to be in line with the position outlined in "Power":

> The gale that wrecked you on the sand,
> It helped my rowers to row;
> The storm is my best galley hand
> And drives me where I go.

According to a journal note from 1852 (*Journals and Miscellaneous Notebooks*, 13:172), these lines are inspired by a passage in Augustin Thierry's *History of the Conquest of England by the Normans*, of which an English version was published in 1841 (London: Whittaker and Co.).

42. As the exact source of Emerson's reference to Norse voyaging cannot be determined, it seems convenient and justifiable here to cite the most accessible modern translation of *Groenlendinga Saga* and *Eiriks Saga: The Vinland Sagas*, translated by Magnus Magnusson and Hermann Pálsson (Penguin Books, 1965). The passages in question will be found in chapter 5 of the latter and chapter 3 of the former text.

43. The error is present already in the corresponding journal entry (*Journals and Miscellaneous Notebooks*, 11:198).

44. *Works*, 6:205. From the *Journals and Miscellaneous Notebooks* (10:342) it is clear that Emerson's source is Laing, *Heimskringla* 1:445 and 1:448.

45. *Works*, 6:20.

46. Primarily from Dasent, *Prose Edda* 35–36 (cf. *Journals and Miscellaneous Notebooks*, 10:109). The journal (10:132) also contains a quotation from the corresponding passage in *Northern Antiquities* (2:93), but Emerson here seems to approach the fable from a rather different angle.

47. The same fable is used more appropriately in a passage in "Wealth" in *English Traits* (*Works*, V.161), in which the telegraph is said to be "the limp band that will hold the Fenriswolf of war" in Europe (except that Ragnarök comes fast in the form of the Franco-Prussian War).

48. *Works*, 6:137–38. Source: Dasent, 25 (cf. *Journals and Miscellaneous Notebooks*, 10:108).

49. *Grimnismál* in the Poetic Edda, which Snorri cites in this context, actually says it has 540 *rooms*, which sounds more like the labyrinth at Knossos.

50. Dasent, *Prose Edda*, 17 (cf. *Journals and Miscellaneous Notebooks*, 6:107.)

51. *Works*, 6:313.

52. Ibid., 6:320–21. The wording does not allow us to trace the reference to a specific translation. "Gylfi's Mocking" is Dasent's title (Mallet-Percy has "Illusions"); on the other hand, the only other journal reference to Thor's adventures in Utgard is to the previously cited passage in *Northern Antiquities*, 2:123 (*Journals and Notebooks*, 10:138).

53. Emerson does get the name right in *English Traits*.

54. A close look at *Society and Solitude* (1870), which features an equal number of Norse references (some of which have already been cited), does not substantially alter the picture. Rather, it confirms in new ways the dangers of the pursuit of literary universality (and perhaps what today is known as "multiculturalism"). In "Books," the reference to genuinely Norse (Icelandic) literature—Snorri's Edda, *Heimskringla*, the second volume of *Northern Antiquities*—is swallowed up and rendered almost unnoticeable in the universal mass of works recommended (*Works*, 7:206). By contrast, "Civilization" contains a long—not particularly apropos—quotation from a Norwegian folk tale attributed to "our Scandinavian forefathers" although very much posterior to the Norse colonization of Britain (*Works*, 7:22). Similarly, in "Success" (*Works* 7:287), Emerson quotes and calls "ancient Norse" a folk ballad about Sven Vondved translated from the Danish by George Borrow and published in the latter's *Romantic Ballads* (Norwich, England: George Borrow, 1826). I suppose, if Bonaparte and the Buddha can be quoted in the same breath, why should folk ballads and the Eddas be kept carefully apart?

CHAPTER 3. THOREAU

1. Adolf B. Benson, "Scandinavian Influences in the Writings of Thoreau" *Scandinavian Studies* 16 (1941):241.

2. The article was published in *Graham's Magazine* 30, no. 3 (March 1847):145–52; 30, no. 4 (April 1847):238–45. According to Walter Harding's *Thoreau Handbook* (New York: New York University Press, 1959), it had been used as a lecture before the Concord Lyceum the year before (p. 49).

3. Walden edition of the *Writings of Henry David Thoreau*, 20 vols. (1906; reprint, New York: AMS Press, 1968), 4:341.

4. This sentence, the imagery in which does sound a bit exaggerated, is omitted in the version printed in *Writings*, and I am quoting from *Graham's Magazine* 30, no. 4 (April 1847):239.

5. *Writings*, 4:343.

6. *A Yankee in Canada* was first published as "An Excursion to Canada" in three successive issues of the first volume of *Putnam's Monthly Magazine*, beginning in January 1853: no. 1, 54–59; no. 2, 170–84; and no. 3, 321–29.

7. *Writings*, 5:28.

8. Chapter 32 in *Olaf Tryggvason's Saga* tells the story of how Olaf is picked as the suitor most to her taste by Queen Gyda over a man whose clothing was very much superior to his. (The event took place in Northumberland, which was then under Norse rule.)

9. Laing, *Heimskringla*, 1:47–48. Apparently he (and Thoreau) got it about right: *odal* (or *udal*) is an umlaut form of *adel*, the former word meaning "inherited land" or "property right," the latter "provenance," "quality," etc. See Elof Hellquist, *Svensk etymologisk ordbok* (Lund, Sweden: Gleerup, 1922). The word *udal* actually appears in the description of the freeholders in *Rigsthula* (The Lay of Rig) in the Poetic Edda (stanza 37). In Romantic literature, one notes the frequent references to "the Udaller" in Scott's *The Pirate*, set in the old Norse colonies of Shetland and Orkneys. (Scott explains the term in a note.)

10. *Writings*, 5:82.

11. "Walking" was first published in the *Atlantic Monthly* 9 (June 1862):657–74.

12. *Writings*, 5:223. Here, Thoreau is echoing a passage in *Cape Cod* (see n. 15) in which he says that the Norsemen "were a hardy race, whose younger sons inherited the ocean."

13. The first four chapters of *Cape Cod* were published in three successive issues of *Putnam's Monthly Magazine* 5 (June 1855):632–40; 6 (July 1855):59–66; and 6 (August 1855):157–64.

14. *Writings*, 4:67.

15. Ibid., 248.

16. For the quoted passage, see *Writings*, 4:140.

17. Ibid., 14.

18. For a fairly complete discussion of the origin of the word *Viking*, see Johannes Brøndsted, *The Vikings*, translated by Kalle Skov (Baltimore: Penguin Books, 1965), 36–39.

19. *Writings*, 4:140. The name of the mountain ridge in central Norway called Kjölen (the Keel), which is frequently mentioned in *Heimskringla*, is actually Dovre Fjell. "Doffrafield Mountains" suggests that Thoreau, perhaps misled by the old-fashioned (Danish) spelling of the word *fjell* as *field*, thought it meant *field* rather than *mountain*.

20. Rafn, *Antiquitates Americanae*, xxxiv.

21. As for the keel image, Thoreau seems to have chosen to pursue it in *Walden* instead: There is a passage in which an old man is said to be so knowledgeable about Nature that you might think he "had helped to lay her keel." I am quoting from *The Variorum Walden*, annotated and with an introduction by Walter Harding (New York: Twayne Publishers, 1962), 245.

22. *Antiquitates Americanae* features parallel texts in these three languages. Professor Rafn divides the written testimony of the Norse discovery into basically two traditions, one deal-

ing with the voyages of the Greenlanders, that is, the sons of Eric the Red, the other (of which he gives two versions) mainly with Thorfinn Karlsefni.

23. In what is nowadays usually referred to as the *Groenlendinga Saga* (chapter 5), Thorvald Eiriksson is said to have named a promontory Kjalarness after erecting a damaged keel as a kind of monument; in what is now commonly called *Eiriks Saga* (chapter 8), Thorfinn Karlsefni finds a ship's keel and names the place after it.

24. *Writings*, 4:187. *Furdustrandas* is the Latinized plural accusative found in the translation of the poem by Thorhall cited below. The correct nominative form, *Furdustrandir*, appears later, in "Provincetown," in a passage culled from Rafn's abstract (*Writings*, 4:248).

25. The other version of the story, ignored by Thoreau, offers a slightly different text, with *cetum* instead of *balaenas*.

26. *The Variorum Walden*, 230–31.

27. *Writings*, 4:191.

28. Thoreau here seems to echo Laing (*Heimskringla*, 1:171.). Laing generally takes a dim view of Rafn's scientific judgment.

29. The incident in question is reported in chapters 3 and 4 of *Groenlendinga Saga*.

30. Benson dwells on this matter at considerable length (*Scandinavian Studies*, 246–49).

31. *Writings*, 4:200–201.

32. Peter Kalm, *Travels into North America*, translated by J. R. Forster, 3 vols. (London, 1770–1771), 1:210–11.

33. In a note, Kalm here refers to Torfaeus's *Historia Vinlandiae*.

34. *Writings*, 4:247.

35. *Writings*, 4:249. Laing expresses the same view in his preliminary dissertation (*Heimskringla*, 1:171). More recently, Helge Ingstad (who directed the excavations of the Norse village at L'Anse aux Meadows in Newfoundland in 1960–66) seems to have reached the same conclusion. But his discovery does not really prove that Vinland was located in Newfoundland and that the Norse never penetrated farther south. Nor has Sven Söderberg's reinterpretation of the word *vin* in Vinland to mean "grassland or pasture" (adduced as support by Ingstad) been generally accepted. The latest word appears to be that Vinland "probably lay south of the Gulf of St. Lawrence, the approximate northern limit of the wild grapes, but north of Cape Cod, the southern limit of the Atlantic salmon" (the Vinland sagas mention salmon). For a convenient overview of the present state of Vinland research, see *The Penguin Atlas of the Vikings* by John Heywood (London: Penguin Books, 1995), 98.

36. *The Variorum Walden*, 171, 239.

37. *The Journal of Henry Thoreau*, edited by Bradford Torrey and Francis H. Allen, 14 vols. bound as two (1906; reprint, New York: Dover Publications, 1962), 3:48.

38. "The milk of Valhalla" is likely to have something to do with the goat Heidrún, from whose udders the mead drunk by the champions flows, according to Snorri's Edda (one sign that Thoreau was acquainted with this work). Yet the image is of real milk from which the yellowish cream is skimmed away, uncovering the "pure" and by comparison actually somewhat bluish milk underneath.

39. Richard Colyer, "Thoreau's Color Symbols" *PMLA* 86, no. 5 (October 1971):1001–2.

40. End of the *Saga of Hákon the Good* in *Heimskringla*, quoted from Lee M. Hollander's translation (Austin: University of Texas Press, 1964), 126.

41. Stanza 8 of *Grimnismál* in Hollander's translation of *Elder Edda* (Austin: University of Texas Press, 1962).

42. Note the Thoreauvian pun on *spiring-aspiring*.

43. Cf. the sudden change of image in the cited journal passage describing the surface

of the Concord River from "milk of Valhalla" to the harder and icier-sounding "panoply of sky-blue plates."

44. See Erik Thurin, *Emerson as Priest of Pan: A Study in the Metaphysics of Sex* (Lawrence: The Regents Press of Kansas, 1981), 27–28.

45. Laing, as noted, makes much of what he sees as the intellectual bent of the Norse. He also emphasizes the masculinity of pagan Scandinavian culture. Apropos of Norse eschatology he says (with only slight exaggeration): "It is remarkable that in the religion of Odin, as in that of Mohamet, women appear to have had no part in the future life. We find no allusion to any Valhalla for the female virtues" (*Heimskringla*, 1:92).

46. *The Variorum Walden*, 243.

47. Ibid., 249.

48. In a letter of 23 April 1861, Thoreau's English friend, Thomas Cholmondeley, drew his attention to this passage (chapter 102 in *Njal's Saga*), in which Thangbrand, while working the western districts of Iceland, is heckled by an old woman who asks him: "Did you not hear how Thor challenged Christ to single combat and that Christ dared not accept the challenge?" See *The Correspondence of Henry David Thoreau*, edited by Walter Harding and Carl Bode (New York: New York University Press, 1958), 613.

49. One might add that the theme also appears in some poems of the time, as, for instance, in Longfellow's "Tegnér's Drapa" (1847).

CHAPTER 4. MELVILLE

1. *Omoo: A Narrative of Adventures in the South Seas*, edited by Harrison Hayford et al. (Evanston, Illinois and Chicago: Northwestern University Press and Newberry Library, 1968), ch. 7, 27–28, 129.

2. *White-Jacket, or, the World in a Man-of-War*, edited by Harrison Hayford et al. (Evanston, Illinois and Chicago: Northwestern University Press and Newberry Library, 1970), 211.

3. *White-Jacket*, 354. The Huns, like the Norse, are a medieval people. In the Poetic Edda, the term *Huns* is sometimes used as a (honorific) synonym for the name of some Scandinavian tribe.

4. In Edda mythology, Jarl, as the son of Riger (Heimdall) and a mortal woman called Modur, is the founder of Norse aristocracy. His son is supposed to have been the first king of Denmark (Konur).

5. *Mardi and a Voyage Thither*, edited by Harrison Hayford et al. (Evanston, Illinois and Chicago: Northwestern University Press and Newberry Library, 1970), 12.

6. Ibid., 97.

7. Ibid., 21.

8. Ibid., 63–64.

9. Ibid., 106.

10. Melville's humorous touch sometimes reminds one of Scott's account of the Norse in *The Pirate*, as does the fact that Jarl hails from one of the islands off the Scottish coast colonized by the Norse. This touch also makes it seem unlikely that Melville was inspired by Tegnér's *Frithiofs Saga* in drawing the portrait of Jarl, a possibility suggested by Merrill Davis in *Melville's Mardi* (New Haven: Yale University Press, 1952), 107. Melville borrowed and read one of the editions of *Frithiofs Saga* early in 1848 (Davis, 64), but Tegnér's touch is not equally humorous.

11. *Mardi*, 29.

12. Ibid., 109.

13. Ibid., 37–38.

14. The whole context ("There are more wonders than the wonders rejected, and more sights unrevealed than you or I ever dreamt of") strongly suggests that this passage is inspired by the discussion of the sea serpent, or *soe-ormen*, in Erik Pontoppidan's *Natural History of Norway* (London: A. Linde, 1755) or, rather, from the extracts printed in John Knox's *A New Collection of Voyages*, 7 vols. (London, 1767). The sea serpent is discussed right before the account of the *Kraken* (4:97–100 and 100–104, respectively, in the latter work), and since Melville was familiar with Pontoppidan's description of the *Kraken* (see n. 27), he cannot possibly have missed the stories about the sea serpent and the eyewitness testimonies that such a creature actually exists.

15. *Mardi*, 482–483, 59.

16. Ibid., 367.

17. Ibid., 482. Torf-Egil, incidentally, is a fictional name and might be part of the humor. There is no such person in Norse annals, although there is a Torf-Einar, Earl of Orkney, who is mentioned in *Heimskringla* and some of the family sagas (he introduced turf heating in his sparsely forested islands).

18. *Mardi*, 603. Such passages call to mind Allen Gutmann's graphic suggestion that *Mardi* (unlike *Moby Dick*) is filled with allusions "filched from Bayle and Brown and Burton, and displayed like stolen jewelry at a pick-pocket's convention." "From *Typee* to *Moby Dick*: Melville's Allusive Art." *Modern Language Quarterly* 24 (September 1963):237–44.

19. Herman Melville, *Moby Dick, or, the Whale*, edited by Charles Feidelson Jr. (New York: Bobbs-Merrill, 1964), 105.

20. *Njal's Saga*, translated by Magnus Magnusson and Hermann Pálsson (Baltimore: Penguin Books, 1960), chapter 119. Melville's immediate source is nevertheless in doubt. He does not mention this text, which, as noted, was not translated into English until 1861. He did little if any reading in other languages, judging by the "check-list of books owned and borrowed" published by Merton Sealts Jr. in *Melville's Reading* (Madison: University of Wisconsin Press, 1966) and again in a revised and enlarged edition with the same title (Columbia: University of South Carolina Press, 1988). The incorrectness of Melville's reference increases the possibility that he knew the passage in question only from hearsay. Melville made friends with a number of possible informants during his years at sea, such as the apparently well-read and Scandinavian-named Nord introduced in chapter 13 of *White-Jacket*.

21. *Moby Dick*, 168.

22. Before the mast, there is an Icelander and a Dane, but they play a most insignificant role compared with other nationalities represented in the crew of the Pequod. They have clearly only been included for the sake of ethnic catholicity.

23. As for the tradition Melville is alluding to, it may have been an oral one so far as he was concerned. It is certainly an obscure one. Sea ivory is a prominent feature in the interior decoration of the palace of the sea king Griper in William Morris's *Sigurd the Volsung*, but it is not mentioned in his sources: the *Volsunga Saga* and the Sigurd cycle in the Poetic Edda.

24. Cf. Glauco Cambon, "Ishmael and the Problem of Formal Discontinuities in *Moby Dick*." *Modern Language Notes* 76 (1961):516–23.

25. Not least intriguing is the fact that Melville does not say *Turf-Egil* but uses the more Norse-sounding form.

26. Sealts, following Davis, identifies two translations of *Frithiofs Saga*, either one of which Melville may have borrowed (no. 122 in the check-list in both editions). *On Heroes and Hero-Worship* is no. 500 in the check-list, likewise in both editions.

27. Carlyle, *On Heroes and Hero-Worship*, 42. Carlyle does not specify what kind of monsters he has in mind. However, among the monsters of the ocean, whales play an important

role in the Norse imagination. In canto 10 of Tegnér's *Frithiofs Saga*, the Norwegian hero, fleeing from the evil brother of his beloved on the ship Ellida, fights and narrowly defeats a whale controlled by two trolls who are the agents of his enemy. Melville must have found this story interesting reading even though he does not cite it in *Moby Dick*, especially as one of the trolls riding the whale is white as snow. Melville does dwell at some length on the Kraken, the immense monster that according to Pontoppidan still lurks in the Norwegian Sea and is said to be capable of stopping a ship "under full sail." Melville identifies this mythological creature with the giant squid and turns it into an alternative symbol of the malevolence lurking at the heart of things: "Almost rather had I seen Moby Dick and fought him, than to see thee, thou white ghost!" says Ahab (*Moby Dick*, 366). The Kraken may well have influenced Melville's conception of the demonic white whale. So may the story of the gigantic and malicious Sea Serpent, a scaled-down version of the Midgard Serpent that, as mentioned, is discussed back to back with the Kraken by Pontoppidan and apparently is alluded to in *Mardi* along with the Midgard serpent itself. According to the Bishop of Bergen, there are actually two kinds of sea serpent, one of which is said to spout like a whale (Knox's *New Collection of Voyages*, 4:99).

28. H. Bruce Franklin, *The Wake of the Gods: Melville's Mythology* (Stanford, California: Stanford University Press, 1963), 204.

29. Ibid., 70.

30. *Moby Dick*, 638. It is true that this thunderstorm is also referred to as a "Typhoon" (336), which gives Franklin leave to call it "an alternative manifestation" of the Typhon fought by Ahab-Osiris (78).

31. As noted, Thoreau compares Carlyle himself to Thor in his 1847 article on the Scottish essayist.

32. Clarel decides to join the group and go traveling after the Zionist American father of a girl he falls in love with in Jerusalem is murdered by an Arab and the girl and her mother, following custom, disappear to mourn him in seclusion for several months.

33. As examples one may mention a parenthesis such as "if we deem / Joel's wild text no Runic dream" (1.20.9–10) or the passage in which Clarel tells himself that a certain Muslim Albanian warrior is certain to be welcome in "Valhalla's hall" (4.2.184). I am quoting from *Clarel: A Poem*, edited byWalter Bezanson (1960; New York: Hendricks House, 1973).

34. Ibid., 2.5.131.

35. Ibid., 2.16.68–70. Sigurd's visit to Jerusalem, where he was received by King Baldwin, is described in chapters 10 and 11 in the *Saga of the Sons of Magnus* in *Heimskringla*. But Melville appears to know about it from his reading of *Early Travels in Palestine*, edited byThomas Wright (1848; reprint, New York: AMS Press, 1969).

36. *Clarel: A Poem*, 2.31.28 (first occurrence).

37. Ibid., 2.34.10–12.

38. Ibid., 2.5.99–102.

39. Ibid., 2.4.72–74.

40. Ibid., 2.31.21–24.

41. Melville's interest in Thor's hammer at this time is also reflected in "Bridegroom Dick," one of the poems in *John Marr and Other Sailors*, which was written in the very year in which *Clarel* was published. Here a drunken Finnish seaman is said be "swaying a fist like Thor's sledge." *Collected Poems of Herman Melville*, edited by Howard P. Vincent (Chicago: Packard and Co., 1947), 176.

42. *Clarel* is not an anti-Semitic poem even though the narrator takes a dim view of the zionism of his love's father and rails at Jewish law when he returns to Jerusalem to find that

both the girl and her mother have died of grief during the long months of secluded mourning. The canto called "Concerning Hebrews" is quite respectful, on the whole.

43. *Clarel: A Poem*, lxxv. Melville was of course aware of the reputation of the Goths. There is an allusion to it in chapter 30 of *Redburn*, edited by Harrison Hayford et al., (Evanston, Illinois, and Chicago: Northwestern University Press and Newberry Library, 1969).

44. This similarity is sometimes alluded to in Norse literature, and there is a tenth-century amulet from Iceland in the form of a hammer, the stylized form of which is influenced by the crucifix. For the amulet, see John Haywood, *The Penguin Historical Atlas of the Vikings*, (London: Penguin Books, 1995), 33.

45. *Clarel: A Poem*, 2.23.8–12.

CHAPTER 5. MINOR KEY

1. Lowell to Charles Eliot Norton, letter printed in *The Complete Poetical Works of James Russell Lowell* (Boston and New York: Houghton, Mifflin and Co., 1896), 285.

2. *Letters of James Russell Lowell*, edited by Charles Eliot Norton, 2 vols. (New York: Harper and Brothers, 1893), 1:171. The date suggests that Lowell may have been prodded by reading James Elliot Cabot's article "The Discovery of America by the Norsemen" in the *Massachusetts Quarterly Review* 6 (1849): 189–214.

3. *Graham's Magazine* 46 (January 1855):72.

4. This part of the letter is also printed in *The Complete Poetical Works* (311).

5. *Gudrida* is a Latinate form of *Gudrid* found in early translations.

6. You might think Lowell had just been reading Emerson's essay on "Power."

7. Here one is reminded of the passage in "The Hero as Divinity" in which Carlyle stresses the idea that the Norse had a strong sense of the dreamlike and evanescent nature of life (*On Heroes and Hero-Worship*, 48).

8. This conception is pretty much in line with the Norse belief that a man's luck or lack of it is part of his constitutional makeup and determines his fate.

9. *Eiriks Saga*, Magnusson and Pálsson, trans., chapter 4. The passage was well known at the time. Scott gives Bartholin's translation of it in note 26 to *The Pirate*.

10. Lowell's journal suggests that the references to whales and phosphorescent water are not exclusively inspired by Norse seafaring but also by observations made during a transatlantic voyage in 1851. See Leon Howard, *Victorian Knight-Errant: A Study of the Early Literary Career of James Russell Lowell* (Berkeley and Los Angeles: University of California Press, 1952), 308.

11. This is one of several passages in American literature predicated on the erroneous notion (originating in the Bartholin-Oláfsson translation of *Krákamál*) that Norse warriors expected to drink mead out of the skulls of defeated enemies in Valhalla. As we have seen, Melville suggests in *Omoo* that they did so in real life. Lowell's purely metaphorical use of the theme must be called elegant compared with the Gothic literalness of his American (and British) colleagues.

12. One may wonder what it *is* that "rays" in Christ's hand. As noted in the section on *Clarel*, Thor's hammer and the cross bear a certain similarity to one other, noticed already by the Norse. But one hesitates to think that Lowell is implying that Christ is carrying a crucifix.

13. The article in question (signed P. A. C.) is called "School of Literature: Poems Illustrative of American History: Whittier's 'The Northmen.'" It can be found in *Poet Lore* 7 (February, 1895):105–9.

14. Albert Mordell, *Quaker Militant: John Greenleaf Whittier* (1933; reprint, Fort Washington, New York: Kennikat Press, 1969). Whitman Bennett, *Bard of Freedom* (1941; reprint, Fort Washington, New York: Kennikat Press, 1972). The reprinting of these works is hardly totally unrelated to the dearth of new studies of this poet.

15. Edward Wagenknecht, *James Russell Lowell: Portrait of a Many-Sided Man* (New York: Oxford University Press), 1971), 134.

16. *Letters of John Greenleaf Whittier*, edited by John B. Pickard, 3 vols. (Cambridge: Harvard University Press, 1975), 1:280, 1:518.

17. Ibid., 538.

18. Ibid., 591.

19. *The Complete Poetical Works of John Greenleaf Whittier*, (Boston and New York: Houghton Mifflin Co., 1894), 9.

20. In an extended sense Lochlin may mean Denmark—and even Scandinavia—in general. Scott uses the name in that sense in *The Pirate*. Cf. *The Poems of Ossian*, edited by Howard Gaskell (Edinburgh, Scotland: Edinburgh University Press, 1996), 421.

21. The references to Praga and Siona are also somewhat puzzling: "Praga of the Runic lay" is likely to be Bragi, the Norse god of eloquence and poetry (called Braga by Klopstock and after him by Longfellow in his translation of *Frithiofs Saga*); "Love-awakening Siona" can only be Sirona, a Celtic goddess of fertility, likewise with a distortion of the name. But Sirona is known only from ancient (Roman) times, and only from the Continent. See Miranda Green, *Celtic Goddesses* (London: British Museum Press, 1995), 102–4.

22. Thule is a name that occurs frequently in *The Pirate*, and in one instance Scott speaks of "the feeble light of the Arctic winter" (16).

23. According to Adam of Bremen (ca. 1075), Odin with his spear and violent temper, is the god of war; he encourages men to fight their enemies and receives the fallen in Valhalla. Thor's hammer is his weapon against trolls and other demonic beings, but he is also associated with thunder, summer rain, and crops, and he appears to have been especially popular among farmers (Brøndsted, 282, 277). As noted, Carlyle stresses that role of Thor's in "The Hero as Divinity." So does Mallet (*Northern Antiquities*, 1:130).

24. Frey, like his sister Freya and father Njord, is not strictly one of the Aesir but one of the *Vanir* who have ended up living in Asgard.

25. Cf. these lines from "The Frost Spirit": "With an unscorched wing he has hurried on, where the fires of Hecla glow / On the darkly beautiful sky above and the ancient ice below" (*Complete Poetical Works of John Greenleaf Whittier*, 141).

26. The description of the spákona's apparel and generally eccentric behavior is part of the inspiration of the Norna in *The Pirate* (51–52).

27. As Emerson also comments on it, Whittier is the third of our authors to allude to the Norse belief that looking into the future is a feminine gift. Whittier was so taken with the idea that he greets Fredrika Bremer, the Swedish novelist and feminist, as "Seeress of the misty Norseland, / Daughter of the Vikings bold," to whose "saga, rune, and song" he and his sister have long listened (*Complete Poetical Works of John Greenleaf Whittier*, 183–84).

28. I shall be quoting "The Norseman's Ride" from *The Poetical Works of Bayard Taylor* (Boston and New York: Houghton, Mifflin and Company, 1899), 17.

29. See Whittier's *Letters*, 2:245, or Elizabeth Vining, *Mr. Whittier* (New York: Viking Press, 1974), 112. Taylor, who was in his early twenties, expresses his appreciation of Whittier's approval in a letter of 16 September 1847: "I fancied I had given it fitting expression, but the friends to whom I showed it did not admire it, and I . . . made up my mind to forget it. Judge then, how grateful and encouraging was your generous commendation. . . . One day, I hope I shall be able to take your hand and tell you what a happiness it is to be understood

by one whom the world calls by the name of poet." The letter is cited in a sale catalogue reprinted in "The Library of John Greenleaf Whittier." See *Emerson Society Quarterly* 34, no. 1 (1964):24–25.

30. Longfellow is quite vague on the issue of his Viking's removal to Valhalla in the final stanza of "The Skeleton in Armor." Whitman, in section 7 of "Salut au Monde," focuses on the equally Norse belief that the dead warriors *inhabited* their mounds:

> I see the burial-cairns of Scandinavian warriors,
> I see them raised high with stones by the marge of restless ocean
>   that the dead men's spirits when they wearied of their
>   quiet graves might rise up through the mounds and gaze on
>   the tossing billows, and be refresh'd by storms, immensity
>   liberty, action.

31. The identity of the central figure is only further obfuscated by a hint that he has had a romantic involvement with a lady called Helva (who was also fond of Surtur). The only known Norse Helva is not Norse at all, but appears in a Danish folk ballad that inspired Whittier's "Kalundborg Church" (*Complete Poetical Works of John Greenleaf Whittier*, 255–56).

32. Complete title: *Northern Travel: Summer and Winter Pictures of Sweden, Den* 33. *Lars: A Pastoral of Norway* was first published by James R. Osgood (Boston, 1873).

34. *The Poetical Works of Bayard Taylor*, 269. While the hero of *Frithiofs Saga* does visit the court of Angantyr (Jarl of the Orkneys), there is no support of any kind for the suggestion that Harald Fairhair harried in the East. There is, in other words, a curious juxtaposition of a fictional and a historical figure.

35. *The Poetical Works of Bayard Taylor*, 277.

36. Taylor was himself of Quaker descent.

37. As Abner's words are clearly abusive, one need not suspect Taylor of actually believing that the Norse drank mead from skulls.

38. *The Poetical Works of Bayard Taylor*, 284.

39. Ruth is not entirely incorrect on that score. Some of the oldest Scandinavian churches bear the marks of pagan architecture and art. Thus the stave church in Sogne, Norway, does not only have shingles "like serpent scales" but dragon-headed spires. (The serpents and dragons were originally part of the decoration of Viking war ships and rune stones, as well as prominent figures in Norse mythology.)

40. *The Poetical Works of Bayard Taylor*, 296.

41. In view of the insistent use of the name Thorsten (for the violent Lars's father, who liked to talk about his Norse ancestry, as well as for Per's violent brother), one may assume an implicit opposition of Thor and Balder and by extension between Thor and Christ.

42. *The Poetical Works of Bayard Taylor*, 299.

43. *Gunnar: A Norse Life* by the minor American novelist Hjalmar Hjort Boyesen, first published by Howells in the *Atlantic Monthly* in 1873, is a more truly pastoral work. But for a book appearing the same year as Taylor's poem it also has an intriguing number of things in common with the latter work. Not only are both works set in nineteenth-century Norway; they both contain suggestions that the old Viking blood is not extinct, and there is a fight involving a knife between two rivals at a third party's wedding. Even some of the names— Lars, Brita, Per—are identical. Brynhilda is mentioned in a ditty sung by the main female character in *Gunnar: A Norse Life*, at the time working as a *saeter* maid, as well as in the conversation of the fisher boy Per in Taylor's poem.

CHAPTER 6. LONGFELLOW

1. Hilen, *Longfellow and Scandinavia*, introductory chapter. As previously noted, this work was published in 1947. It is a measure of Professor Hilen's success that he could say in "Longfellow and Scandinavia Revisited," one of the papers read at the Longfellow Commemorative Conference in April 1982: "I break no new trails, make no new claims, alter no old conclusions. I simply revisit an old interest" (p. 1).

2. One indication that Longfellow had read Mallet is his obvious confusion of Celtic and Norse in the account of his visit to Sweden in the summer of 1835: he refers to the monuments of Old Uppsala as "Druidic" (Hilen, *Longfellow and Scandinavia*, 101).

3. Rasmus K. Rask, *A Grammar of the Icelandic or Old Norse Tongue*, translated by George W. Dasent (London: William Pickering, 1843).

4. The inscription is given in a note to the poem: *Oft war ek dasa den eck dro thick* (I was often weary when I pulled at you). It appears that it first struck Longfellow's fancy as an emotional parallel to his feeling during the tedious work of revising his Dante translation (Hilen, *Longfellow and Scandinavia*, 104).

5. Ibid., 88–89.

6. Not least interesting is the suggestion in chapter 3 of *Hyperion* that Paul Fleming—the author's alter ego—"both in person and character" resembles the young Harald Fairhair (incidentally portrayed as fond of the company of maidens and handsome widows).

7. One may add that Longfellow, in addition to the pieces actually written and published, regularly projected "Norse" works that were never completed. For instance, after his review of *Frithiofs Saga* he planned a series of ballads on the voyages of the Norsemen (in which "The Skeleton in Armor" would have been a good fit). He did research for a "lively" book on Norse mythology. Possibly inspired by Oehlenschläger, he planned a "Saga of Hakon Jarl," the outline for which was later used for *The Saga of King Olaf*, and, finally, after the successful publication of the latter work, a long poem about Olaf Haraldsson (Hilen, *Longfellow and Scandinavia*, 91ff.).

8. I will leave out "The Broken Oar," further discussion of which would seem anticlimactic after dealing with *The Saga of King Olaf*.

9. *The Letters of Henry Wadsworth Longfellow*, edited by Andrew Hilen, 2 vols., (Cambridge, Massachusetts: Harvard University Press, 1966), 1:505.

10. Longfellow's review was published in *North American Review* 45 (1837):149–85.

11. *Blackwood's Edinburgh Magazine* 23 (1828):137–61. *Foreign Quarterly Review* 3 (1829):254–82.

12. For Higginson, see his *Cheerful Yesterdays* (1898; reprint, New York: Arno Press, 1968), 101. Emerson's letter is not in Rusk's edition of his *Letters* but is printed in Samuel Longfellow's *Life of Henry Wadsworth Longfellow*, 3 vols. (Boston and New York: Ticknor and Co., 1886), 2:402–3.

13. The Swedish text is quoted from the second illustrated edition (Stockholm: P. A. Nordstedt, 1876), 160.

14. This letter is cited by Hilen both in Swedish and in English translation (*Letters*, 51–52).

15. Cf. letter of 2 June 1841 to Sam Ward, who had been prodding him to complete the translation (*Letters*, 2:304).

16. "The Tower in Newport, Rhode Island," was published in *The Annals of the Royal Society of Northern Antiquaries* (Copenhagen, 1838).

17. Herbert S. Gorman, *A Victorian American: Henry Wadsworth Longfellow* (New York: George H. Doran Co., 1926), 279.

18. Robert Spiller et al., *Literary History of the United States*, 4th ed., rev. (New York: Macmillan, 1974), 590. Newton Arvin, *Longfellow: His Life and Work* (Boston: Little, Brown and Co., 1963), 70.

19. *Graham's Magazine* 20 (March 1842):189.

20. Longfellow to his father, 13 December 1840 (*Letters*, 2:209). Longfellow also tells his father he has seen the skeleton himself.

21. J. T. Smith follows Rafn slavishly in *The Northmen in New England*, but Laing already accuses "the Northern antiquaries" of wanting to "prove too much" and is particularly vexed by the affair involving "the old stone mill" in Newport (*Heimskringla*, preliminary dissertation, 160 and 182–85). See also P. A. Means' *Newport Tower* (New York: H. Holt and Co., 1942).

22. *The Complete Poetical Works of Henry Wadsworth Longfellow* (Boston and New York: Houghton Mifflin and Co., 1899), 652.

23. *The Poetical Works of John Greenleaf Whittier*, 255. If testimony from Norse times is needed, there is Adam of Bremen, who stresses the unusual fertility of Zealand (*opulentia frugum celeberrima*) and classifies Skåne with its open country among provinces *frugibus plenae* (Brøndsted, 226).

24. *The Complete Poetical Works of Henry Wadsworth Longfellow*, 25–26.

25. Haki the Berserker falls on his spear after losing his bride-*in-spe* in chapter 5 of the *Saga of Halfdan the Black* in *Heimskringla*.

26. The toast is also anachronistic. Even granting that the Vikings toasted in this way, they would not have used the modern Scandinavian pronunciation of the word *skål*. It is used in *Frithiofs Saga*, but Tegnér has the excuse that he is writing in modern Swedish. The way Longfellow changes the spelling of the word (*skoal*) is also unfortunate. He says in a note that he has changed the orthography slightly "in order to preserve the correct pronunciation," but if that was his intention it would have been better to write *skawl*, which is more nearly accurate; Longfellow's spelling falsely suggests that *skål* rhymes with *coal* and *shoal*, which are pronounced with a diphthong. Longfellow is no doubt responsible for the misguided spelling *skoal!* of current beer and liquor advertising.

27. Hilen, *Longfellow and Scandinavia*, 61.

28. Gerald R. Griffin also ignores these facts about the Swedish poet in his attempt to explain Longfellow's "intentions" with exclusive reference to Tegnér's allegedly saintly and single-mindedly religious disposition in "Longfellow's 'Tegnér's Drapa': A Reappraisal," *American Transcendental Quarterly* 40 (1978): 379–382.

29. *The Complete Poetical Works of Henry Wadsworth Longfellow*, 34.

30. Carlyle, *On Heroes and Hero-Worship*, 72–73.

31. Longfellow recycles the image as he describes the departure of Hiawatha for "the land of the Hereafter" (*The Complete Poetical Works of Henry Wadsworth Longfellow*, 191):

> Westward, westward Hiawatha
> Sailed into the fiery sunset,
> Sailed into the purple vapors,
> Sailed into the dusk of evening.

In this case there is probably also an echo of Väinömöinen's departure in a boat (also a metaphor of his death) in the final *runo* of *Kalevala*, the Finnish epic put together by Elias Lönnrot that Longfellow read in M. A. Castrén's Swedish translation and from which he borrowed the meter for his "Indian Edda." By a remarkable coincidence, *Hiawatha* was published the same year (1855) as Arnold's "Balder Dead," in which the departure of Balder's funeral ship is described in very similar terms (see chapter 1).

32. Cecil B. Williams, in defiance of the mythological pattern, states that this poem is largely devoted to "a comparative description of the old warlike mythology of the Scandi-

navians and the new poetry of human love and brotherhood" and that within this framework Balder stands for the former, Tegnér for the latter. See *Henry Wadsworth Longfellow* (New York: Grossett and Dunlap, 1964), 142.

33. Hilen, *Longfellow and Scandinavia*, 61.

34. In a sense Tegnér drew his "curtain" chiefly by choosing the Norse tale he did. "Frithiof the Bold" is remarkably free from the kind of graphic descriptions of killings one typically finds in older sagas. One will look in vain in it for the potentially fatal single combat between Frithiof and a berserk at the court of Angantyr so vividly described by Tegnér. The reference to Frithiof's activities as a property-collecting Viking is charitably brief compared with canto 15 in *Frithiofs Saga*. The ancient Norse author does not have King Ring barbarically bleed himself to death by committing geir-odd; he makes him to die from sickness in bed.

35. *North American Review*, 151.

36. Longfellow depended on the whole on Samuel Laing's translation of *Heimskringla*, although he may also (Hilen, *Longfellow and Scandinavia*, 99) have looked at the Danish translations of some other sagas touching on the same events in his copy of P. E. Mueller's *Sagabibliothek* (Copenhagen: J. F. Schultz, 1817–1824) and had earlier cut open the pages of the first volume of a Swedish translation of *Heimskringla: Konunga-sagor, en översättning*, by J. G. Richert, A. J. D. Cnattingius, and G. Guldberg, 3 vols. (Stockholm: Marquardska tryckeriet, 1816–1829).

37. *The Complete Poetical Works of Henry Wadsworth Longfellow*, 246.

38. Hilen says Longfellow "undoubtedly" looked at *Njal's Saga* in the Harvard library (p. 99).

39. Runes apart, Icelandic writing began with legal codes, in the winter of 1117–1118 (Gordon, *Introduction to Old Norse*, lxiii).

40. The list of books in Longfellow's library given by Hilen (appendix D) includes a German and even a French work about Scandinavian folk ballads as well as standard Swedish and Danish collections such as E. G. Geijer and A. A. Afzelius, *Svenska folkvisor från forntiden*, 3 vols. (Stockholm: Strinnholm och Häggström, 1814–16) and V. H. E. Abrahamson, Rasmus Nyerup, and K. L. Rahbek, *Udvalgte danske Folkeviser fra Middelalderen*, 5 vols. (Copenhagen: J. F. Schultz, 1812–14).

41. In "To an Old Danish Songbook," written in 1845 (*The Complete Poetical Works of Henry Wadsworth Longfellow*, 88), Longfellow recalls how during his 1835 stay in Copenhagen he "paused to / The old ballad of King Christian / Shouted from suburban taverns" and adds:

> Once some ancient Scald
> In his bleak, ancestral Iceland,
> Chanted staves of these old ballads
> To the Vikings.

42. This phenomenon was first analyzed by Hermann Varnhagen in *Longfellows Tales of a Wayside Inn und ihre Quellen* (Berlin: Weidmann, 1884), 69–73.

43. This refrain is a word-for-word equivalent of the refrain of a Danish folk ballad, "Herr Morten af Fogelsang," which, as noted by Varnhagen, was available to Longfellow in Abrahamson, Nyerup and Rahbek's *Udvalgte danske Folkeviser fra Middelalderen* (1:215).

44. The context of the original, Danish refrain (*Min Hjertens allerkjaereste hvorfor sørge I saa*) is quite different. (See Abrahamson, Nyerup, and Rahbek, 1:326).

45. Michel Foucault, *The History of Sexuality*, translated by Robert Hurley, 3 vols. (1976; reprint, New York: Vintage Books, 1990), 1:121.

46. Jenny Jochens argues in *Women in Old Norse Society* (Ithaca: Cornell University Press, 1995) that the tough women of the sagas "did not represent flesh-and-blood women . . . but . . . were images in men's imagination" (ix). If so, Longfellow might be closer to historical reality than to the literary tradition from which he sometimes chooses to deviate.

47. One cannot exclude the possibility that this trait was what kept Longfellow from realizing his plan of emulating Oehlenschläger by composing a "Hakon Jarl."

CHAPTER 7. THE WOMEN WRITERS

1. *The Complete Poems of Emily Dickinson*, edited by Thomas H. Johnson (Boston and Toronto: Little, Brown and Co., 1960).

2. *Uncle Tom's Cabin* (1852; reprint Garden City, New York: Dolphin Books, 1960); *Dred* (1856; reprint, Grosse Pointe, Michigan: Scholarly Press, 1968); *The Minister's Wooing* (1859; reprint, Hartford, Connecticut: Stowe-Day Foundation, 1994); *Agnes of Sorrento* (1862; reprint, Boston: Houghton Mifflin Co., 1967); *The Pearl of Orr's Island* (1862; reprint Boston and New York: Houghton Mifflin Co., 1983); *Oldtown Folks* (1869; reprint New Brunswick, New Jersey: Rutgers University Press, 1987).

3. *The Years and Hours of Emily Dickinson*, edited by Jay Leyda, 2 vols. (New Haven: Yale University Press, 1960).

4. *The Letters of Emily Dickinson*, edited by Thomas H. Johnson, 3 vols. (Cambridge: Harvard University Press, Belknap Press, 1965).

5. *The Complete Poems*, nos. 1696, 1048, and 525.

6. *The Complete Poems*, no. 526.

7. New York: William Morrow and Co., 1975.

8. *Moods* was published by Loring (Boston, 1865).

9. *Little Women* (Boston: Roberts Brothers, 1868–69; reprint, New York: Modern Library, 1983).

10. *Little Men* (1871; reprint, New York: E. P. Dutton and Co., 1967).

11. *Little Men*, 17.

12. *Jo's Boys* (Boston: Roberts Brothers, 1886).

13. Baron Friedrich de la Motte Fouqué, *Undine and Other Stories* (Boston and New York: Houghton, Mifflin Co., 1867.

14. The other children's books I have checked, all published in Boston by Roberts Brothers, are *An Old-Fashioned Girl* (1870), *Eight Cousins* (1875), *Rose in Bloom* (1876), *Under the Lilacs* (1877), and *Jack and Jill* (1880). One may add that in the last-mentioned volume, Alcott does make use of the old nursery rhyme "Jack and Jill went up the hill / To fetch a pail of water" but passes up the chance to do something with Jack and Jill's background in Norse myth, in which Mani (the Moon) snatches away Hiuki and Bil from their cruel father who makes them carry water all night (Hiuki is identified as the waxing, Bil the waning moon).

15. Margaret Fuller, *Summer on the Lakes* (Boston and New York: C. C. Little and James Brown, 1844).

16. Ibid., 40.

17. Ibid., 63–64.

18. Ibid., 68.

19. Ibid., 29.

20. Ibid., 75.

21. *Woman in the Nineteenth Century* was first published in 1845 (New York: Greeley and McElrath) then reprinted along with "kindred papers relating to the sphere, condition, and

duties of woman" in an edition issued by her brother, Arthur B. Fuller and prefaced by Horace Greeley (Boston: Roberts Brothers, 1878). I am using the Greenwood Press reprint of the latter volume (New York, 1968).

22. *Woman in the Nineteenth Century*, 156–57.

23. Ibid., 161.

24. *Nibelungenlied*, 7th *aventiure*.

25. *Dial*, 4, no. 1 (July 1843):1–47.

26. Ibid., 157.

27. There are no signs at all of such an interest in the six volumes of the *Letters of Margaret Fuller*, edited by Robert N. Hudspeth (Ithaca: Cornell University Press, 1983–84).

28. I am quoting from *Margaret Fuller: American Romantic*, edited by Perry Miller (Garden City, New York: Doubleday and Co., 1963), 258.

29. *Cleopatra* (San Francisco: the Bancroft Co., 1889).

30. *Our Roll of Honor, or, Poems of the Revolution* (New York: Knickerbocker Press, 1894)

31. *Valhalla, the Myths of Norseland: A Saga in Twelve Parts* (San Francisco: Edward Bosqui, 1878; reprint, New York: R. Worthington, 1880).

32. Anderson refers to Laing and Carlyle, as well as to Oehlenschläger and Grundtvig, and he uses the words *Goths* and *Gothic* in the same loose sense as Jones does. One also notes Anderson's stress on the influence of the Northern landscape, the purity and chastity of the "Goths," and their invention of the concept of freedom. Even Anderson's handling of the relation between Norse religion and Christianity sometimes reminds one of Jones.

33. *Valhalla*, 7.

34. Ibid., 9, 11.

35. Ibid., 11.

36. Ibid., 12.

37. Ibid., 15.

38. Ibid.

39. Apparently Longfellow does not sufficiently explain the meaning since Jones, judging by her glossary, thinks the word signifies "'hail,' an expression of greeting."

40. Bragi's Song" is found on pp. 44–47 in *Valhalla*.

41. See *Valhalla*, 94.

42. Ibid., 50.

43. There is an echo of *Paradise Lost* in the portrayal of the fallen Loki in "King Aegir's Feast": "Yet still, tho' lost, upon his face / at times a grace / Faint glimmered of the ancient day," etc.

44. *Valhalla*, 131, 145.

45. Ibid., 45–46.

Bibliography

Abrahamson, W. H. F., Rasmus Nyerup, and K. L. Rahbek. *Udvalgte danske Folkeviser fra Middelalderen.* 5 vols. Copenhagen: J. F. Schultz, 1812–14.

Alcott, Louisa May. *An Old-Fashioned Girl.* Boston: Roberts Brothers, 1870.

———. *Behind a Mask: The Unknown Thrillers of Louisa May Alcott,* edited by Madeleine Stern. New York: William Morrow and Co., 1975.

———. *Eight Cousins.* Boston: Roberts Brothers, 1875.

———. *Jack and Jill.* Boston: Roberts Brothers, 1880.

———. *Jo's Boys.* Boston: Roberts Brothers, 1886.

———. *Little Men.* 1871. Reprint, New York, E. P. Dutton and Co., 1967.

———. *Little Women.* 1868–69. Reprint, New York: Modern Library, 1983.

———. *Moods.* Boston: Loring, 1865.

———. *Rose in Bloom.* Boston: Roberts Brothers, 1876.

———. *Under the Lilacs.* Boston: Roberts Brothers, 1877.

Allen, R. B. *Old Icelandic Sources in the English Novel.* 1933. Reprint, Folcroft, Pennsylvania: Folcroft Library Editions, 1977.

Anderson, R. B. *America Not Discovered by Columbus: A Historical Sketch of the Discovery of America by the Norse in the Tenth Century.* Chicago: S. C. Griggs and Co., 1874.

———. *Norse Mythology; or, the Religion of our Forefathers.* 1875. Reprint, Chicago: S. C. Griggs and Co., 1879.

Arnold, Matthew. *The Poems of Matthew Arnold.* 2d ed., edited by Miriam Allott. London and New York: Longman, 1979.

Arvin, Newton. *Longfellow: His Life and Work.* Boston: Little, Brown and Co., 1963.

Asbjornsen, Peter C. *Popular Tales from the Norse.* New York: Appleton, 1859.

Avallone, Charlene. "What American Renaissance? The Gendered Genealogy of a Critical Discourse." *PMLA* 112 (October 1997): 1102–20.

Baker, Houston. "Figurations for a New American Literary History." In *Ideology and Classic American Literature,* edited by Sacvan Bercovitch and Myra Jehlen. Cambridge, England: Cambridge University Press, 1986.

Barnason, C. F. *The Revival of Old Norse Literature.* PhD. diss., Harvard University, 1936.

Bartholin, Thomas [Bartholinus]. *De causis contemptae mortis a Danis adhuc gentilibus.* Copenhagen: J. P. Brockenhauer, 1689.

Bennett, Whitman. *Bard of Freedom.* 1941. Reprint, New York: Kennikat Press, 1972.

Benson, Adolf B. "Scandinavian Influences in the Writings of Thoreau." *Scandinavian Studies* 16 (1941): 201–11, 241–56.

Björner, Erik. J. *Nordiska kämpadater.* Stockholm: J. L. Horn, 1737.

Borrow, George. *Romantic Ballads.* Norwich, England: George Borrow, 1826.

Boyesen, Hjalmar Hjort. *Gunnar: A Tale of Norse Life.* Boston: J. R. Osgood, 1874.

Bradish, Sarah Powers. *Old Norse Stories.* New York: American Book Co., 1900.

Brøndsted, Johannes. *The Vikings.* Translated by Kalle Skov. Baltimore: Penguin Books, 1965.

Bryant, William Cullen. *Poems.* London and New York: Oxford University Press, 1914.

Cabot, James Elliott. "The Discovery of America by the Norsemen." *Massachusetts Quarterly Review* 6 (1849): 189–214.

Cambon, Glauco. "Ishmael and the Problem of Formal Discontinuities in *Moby Dick.*" *Modern Language Notes* 76 (1961): 516–23.

Cambridge History of American Literature. Edited by Sacvan Bercovitch. Cambridge, England: Cambridge University Press, 1995.

Carlyle, Thomas. *On Heroes and Hero-Worship.* 1841. Reprint, London: Oxford University Press, 1959.

————. *Early Kings of Norway.* London: Chapman and Hall, 1875.

Collins, William. *The Works of William Collins,* edited by Richard Wendorf and Charles Ryskamp. Oxford, England: Clarendon Press, 1979.

Colyer, Richard. "Thoreau's Color Symbols." *PMLA* 86, no. 5 (October 1971): 999–1008.

The Correspondence of Emerson and Carlyle, edited by Joseph Slater. New York: Columbia University Press, 1964.

Dalin, Olof von. *Svea rikes historia.* 4 vols. Stockholm, 1747–65.

Davis, Merrill. *Melville's Mardi.* New Haven: Yale University Press, 1952.

Decosta, Benjamin Franklin. *The Pre-Columbian Discovery of America by the Northmen, Illustrated by Translations from the Icelandic Sagas.* Albany, New York: J. Munsell, 1868.

Dickinson, Emily. *The Complete Poems of Emily Dickinson,* edited by Thomas H. Johnson. Boston and Toronto: Little, Brown, and Co., 1960.

————. *Letters of Emily Dickinson,* edited by Thomas H. Johnson. 3 vols. Cambridge: Harvard University Press, The Belknap Press, 1965.

Edda (the "Elder" or "Poetic" or "Saemund's"). Translated by Lee M. Hollander. Austin: University of Texas Press, 1962.

————. Translated by Karl Simrock. Stuttgart, Germany: J. Gotta, 1854.

————. *Lieder der alten Edda.* Translated by Jakob and Wilhelm Grimm. Berlin: Realschulbuchhandlung, 1815.

Edda (the "Younger" or "Prose" or "Snorri's"). See Sturluson, Snorri.

Eiriks Saga. See *Vinland Sagas.*

Emerson, Ralph Waldo. *Complete Works of Ralph Waldo Emerson,* edited by E. W. Emerson. 12 vols. Boston and New York: Houghton, Mifflin and Co., 1903.

———. *The Early Lectures of Ralph Waldo Emerson,* edited by Stephen E. Whicher and Robert E. Spiller. Cambridge: Harvard University Press, Belknap Press, 1959.

———. *English Traits,* edited by Howard Mumford Jones. Cambridge: Harvard University Press, 1966.

———. *Journals and Miscellaneous Notebooks of Ralph Waldo Emerson,* edited by William H. Gilman et al. 16 vols. Cambridge: Harvard University Press, Belknap Press, 1960–82.

Everett, Edward. Review of *Antiquitates Americanae: Scriptures septentrionales rerum antecolumbiarum in America,* edited by Carl Christian Rafn. *North American Review* 46(1838): 161–203.

Fales, Ernest. *History of the Northmen's Visits to Rhode Island and Massachusetts in the Tenth Century.* Providence: F. N. Shaw, 1888.

Farley, Frank E. *Scandinavian Influences in the English Romantic Movement.* 1903. Reprint, Boston: Ginn, 1980.

Farnum, Alexander. *Visits of the Northmen to Rhode Island.* Providence: S. S. Rider, 1877.

Five Pieces of Runic Poetry. Edited by Thomas Percy. London: Thomas Percy, 1765.

Foucault, Michel. *The History of Sexuality.* Translated by Robert Hurley. 3 vols. 1976. Reprint, New York: Vintage Books, 1990.

Fouqué, Baron Friedrich de la Motte. *Undine and Other Stories.* Boston and New York: Houghton, Mifflin and Co., 1867.

Franklin, H. Bruce. *The Wake of the Gods: Melville's Mythology.* Stanford, California: Stanford University Press, 1963.

"Frithiof the Bold." See *Three Northern Love Stories.*

Fuller, Margaret. *Letters of Margaret Fuller,* edited by Robert N. Hudspeth. 6 vols. Ithaca: Cornell University Press, 1983–84.

———. *Summer on the Lakes.* Boston and New York: C. C. Little and James Brown, 1844.

———. *Woman in the Nineteenth Century.* New York: Greeley and McElrath, 1845.

———. *Woman in the Nineteenth Century* (and "kindred papers relating to the sphere, condition, and duties of woman"), edited by Arthur B. Fuller. With a preface by Horace Greeley. 1878. Reprint, New York: Greenwood Press, 1968.

Geijer, E. G. and A. A. Afzelius. *Svenska folkvisor från forntiden.* 3 vols. Stockholm: Strinnholm och Häggström, 1814–16.

Geijer, E. G. *Dikter.* Second edition. Stockholm: P. A. Nordstedt, 1926.

Gordon, E. V. *Introduction to Old Norse.* 2d ed. Revised by A.R. Taylor. Oxford, England: Clarendon Press, 1957.

Gorman, Herbert S. *A Victorian American: Henry Wadsworth Longfellow.* New York: George H. Doran, 1926.

Green, Miranda. *Celtic Goddesses.* London: British Museum Press, 1995.

Greenway, John L. *The Golden Horns.* Athens: University of Georgia Press, 1977.

Griffin, Gerald R. "Longfellow's 'Tegnér's Drapa': A Reappraisal." *American Transcendental Quarterly* 40 (1978): 379–87.

Groenlendinga Saga. See *Vinland Sagas.*

Grundtvig, N. F. S. *Nordens mytologi, eller Udsigt over Eddalaeren for dannede Maend der ei selve ere Mytologer.* Köbenhavn: T. H. Schubotes Forlag, 1808.

Gustafson, Alrik. *History of Swedish Literature.* Minneapolis: University of Minnesota Press, 1963.

Gutmann, Allen. "From *Typee* to *Moby Dick*: Melville's Allusive Art." *Modern Language Quarterly* 24 (September 1963): 237–44.

Hall, Richard A. *Viking Age Archeology in Britain and Ireland.* Princes Risborough, England: Shire, 1990.

Harding, Walter. *A Thoreau Handbook.* New York: New York University Press, 1959.

Hellquist, Olof. *Svensk etymologisk ordbok.* Lund, Sweden: Gleerup, 1922.

Herbert, William. *Select Icelandic Poetry Translated from the Originals.* 2 vols. 1804–6. Reprint. Folcroft, Pennsylvania: Folcroft Press, 1970.

Herford, C. H. *Norse Myth in English Poetry.* Manchester, England: Manchester University Press, 1919.

Heywood, John. *The Penguin Historical Atlas of the Vikings.* London: Penguin Books, 1995.

Higginson, Thomas Wentworth. *Cheerful Yesterdays.* 1898. Reprint. New York: Arno Press, 1968.

———. "The Visit of the Vikings." *Harper's* 65 (September, 1882):515–27.

Hilen, Andrew. *Longfellow and Scandinavia.* New Haven: Yale University Press, 1947.

———. "Longfellow and Scandinavia Revisited." Papers submitted at the Longfellow Commemorative Conference, Washington, D.C., 1–3 April, 1982. Washington, D. C. U.S. Government Printing Office, 1982. 1–12.

Horsman, Reginald. *Manifest Destiny.* Cambridge: Harvard University Press, 1981.

Howard, Leon. *Victorian Knight-Errant: A Study of the Early Literary Career of James Russell Lowell.* Berkeley and Los Angeles: University of California Press, 1952.

Ideology and Classic American Literature, edited by Sacvan Bercovitch and Myra Jehlen. Cambridge, England: Cambridge University Press, 1986.

Illustrations of Northern Antiquities, edited by Robert Jamieson, Henry Weber, and Sir Walter Scott. Edinburgh, Scotland, and London: Longman, Hurst, Rees, Orme, and Brown, 1814.

Irving, Washington. "Wheaton's *History of the Northmen.*" *The North American Review* 35 (1832): 342–71.

Jehlen, Myra. "Introduction: Beyond Transcendence." In *Ideology and Classic American Literature,* edited by Sacvan Bercovitch and Myra Jehlen. Cambridge: Cambridge University Press, 1986.

Jones, Julia Clinton. *Valhalla, the Myths of Norseland: A Saga in Twelve Parts.* San Francisco: Edward Bosqui, 1878.

Jones, William Powell. *Thomas Gray, Scholar.* New York: Russell and Russell, 1965.

Kalevala. Translated into Swedish by M. A. Castrén. 2 vols. Helsinki: J. Simelii enka, 1841.

Kalm, Peter. *Travels into North America.* Translated by J. R. Forster. 3 vols. London, 1770–71.

Keyser, Rudolph. *The Religion of the Northmen.* Translated by B. Pennock. New York: C. B. Norton, 1854.

Klopstock, Friedrich G. *Hermanns Tod.* Hamburg, Germany: B. J. Hoffmann, 1787.

Knox, John, ed. *A New Collection of Voyages.* 7 vols. London: John Knox, 1767.

Knox, Robert. *The Races of Men.* London: H. Renshaw, 1850.

Larned, Augusta. *Tales from the Norse Grandmother: The Elder Edda.* New York: Phillips and Hunt, 1884.

Leighton, Robert. *The Thirsty Sword: A Story of the Norse Invasion of Scotland (1262–1263).* New York: Scribner's Sons, 1892.

Levin, David. *Forms of Uncertainty.* Charlottesville: University Press of Virginia, 1994.

Leyda, Jay. *The Years and Hours of Emily Dickinson.* 2 vols. New Haven: Yale University Press.

"Library of John Greenleaf Whittier." *Emerson Society Quarterly* 34(1) (1964):1–76.

Lieder, P.R. Scott and Scandinavian Literature." *Smith College Studies in Modern Languages* 2, no. 1 (1920): 8–57.

Litchfield, Mary Elizabeth. *The Nine Worlds: Stories from Norse Mythology.* Boston: Ginn, 1890.

Literary History of the United States. Robert E. Spiller et al. 4th edition, revised. New York: Macmillan, 1974.

Litzenberg, Karl. *The Victorians and the Vikings: A Bibliographical Essay on Anglo-Norse Literary Relations.* Ann Arbor: University of Michigan Press, 1947.

Lohenstein, D. K. von. *Arminius.* Leipzig, Germany: J. F. Bledisch, 1689–90.

Longfellow, Henry Wadsworth. *Ballads and Other Poems.* Cambridge, Massachusetts: J. Owen, 1842.

———. *The Complete Poetical Works of Henry Wadsworth Longfellow.* Household ed. Boston and New York: Houghton, Mifflin and Co., 1899.

———. *Hyperion: A Romance.* Boston: Ticknor and Co., 1848.

———. *The Letters of Henry Wadsworth Longfellow.* 2 vols. Edited by Andrew Hilen. Cambridge, Massachusetts: Harvard University Press, 1966.

———. "Tegnér's *Frithiof's Saga.*" *North American Review* 45 (1837): 149–85.

Longfellow. Samuel. *The Life of Henry Wadsworth Longfellow.* 2 vols. Boston and New York: Ticknor and Co., 1886.

Lowell, James Russell. *Complete Poetical Works of James Russell Lowell.* Boston and New York: Houghton, Mifflin and Co., 1896.

———. "Hakon's Lay." *Graham's Magazine* 46 (January 1855): 72.

———. *Letters of James Russell Lowell.* Edited by Charles Eliot Norton. 2 vols. New York: Harper and Brothers, 1893.

Magnus, Johannes. *Historia de omnibus Gothorum Sueonumque regibus.* Rome: de Viottis, House of Birgittine Order, 1554.

Marsh, George Perkins. *The Goths in New England.* Middlebury, Vermont: Philomathesian Society of Middlebury College, 1843.

Mallet, Jean-Paul. *Introduction à l'histoire de Dannemarc.* Copenhagen: (impr. des héritiers de Berling, par H. L. Lillie), 1755.

————. *Monuments de la mythologie et de la poésie des Celtes, et particulièrement des anciens Scandinaves.* Copenhagen: C. Philibert, 1756.

Means, P. A. *Newport Tower.* New York: H. Holt and Co., 1942.

Melville, Herman. *Clarel: A Poem.* Edited by Walter Bezanson. 1960. Reprint, New York: Hendricks House, 1973.

————. *Collected Poems of Herman Melville.* Edited by Howard P. Vincent. Chicago: Packard and Co., 1947.

————. *Mardi and a Voyage Thither.* Edited by Harrison Hayford et al. Evanston, Illinois and Chicago: Northwestern University Press and Newberry Library, 1970.

————. *Moby Dick, or, the Whale,* edited by Charles Feidelson Jr. New York: Bobbs-Merrill, 1964.

————. *Omoo: A Narrative of Adventures in the South Seas.* Edited by Harrison Hayford et al. Evanston, Illinois and Chicago: Northwestern University Press and Newberry Library, 1968.

————. *Redburn,* edited by Harrison Hayford et al. Evanston, Illinois and Chicago: Northwestern University Press and Newberry Library, 1969.

————. *Typee: A Peep at Polynesian Life,* edited by Harrison Hayford et al. Evanston, Illinois and Chicago: Northwestern University Press and Newberry Library, 1968.

————. *White-Jacket, or, the World in a Man-of-War,* edited by Harrison Hayford et al. Evanston, Illinois and Chicago: Northwestern University Press and Newberry Library, 1970.

Micek, Margrethe Schioler. "Scandinavian Antiquity in German Literature from 1745 to 1773." Ph.D. diss., University of California, 1962.

Miller, Perry, ed. *Margaret Fuller: American Romantic.* Garden City, New York: Doubleday and Co., 1963.

Milton, John. *The Poetical Works of John Milton.* London: Oxford University Press, 1958.

Mitchell, P. M. "Old Norse-Icelandic Literature in Germany 1789–1849, with a Critical Bibliography." Ph.D. diss., University of Illinois, 1942.

Mjöberg, Jöran. *Drömmen om sagatiden.* 2 vols. Stockholm: Natur och kultur, 1969–70.

Mordell, Albert. *Quaker Militant: John Greenleaf Whittier.* 1933. Reprint, Fort Washington, New York: Kennikat Press, 1969.

Morris, William. *The Lovers of Gudrun: A Poem.* Boston: Roberts Brothers, 1870.

————. *Sigurd the Volsung and the Fall of the Niblungs.* 1876. Reprint, London: Longmans, Green, and Co., 1904.

Mueller, P. E. "The Origin and Decline of Icelandic Historical Literature." Translated by George Perkins Marsh. *The American Eclectic* 1 (May 1841):446–66 and 2 (July 1841):131–46.

————. Ed. *Sagabibliothek.* 3 vols. Copenhagen: J. F. Schulz, 1817–20.

Das Nibelungenlied. Nach der Ausgabe von Karl Bartsch herausgegeben von Helmut de Boor. Mannheim, Germany: F. A. Brockhaus, 1988.

Nicoloff, Philip L. *Emerson on Race and History: An Examination of English Traits.* New York: Columbia University Press, 1961.

Njal's Saga. Translated by Magnus Magnusson and Hermann Pálsson. Baltimore: Penguin Books, 1960.

———. *The Story of Burnt Njal, or Life in Iceland at the End of the Tenth Century.* Translated by George W. Dasent. 2 vols. Edinburgh, Scotland: G. Richards, 1861.

Nordby, C. H. *The Influence of Old Norse Literature Upon English Literature.* 1901. Reprint, New York: AMS Press, 1966.

Northern Antiquities, edited by Thomas Percy. 2 vols. London: T. Carnan and Co., 1770.

Oehlenschläger, Adam G. *Amleth, en Tragedie.* Copenhagen: 1847. Reprint, Aarhus, Denmark: Arkona, 1979.

———. *Balder hin Gode.* 1806. Reprint, Copenhagen: P. G. Philipsen, 1887.

———. *The Gold Horns.* London: Thomas Wise, 1913.

———. "Guldhornene." In *Digte.* 1803. Reprint, Copenhagen, 1966.

———. *Hakon Jarl hin rige.* 1807. Reprint, Copenhagen: Gyldendal, 1960.

———. *Ragnar Lodbrok.* Copenhagen: A. F. Host, 1849.

P.A.C. "School of Literature: Poems Illustrative of American History: Whittier's 'The Northmen.'" *Poet Lore* 7 (February 1895): 105–9.

Pigott, Grenville. *A Manual of Scandinavian Mythology.* London: W. Pickering, 1893.

Poe, Edgar Allan. Review of Longfellow's *Ballads and Other Poems. Graham's Magazine* 20 (March 1842): 189–91.

Poems of Ossian, edited by Howard Gaskell. Edinburgh, Scotland: Edinburgh University Press, 1996.

Pontoppidan, Erik. *Natural History of Norway.* 2 vols. in 1. London: A Linde, 1755.

Rafn, Carl Christian. *America Discovered in the Tenth Century.* New York: W. Jackson, 1838.

———. Ed. *Antiquitates Americanae, sive: scriptores septentrionales rerum ante-columbiarum in America.* Copenhagen: J. F. Schulz. 1837.

———. "The Round Tower in Newport, Rhode Island." *Annals of the Royal Society of Northern Antiquaries.* Copenhagen: The Royal Society of Northern Antiquaries. 1838–1839.

Rask, Rasmus K. *A Grammar of the Icelandic or Old Norse Tongue.* Translated by W. G. Dasent. London: William Pickering, 1843.

Richards, J. D. *Viking Age England.* London: B. T. Batsford, 1991.

Ritchie, A. *Viking Scotland.* London and Edinburgh, Scotland: B. T. Batsford, 1993.

Rudbeck, Olof. *Atlantica sive Manheim.* 4 vols. Uppsala, 1679–1704.

Saxo Grammaticus. *History of the Danes.* 2 vols. in 1. Woodbridge, Suffolk, and Rochester, New York, 1996.

Scott, Sir Walter. *Complete Poetical Works of Sir Walter Scott.* Boston and New York: Houghton Mifflin, 1924.

———. *The Pirate*. Vol. 15 of *The Waverley Novels*. 1822. Reprint, New York and London, undated.

Sealts, Morton, Jr. *Melville's Reading*. Madison: University of Wisconsin Press, 1966; rev. and enl., Columbia, S.C.: University of South Carolina Press, 1988.

Smith, J. T. *The Northmen in New England or America in the Tenth Century*. Boston: Hilliard, Gray, and Co., 1839.

Stowe, Harriet Beecher. *Agnes of Sorrento*. 1862. Reprint, Boston: Houghton Mifflin, 1967.

———. *Dred*. 1856. Reprint, Grosse Pointe, Michigan: Scholarly Press, 1968.

———. *The Minister's Wooing*. 1859. Reprint, Hartford, Connecticut: Stowe-Day Foundation, 1994.

———. *Oldtown Folks*. 1869. Reprint, New Brunswick, N.J.: Rutgers University Press, 1987.

———. *The Pearl of Orr's Island*. 1862. Reprint, Boston and New York: Houghton Mifflin, 1983.

———. *Uncle Tom's Cabin*. 1852. Reprint, Garden City, New York: Doubleday and Co., 1960.

Sturluson, Snorri. *Heimskringla, or, Chronicle of the Norse Kings*. Translated by Samuel Laing. London: Longmans, Brown, Green, and Longmans, 1844.

———. *Heimskringla*. Translated by Lee M. Hollander. Austin: University of Texas Press. 1964.

———. *Konunga-sagor: en översättning*. Translated by J. G. Richert, A. J. D. Cnattingius, and G. Guldberg. 3 vols. Stockholm: Marquardska tryckeriet, 1816–1829.

———. *The Prose or Younger Edda Commonly Assigned to Snorri Sturluson*. Translated by G. W. Dasent. Stockholm and London: W. Pickering, 1842.

Swannell, J. N. *William Morris and Norse Literature*. London: William Morris Society, 1962.

Tacitus. *Germania*. Translated by M. Hutton. London and New York: Loeb Classical Library, 1920.

Taylor, Bayard. *Lars: A Pastoral of Norway*. Boston: J. R. Osgood, 1873.

———. *Northern Travel: Summer and Winter Pictures of Sweden, Denmark, and Lapland*. New York: G. P. Putnam, 1857.

———. *The Poetical Works of Bayard Taylor*. Boston and New York: Houghton, Mifflin and Co., 1899.

Tegnér, Esaias. *Frithiofs Saga*. 1825. Reprint, Stockholm: P. A. Nordstedt, 1876.

———. *Frithiof's Saga*. New York: Exposer Press, 1960.

Thierry, Augustin. *History of the Conquest of England by the Normans*. Translated from the French. London: Whittaker and Co., 1841.

Thoreau, Henry. "An Excursion to Canada" [A Yankee in Canada]. Parts 1–3. *Putnam's Monthly Magazine* 1, no. 1 (1853):54–59, 1, no. 2 (1853): 170–84, and 1, no. 3 (1853): 321–29.

———. *Cape Cod* (first four chapters). Parts 1–3. *Putnam's Monthly Magazine* 3, no. 5 (1855): 632–40, 3, no. 6 (1855): 59–66 and 157–64.

———. "Carlyle and His Works." *Graham's Magazine* 30, no. 3 (1847): 145–52; 30, no. 4 (1847): 238–45.

———. *The Correspondence of Henry David Thoreau.* Edited by Walter Harding and Carl Bode. New York: New York University Press, 1958.

———. *The Journal of Henry Thoreau.* Edited by Bradford Torrey and Francis H. Allen. 14 vols. bound as 2. 1906. Reprint, New York: Dover Publications, 1962.

———. *The Variorum Walden.* Annotated and with an introduction by Walter Harding. New York: Twayne Publishers, 1962.

———. "Walking." *Atlantic Monthly* 9 (June 1862):657–74.

———. *A Week on the Concord and Merrimack Rivers.* Boston: Houghton Mifflin, 1961.

———. *Writings of Henry David Thoreau.* Walden edition. 20 vols. 1906. Reprint, New York: AMS Press, 1968.

Three Northern Love Stories. Translated from the Icelandic by Eiríkr Magnússon and William Norris. 1875. Reprint, London: Longmans, Green, and Co., 1901.

Thurin, Erik. *Emerson As Priest of Pan: A Study in the Metaphysics of Sex.* Lawrence: The Regents Press of Kansas, 1981.

Torfason, Thormódur (Torfaeus). *Orcades, sive rerum Orcadensium historia.* Hafniae (Copenhagen): J. Hog, 1697.

———. *Historia Vinlandiae antiquae.* Hafniae (Copenhagen): apud Hieron, 1715.

———. *The History of Ancient Vinland.* Translated from the Icelandic. New York: John G. Shea, 1891.

Tovey, D.C. *Gray's English Poems.* Cambridge: Cambridge University Press, 1898.

Turner, Sharon. *A History of the Anglo-Saxons.* 6th edition. London: Longman, Rees, Orme, Brown, and Green, 1836.

Varnhagen, Hermann. *Longfellows Tales of a Wayside Inn und ihre Quellen.* Berlin: Weidmann, 1884.

Vining, Elizabeth. *Mr. Whittier.* New York: Viking Press, 1974.

Vinland Sagas. Translated by Magnus Magnusson and Hermann Pálsson. Harmondsworth, England: Penguin Books, 1965.

Volsunga Saga. Translated by William Morris. 1870. Reprint, London: Longmans, Green and Co., 1901.

Wagenknecht, Edward. *James Russell Lowell: Portrait of a Many-Sided Man.* New York: Oxford University Press, 1971.

Wheaton Henry. *History of the Northmen, or Danes and Normans, from the Earliest Times to the Conquest of England by William of Normandy.* London: George Mussan, 1831.

———. "Scandinavian Mythology, Poetry, and History." *The North American Review* 38 (January, 1829):18–37.

Whitman, Walt. *Leaves of Grass.* Edited by Sculley Bradley and Harold W. Blodgett. New York: W. W. Norton and Co., 1973.

Whittier, John Greenleaf. *Complete Poetical Works of John Greenleaf Whittier.* Boston and New York: Houghton Mifflin Co., 1894.

———. *Letters of John Greenleaf Whittier.* Edited by John B. Pickard. 3 vols. Cambridge, Massachusetts: Harvard University Press, 1975.

Williams, Cecil B. *Henry Wadsworth Longfellow*. New York: Grossett and Dunlap, 1964.

Worm, Ole [Wormius]. *Runir, seu Danica literatura antiquissima, vulgo Gothica dicta*. Amsterdam: apud Joannes Jansonium, 1636.

Wright, Thomas, ed. *Early Travels in Palestine*. 1848. Reprint, New York: AMS Press, 1969.

Index

177